Restoring ~~~~~~ ~~~~~~~

Restoring At-Risk Communities

Doing It Together
and Doing It Right

Edited by John M. Perkins

 Baker Books

A Division of Baker Book House Co
Grand Rapids, Michigan 49516

© 1995 by John M. Perkins

Published by Baker Books
a division of Baker Book House Company
P. O. Box 6287, Grand Rapids, MI 49516-6287

Printed in the United States of America

Library of Congress Cataloging-in-Publication Data

Restoring at-risk communities : doing it together and doing it right / edited by John M. Perkins.
  p. cm.
Includes bibliographical references.
ISBN 0-8010-5463-X (paper)
  1. Church work with the poor—United States. 2. City churches—United States. 3. City missions—United States. 4. Community development—Religious aspects—Christianity. 5. Community development—United States. 6. Evangelicalism—United States. I. Perkins, John, 1930–.
BV639.P6R47 1995
261.8′0973—dc20   95-35456

Unless otherwise indicated, Scripture is taken from the HOLY BIBLE, NEW INTERNATIONAL VERSION®. NIV®. Copyright © 1973, 1978, 1984 by International Bible Society. Used by permission of Zondervan Publishing House. All rights reserved.

Verses marked LB are taken from *The Living Bible,* copyright © 1971 by Tyndale House Publishers, Wheaton, Illinois. Used by permission.

Scripture quotations marked NASB are from the New American Standard Bible, © the Lockman Foundation 1960, 1962, 1963, 1968, 1971, 1972, 1973, 1975, 1977.

Chapter 4, "The Character of a Developer" is adapted from *With Justice for All* by John Perkins. Copyright 1982. Used by permission of Regal Books.

Chapter 6, "Reconciliation" is adapted from *More Than Equals* by Spencer Perkins and Chris Rice. Copyright 1993 by Spencer Perkins and Chris Rice. Used by permission of InterVarsity Press.

Contents

Acknowledgments

Although my name is on the cover of this book as its editor, more of the credit for bringing this project to fruition should go to several friends and co-workers.

First, I must thank the board members of the Christian Community Development Association. Much of the heart of the book has come out of our meetings together in the boardroom. Thanks are also in order to the advisory committee who gave generously of their time and, at their own expense, met together to give vision to this book: George Neau of the New Orleans School of Urban Ministries; Virgil Tolbert of Restoration Ministries in Harvey, Illinois; and Ron Potter, professor of theology at Center for Urban Theological Studies in Philadelphia, Pennsylvania (now living in Jackson, Mississippi).

Second, I would like to thank the writers of each of the chapters. The fact that so many extremely busy people took the time to work on this book is a testimony to the strength of their belief in the important work of Christian Community Development.

Thanks also to the *Urban Family* magazine staff, especially Chris Rice and my son Spencer. They are the ones who coordinated the project from the beginning and saw it through to completion. Also thanks to Phil Reed of Voice of Calvary Fellowship in Jackson, Mississippi, who took the point in the book's initial stages.

A very special thanks to Bob Smith for the many hours of day-to-day, hands-on editing and coordinating of this book. In the end, it was Bob who drove all of us to meet our deadlines and who pulled this project together. I must also thank his wife, Ardes, for bearing with Bob while he worked on this project.

My wife Vera Mae's chapter on CCD and the Family was ghost-written by Jennifer Parker from *Urban Family* magazine. Jennifer has incredible talent and did a tremendous job putting Vera Mae's stories and thoughts on paper. And Alexis Spencer-Byers did finishing touches that improved the final product.

Finally, I thank God for the growing number of co-laborers who are demonstrating God's love in some of the toughest communities of our nation. For years I have said that we are staging a "quiet revolution." As our numbers are multiplying, I'm not so sure we will be able to call this movement "quiet" much longer.

John M. Perkins

Introduction

John M. Perkins

Questions are being asked from every sector of American society about the direction we should head as a nation. Everyone from powerful politicians to the average person on the street seems to be confused about solutions for our declining inner cities.

Thirty years after the successes of the civil rights movement of the fifties and sixties, we stand at another crossroads. The civil rights era was probably the most important social movement of this century. Voting rights legislation that accompanied it brought the Black community into full citizenship. Poverty and affirmative action programs did much to create a large and thriving middle class, and minority elected officials are at an all-time high. Much progress has been made.

But at the same time that all this progress was being made, a new phenomenon was developing. This phenomenon has been dubbed the "underclass." This stubborn new form of poverty is a by-product of Black economic and political/legislative success, well-intentioned poverty programs gone awry, and of course, the persistence of racism.

With the new freedom of movement afforded to African Americans by the fair housing laws combined with new economic independence, Blacks migrated up and out of traditional Black neighborhoods, leaving behind only those too poor to escape. In many inner city neighborhoods, when Blacks moved in, Whites moved out. Along with this, there has been a loss of skills that could have provided goods and services and employment. These goods and services are now being provided by new immigrants. While I do not fault immigrants, there needs to be a new Black leadership to provide some of our own goods and services. Instead, in many of these poor urban neighborhoods, the economy revolves around welfare benefits and drug markets that have created a subculture of permanent dependency and violence. Compounding this, government welfare programs have subtly enabled the development of a new single-parent norm for the family. Add to that a big city educational system that is inept and insufficient. The results have been devastating.

But in every crisis there is opportunity. Much of the credit for the success of the civil rights movement must go to Black clergy and White northern liberal churches. For the most part, White evangelicals stood on the sidelines as their Black brothers and sisters struggled through this critical period in American history. This is a matter of fact, not blame. However, the game is not over. There is still much unfinished business. The moral crisis that we are facing in this country is crying out for spiritual leadership. It offers evangelicals the opportunity to put our faith to work—to roll up our sleeves and become players instead of sitting on the sidelines.

There are already signs that the evangelical community, which has been faithful in preaching a bold message of salvation but long silent on social issues like poverty and race, is beginning to make its presence felt. I am encouraged by what I see happening in movements across the country. For instance, almost every place I go where there is a spark of renewal, David Bryant's Concert of Prayer is very active.

I am greatly encouraged by Promise Keepers, the men's movement that was started just five years ago by Bill McCartney, former football coach of the University of Colorado, and Dr. Dave Wardell and is being led by my dear friend Randy Phillips. Promise Keepers has made a powerful commitment to the development and discipleship of men across racial and cultural boundaries. Last year over 230,000 men attended six sold-out conferences around the country proclaiming the seven promises of a Promise Keeper:

1. A Promise Keeper is committed to honoring Jesus Christ through prayer, worship, and obedience to his Word, in the power of the Holy Spirit.

2. A Promise Keeper is committed to pursuing vital relationships with a few other men, understanding that he needs brothers to help him keep his promises.
3. A Promise Keeper is committed to practicing spiritual, moral, ethical, and sexual purity.
4. A Promise Keeper is committed to building strong marriages and families through love, protection, and biblical values.
5. A Promise Keeper is committed to supporting the mission of his church by honoring and praying for his pastor and by actively giving his time and resources.
6. A Promise Keeper is committed to reaching beyond any racial and denominational barriers to demonstrate the power of biblical unity.
7. A Promise Keeper is committed to influencing his world, being obedient to the Great Commandment (Mark 12:30–31) and the Great Commission (Matt. 28:19–20).

InterVarsity has been doing some wonderful work with their urban projects, reaching minorities, especially Asians. InterVarsity has developed a marketplace ministry led heavily by Pete Hammon and his staff. More than half of the college students who go into the inner city as volunteers with these summer urban projects relocate to the urban site after graduation.

Campus Crusade, a movement started by Dr. Bill Bright many years ago to reach out to high school and college students, is now the largest mission organization in the world. Out of this movement is blossoming an effort to reach urban children, headed by Dan Pryor, called SAY (*Save America's Youth*) Yes. Dan is working with churches to make their facilities and resources available for after-school tutoring programs.

In 1977 I joined the board of directors of World Vision and have been encouraging them to bring the skills they are teaching around the world to America's inner cities. Praise God that this is beginning to happen under the leadership of World Vision President Bob Sieple, as they are now putting more time and resources into tackling America's persistent form of urban poverty.

The National Association of Evangelicals (NAE), which has for many years been championing the cause of biblical foundations during changing times, has had trouble breaking racial barriers. In 1963, the National Black Evangelical Association (NBEA) was formed. Recently, racial reconciliation has become a major priority among these two associations as well as NAE's Hispanic Commission.

The Pentecostals have made racial reconciliation a similar priority. Historically, this denomination's roots go back to 1906, to an African American pastor, William Joseph Seymour, who had a mission church on Azusa Street in Los Angeles. Pentecostals have long been separated by race but have recently begun to tear down some old walls of separation through confession and repentance.

Doug Coe, former Young Life leader, has started the Fellowship, a worldwide movement of governors' and mayors' prayer breakfasts, including the National President's Prayer Breakfast in Washington, D.C. This prayer movement is doing some wonderful work around the country.

Young Black intellectuals like Eugene Rivers and Tony Evans are taking the gospel to the streets and serving as models for others to follow.

Then there is the Christian Community Development Association (CCDA) movement, which has grown to over three hundred organizational members in six short years. It represents thousands of grassroots workers, African American, Anglo, Asian, and Latino who are doing some of the most creative work in the toughest communities of our nation. There are also many other positive urban models that are growing out of the church and impacting our cities.

Although there are many positive things happening, more can and must be done. It is time that we demand more of ourselves as Christians. We are the hands and feet of Jesus Christ, and if the world is going to see, feel, and touch him, it will have to be through us.

We need more troops who are willing to give up their personal ambitions and maybe even risk their lives by going into our inner cities—the frontlines. We need more troops on the supply lines offering their love and volunteering their time and skills to those at the front. And we need more support from the home front—concerned Christians providing prayer support and making sure that the emotional and physical needs of those in the trenches are being met.

For more than thirty years I have crisscrossed this nation challenging and exhorting Christians to make God's love visible to the poor. I have written extensively on justice issues and on God's concern for racial reconciliation. Nearly twenty years ago, in my books *Let Justice Roll Down* and *A Quiet Revolution,* I told how God called me and my family to the town of Mendenhall in rural Mississippi, how we began to work with the kids, and how God protected us through some sticky times. In my book *With Justice for All* we built upon what we had learned in Mendenhall and applied it to the urban setting in Jackson, at the same time laying out a strategy for Christian community development. Then in my book *Beyond Charity* we described the growing movement of Christian community development and outlined how our response to the poor must be personal.

Still, as I travel all over this country and talk with Christians who are beginning to hear the call of God on their lives, they are asking for more instruction. Many have said that they need a comprehensive "how-to" manual to guide their efforts. So together with some of my dear friends and co-workers in the Christian Community Development Association, we have put together this handbook that describes not only the theology, principles, and strategy that guide what we are doing, but also offers more practical how to's—lessons learned from years of struggle and triumph in some of America's toughest neighborhoods.

Read and reread this book. It is meant to be used as a reference, as a guide that you can go back to time and time again to gain encouragement and fresh insight that will help you negotiate the pitfalls and mine fields associated with doing ministry with integrity among our nation's poor. This book is to be used as a manual and a textbook for small group Bible studies, Sunday school classes, and a guide for church and organization staff.

God is definitely at work. He is drawing more and more believers into areas that have been, until recently, feared and avoided. Maybe he's speaking to you.

Whether you are already deeply involved with the poor or whether you are just beginning to hear God's call, we trust that this book will not only give you encouragement, but that it can serve as a companion as you do your part to make the gospel truly good news to the poor.

Part 1
Foundations of Christian Community Development

The four chapters in this section describe both what Christian community development is and the "under-girdings" necessary for a Christian community development ministry to proceed in carrying out its mission.

1

What Is Christian Community Development?

John M. Perkins

The desperate conditions that face the poor call for a revolution in our attempts at a solution. Through years of experience among the poor, I have come to see these desperate problems cannot be solved without strong commitment and risky actions on the part of ordinary Christians with heroic faith.

The most creative long-term solutions to the problems of the poor are coming from grassroots and church-based efforts—people who see themselves as the agents of Jesus here on earth in their own neighborhoods and communities.

This specific calling is one we have come to call Christian community development (CCD). It is not a concept that was developed in a classroom, nor formulated by people foreign to the poor community. These are practical biblical principles evolved from years of living and working among the poor.

Meeting Felt Needs

The great question is, How do we affirm the dignity of people, motivate them, and help them take responsibility for their own lives?

By beginning with the people's felt needs we establish a relationship and a trust, which then enable us to move to deeper issues of development. This idea of beginning with people's felt need is what is called the felt need concept. It is summed up in a Chinese poem:

> Go to the people
> Live among them
> Learn from them
> Love them
> Start with what they know
> Build on what they have:
> But of the best leaders
> When their task is done
> The people will remark
> "We have done it ourselves."

Jesus' encounter with the Samaritan woman at the well (John 4) shows us a pathway to a deeper relationship with the poor.

For a Jew, the Samaritans were the outcasts, the throwaways of society much like the ghetto dwellers of today. When Jews went up to Galilee from Jerusalem, instead of taking the more direct route that led through Samaria, they would take the long way around. But Jesus chose to go directly into Samaria. The challenge is for us to ask God, Is there a Samaria that you are calling me to go into?

When Jesus meets the Samaritan woman at the well, he knows her immediate (felt) need is for water from the well, and he does not ignore this need in order to meet her spiritual need for eternal life. His first words to her were not, "You are a sinner; you need to accept me into your life"; or "God loves you and has a wonderful plan for your life."

Instead, Jesus says to her, "Give me a drink of water." He did not start by saying, "I can help you." He wanted her to know that she could help him. The Jews despised and separated themselves from the Samaritans, so by talking to her and asking her for help—demonstrating she had something of value that she could share with him—Jesus affirmed her dignity and broke down the wall of distrust.

There is a great barrier of distrust between the rich and poor today, which can be overcome only by affirming the dignity of people and loving them around their needs. During more than thirty-five years of ministry, we have discovered that one of the needs we can love people around is their children. As we love their children, the parents begin to respect us and to look to our spiritual motives.

Now this Samaritan woman, who understood the historical relationship between the Jews and Samaritans, needed to understand Jesus' motives. Motives are very important to the people who are being helped. What drives us to go out of our way and show compassion for someone in need? The poor are experts at sniffing out guilt, and they exploit it. She asks, "How is it that you, being a Jew, ask drink of me who am a woman of Samaria, for the Jews have no dealings with the Samaritans." She raised the race issue, and believe me, if she had smelled guilt motivating Jesus, she would have exploited it. But because Jesus won her trust by going out on a limb and talking to her and affirming her, he was able to cut through the old racial garbage. He says, "If you knew the gifts of God and who it is that asks you for a drink, you would have asked him and he would have given you living water."

When she hears "living water" she replies, "Sir, you have nothing to draw with and the well is deep. Where can you get this living water?" Jesus has identified her felt need. Now he will show her that she has a deeper need. He will not say to her, "You are a sinner," but rather will love her into discovering her need herself.

Jesus replies, "Everyone who drinks this water will be thirsty again, but whoever drinks the water I give him will never thirst. Indeed the water I give him will become in him a spring of water welling up to eternal life." She responds, "Sir, give me this water so that I won't get thirsty and have to keep coming here to draw water." Once Jesus affirmed her around her felt need, he was then in a position to show her her deeper spiritual need. Because Jesus had won her trust and belief in his love and compassion for her, they could get down to the heart of the matter. It is at this point that Jesus says, "Go, call your husband." When she answers that she has no husband, and Jesus acknowledges that she has had five and is now living with a man who is not her husband, he takes her to a deeper level of understanding, leading her to say, "I know that Messiah is coming." Answers Jesus: "I who speak to you am he." The woman returned to her city and brought many people back with her to meet Jesus; many of the Samaritans believed in him.

Jesus goes directly to the people and loves and affirms them. Because they trust him, many come to believe in him. Jesus' method of ministering to people around their needs offers us a powerful example. Jesus met the Samaritan woman around her felt need (having her dignity affirmed), loved her around that need (by boldly initiating a dialogue), made her need his very own (by asking for a drink), then shared with her the "wonderful plan" by helping her discover for herself her spiritual need.

Three Universal Felt Needs

Of course, felt needs are different from person to person and place to place. In order to do ministry effectively you will need to discover and identify these needs. Over the years we have found, however, that there are three inherent needs that are universal. The extent to which a person has these needs met is the extent to which that person develops, grows, and secures a sense of dignity.

The first need is the need to belong. We all have a need to belong to someone and to something. In the poorer areas of our nation, families are often torn apart, love is scarce, and people live with a sense of hopelessness and a bitterness toward life. They want to belong but feel like the world all around them, on the streets and in the home, is a hostile place. This need to belong is at the heart of the urban gang problem.

The second need is the need to be significant and important—to be somebody. As we develop indigenous leaders we do it in a way that affirms the dignity of a person. We try to motivate people to take responsibility for their own lives. It is the opposite of the welfare mentality, which cripples people and makes them dependent on others. It is amazing how these children, who hear and experience so much negative reinforcement, thrive when they begin to believe that they are special.

The third need is the need for a reasonable amount of security. Many of our cities, like Northwest Pasadena, are not secure places to live. Shortly after returning from the Persian Gulf, a young soldier was killed by a stray bullet from a drive-by shooting in Los Angeles. Our cities are in terrible shape when a soldier is safer on the front lines of a war than he is in his own home. If our Christian community development is to be successful, then a major focus of our work must be to make our families feel secure in their own neighborhoods. One of the most gratifying things for me is to see the children, who used to live in terror, begin to play on the streets again.

The Gospel

Wholistic: Evangelism and Social Action

The gospel, rightly understood, is wholistic. It responds to people as whole people; it doesn't single out just spiritual or just physical needs and speak to those. Christian community development begins with people transformed by the love of God, who then respond to God's call to share the gospel with others through evangelism, social action, economic development, and justice. These groups of Christians start both churches and community development corporations, evangelism outreaches and tutoring programs, discipleship groups and housing programs, prayer groups and businesses. However, the next principle is an additional commitment that distinguishes this movement from traditional approaches.

Relocation: Living among the Poor

Living the gospel means desiring for your neighbor and your neighbor's family that which you desire for yourself and your family. Living the gospel means bettering the quality of other people's lives—spiritually, physically, socially, and emotionally—as you better your own. Living the gospel means sharing in the suffering and pain of others.

How did Jesus love? "The Word became flesh and dwelt among us, and we beheld his glory, the glory as of the only begotten from the Father, full of grace and truth" (John 1:14). Jesus relocated. He became one of us. He didn't commute back and forth to heaven.

Similarly, the most effective messenger of the gospel to the poor will also live among the poor.

By relocating, we will understand most clearly the real problems facing the poor; then we may begin to look for real solutions. For example, if our children are a part of that community, you can be sure we will do whatever we can to make sure that the children of our community get a good education. Relocation transforms "you, them, and theirs" to "we, us, and ours." Effective ministries plant and build communities of believers that have a personal stake in the development of their neighborhoods.

Reconciliation: People to God, Neighbor to Neighbor

Reconciliation is at the heart of the gospel. Jesus said that the essence of Christianity could be summed up in two inseparable commandments: love God and love thy neighbor.

First, Christian community development is concerned with reconciling people to God and bringing them into a church fellowship where they can be discipled in their faith.

But can a gospel that reconciles people to God without reconciling people to people be the true gospel of Jesus Christ? Our love for Christ should break down every racial, ethnic, or economic barrier. As Christians come together to solve the problems of their community, the great challenge will be to partner and witness together across these barriers. Christian community development recognizes that the task of loving the poor is shared by the entire body of Christ, black and white, brown and yellow, rich and poor, and urban and suburban.

Redistribution: Empowering the Poor

When the body of Christ is visibly present and living among the poor (relocation) and when we are loving our neighbor and our neighbor's family the way we love ourselves and our own family (reconciliation), the result is redistribution. It is not taking away from the rich and giving to the poor. Rather, it is when God's people with resources are living in the poor community and are a part of it, applying skills and resources to the problems of that community, thereby allowing a natural redistribution to occur. Redistribution is putting our lives, our skills, our education, and our resources to work to empower people in a community of need. Christian community development ministries find creative avenues to create jobs, schools, health centers, home ownership, and other enterprises of long-term development.

Leadership Development

The primary goal of redistribution is to fill the vacuum of moral, spiritual, and economic leadership that is so prevalent in poor communities. This is most effectively done by raising up Christian leaders from the community of need who will remain in the community. Most Christian community development ministries put a strong accent on youth development, winning youth to Christ as early as kindergarten, following them all the way through college with spiritual and educational nurturing, and creating opportunities for leadership upon their return to their community.

Church-Based

The people of God functioning as a church community is the best means of affirming the dignity of the poor and empowering them to meet their own needs. It is practically impossible to do effective wholistic ministry apart from the local church. A nurturing community of faith can best provide the thrusts of evangelism, discipleship, spiritual accountability, and relationship by which disciples grow in their walk with God.

Time-Tested Principles

Our work and a growing understanding of the effectiveness of these principles began in 1960 when our family returned to our hometown of rural Mendenhall, Mississippi, a town caught in the vice-grip of racism and poverty. Saddened and concerned by the great number of young people leaving this little ghetto for the "big city," we recognized that long-term development had to begin with introducing these young people to God and nurturing them in their faith, continue with encouraging them to go to college, and end with these young leaders returning with valuable education and skills to start programs that will continue to develop their communities.

In Mendenhall, we saw many homegrown leaders such as Dolphus and Rosie Weary and Artis and Carolyn Fletcher return to their community to begin a health center, businesses, a Christian school, a law office, and a church. Also, they started a pastor development program, which is nurturing Black church leadership throughout the state of Mississippi. These programs in turn led to economic development and job opportunities for many others in Mendenhall.

The development of indigenous leaders in Mendenhall enabled us to move on to Jackson, where we planted a similar work, Voice of Calvary Ministries. Melvin Anderson, VOC's leader today, is another disciple who grew up in Mendenhall, went off to college, and moved into Jackson's inner city. Voice of Calvary includes a church, a home ownership/family development program, a health center, and a thrift store. The same process of indigenous development is now taking place in Northwest Pasadena, where we moved in 1982 after ten years in Jackson.

During the years in Jackson, we started an International Study Center and began to share our vision and principles through workshops and conferences. Other ministries began to sprout up during this same time, led by people committed to living among and making God's love visible to the poor.

Bob Lupton went to Atlanta and became burdened by the plight of young Black boys. Out of that burden came FCS Urban Ministries, which is pioneering in the "re-neighboring" of the deteriorating Summerhill community, site of the 1996 Olympics.

Ted Travis, a young Black musician, moved into Denver's Five Points community and began Neighborhood Ministries.

Kathy Dudley, a young White woman mentored by Dolphus Weary, moved into west Dallas and began working with children there, starting Voice of Hope.

A young White Moody Bible Institute graduate named Glen Kehrein relocated into the Austin neighborhood of Chicago and started Circle Urban Ministries. He was later joined by a Black pastor, Raleigh Washington.

Noel Castellanos, a Mexican American, moved into a Latino neighborhood in Chicago and began a Mexican/Anglo Church and ministry called La Villita.

Wayne Gordon, a White Wheaton College graduate, moved into one of Chicago's more severe ghettos and started a church, more than fifty youngsters from which have graduated from college, many returning to their community to head up ministries there. He was later joined by a dynamic young Black pastor, Carey Casey.

Elizar Pagan, a Puerto Rican American, moved into a Brooklyn, New York, neighborhood and is now a powerful leader in his community. Other ministries were started in Detroit, Denver, Baltimore, and Seattle and are still popping up all over the country.

With these men and women and many others attempting to live out the reconciling love of God among the poor, we began to recognize more and more our need to encourage and learn from each other. Therefore, in 1989 the Christian Community Development Association (CCDA) was born. Now CCDA has nearly three hundred member organizations in over one hundred cities and thirty-five states. These churches and ministries are showing that it is possible for the church to live out the love of God in the world; that black and white, yellow and brown, and rich and poor together can be reconciled; and that we can make a difference—we can rescue the ghettoes and barrios of this nation.

The vision has also been seeded beyond the United States through leaders from other nations who visited Voice of Calvary and other CCDA members and transplanted the principles of Christian community development back into their own cities and communities. Jean and Joy Thomas relocated to Jean's native country of Haiti. They are heading up one of the most significant efforts of church-based community development in the Western Hemisphere's poorest nation. Graham and Dorcas Cyster returned to Capetown, South Africa, to begin a ministry of reconciliation and development there. There are many others: Patrick Sookdeo in London; Sam Chapman, a native New Zealand Maori; Australian Aborigines; and ministries in Mexico and Kenya.

In hundreds of communities and cities across the world, these defining principles of Christian community development are proving that grassroots, community-based ministries, led by people who have made these communities their homes, are the most effective agents for spiritual transformation and socioeconomic development for the poor.

The Key Elements of Christian Community Development

Christian community development is a church-based ministry among the poor, which

- begins with felt needs of the people in the community
- responds to those needs in a wholistic way
- is based on clear biblical principles
- is "time-tested"
- develops and utilizes leaders from within the community
- encourages relocation—living among the poor
- demands reconciliation—people to God and people to people
- empowers the poor through redistribution—all community members sharing their skills, talents, education, and resources to help each other

2

Toward a Theology of Christian Community Development

Phil Reed

It is not difficult to get agreement on the fact that American society and culture are in a state of crisis. Most people would acknowledge that our institutions, communities, and personal lives are experiencing an unprecedented social and moral breakdown. Even those who don't live in the inner city or don't have firsthand exposure to the unraveling of the moral fabric of our nation and world have the media's all-too-vivid exhibition of the problems.

The Christian Community Development Association, along with many other civic and religious groups, is attempting to address America's urban crisis. One of the distinctives of CCDA is a commitment to a specifically biblical approach to urban community development. The goal of this chapter is to provide for the reader of this handbook a theology that undergirds the life and practice of Christian community development. We have made an effort to get at the big picture of what is contained in the Bible in terms of principles, rather than pulling out isolated "proof texts."

The chapter is divided into two main parts: the theological basis for the vision of CCD, and the theological basis for its method, particularly the three Rs (reconciliation, redistribution, and relocation) and the "wheel of ministry."

The Vision of Christian Community Development

George Barna has defined vision as "a clear mental image of a preferable future imparted by God to His chosen servants and based upon an accurate understanding of God, self, and circumstances."[1] Christian community development should help us attain a mental image of how our community will look in the future when God is in control, when his kingdom has come "on earth as it is in heaven." We should not just have goals and objectives or a set of isolated programs we are operating for the betterment of society. We should have an overall picture of what God wants to do in the inner city, based upon his desire for his people as revealed in the Word of God.

One place in Scripture where we can see what God views as best for his creation is the picture of Paradise, the Garden of Eden, in Genesis 1 and 2. The first mention of mankind in Holy Scripture is in Genesis 1:26–27 when God created man in his own image, male and female he created them. Being created in God's image has many implications, one of which is the close relationship that God had with human beings. Genesis 3:8 says that God habitually walked in the Garden in the cool of the day, presumably to spend time with his creation. Unfortunately, God did not find man and woman in their usual place. They were hiding behind a tree, having already eaten the forbidden fruit and now ashamed of their nakedness.

This story in Genesis gives us the biblical principle of CCD that mankind's deepest needs are for spiritual change. Mankind was created to have fellowship with God and cannot be truly human otherwise. Yet sin has destroyed our relationship with God, so that we desire to hide from him. Through it all, our loving and compassionate God continues to seek us out, even in our sinful and rebellious states. Finally God showed the full extent of his love for us by sending Jesus Christ to restore the relationship that was destroyed in the Garden: "For if, by the trespass of the one man, death reigned through that one man, how much more will those who receive God's abundant provision of grace and of the gift of righteousness reign in life through the one man, Jesus Christ" (Rom. 5:17).

The implication for ministry is simply this: Christian community development must address spiritual needs. We can rebuild houses, provide food and clothing, tutor children, and establish all manner of programs, but if we are not helping people find a relationship with Jesus Christ that leads to eternal life, then we are not meeting the true needs.

An accompanying principle to the importance of meeting spiritual needs is that Christian community development is most effectively done through the church. In Matthew 16:13–19, Jesus authorizes the church to tear down the spiritual strongholds of hell, which have been established in our inner cities. In Matthew 28:18–20, Jesus commissions the church to make disciples of all nations. This is not to say that it is impossible to do ministry in the inner city through organizations not tied to a local church; however, as Glen Kehrein argues convincingly in the chapter on "The Local Church and Christian Community Development," we do believe that spiritual needs will best be addressed by the organization that is tied to a church.

As we return to God's perfect plan for his creation in Paradise, we find that not only did Adam and Eve have a relationship with God, but they also had a relationship with each other. The second chapter of Genesis closes with a wedding picture of Adam and Eve standing before God to become "one flesh." In Matthew 19, Jesus refers to this created order to speak about the sacredness of the marriage bond: "What God has joined together, let man not separate" (v. 6). In Genesis 3, this relationship also became a casualty of the fall. When confronted with his sin, Adam blamed Eve for his failure. The principle for Christian community development is that our efforts have to build up the family unit if we envision our communities as places where we are to experience some of God's provisions in Paradise.

Couples continue to be torn apart to this day as husband and wife are set at odds with each other, instead of being the partners in ministry that they were created to be. As early as 1939, E. Franklin Frazier began to sound the alarm about how slavery had undermined the Black family. In 1965, the Moynihan Report said that the rising rates of broken marriages, female-headed households, out-of-wedlock births, and welfare dependency was one of the central problems among the Black lower class. William J. Wilson points out that the problems described by Frazier and Moynihan began to accelerate in the mid-seventies and reached catastrophic proportions in the eighties. "To be more specific, one-quarter of all black births occurred outside of marriage in 1965, . . . and by 1980, 57 percent [did]; in 1965, nearly 25 percent of all black families were headed by women, and by 1980, 43 percent were. . . ."[2] Wilson goes on to point out that although some of the statistics in the Black community show signs of improving, other minority communities of Hispanics and Asians are demonstrating the same rapid increase in social problems true of the Black community of the mid-seventies. The church has a biblical and practical mandate to ensure that family development is at the center of all that we do.

One more peek at the picture in Paradise reveals a third element of God's plan for his people: fruitful labor. When the alarm clock goes off at 5:30 A.M. to rouse us from sleep to get ready to go to work, many of us might think that surely labor was part of the curse of the fall and not part of Paradise. But God created man and woman and put them in the Garden, giving them the job "to work it and take care of it" (Gen. 2:15). Their work for God was part of the created order. However, after the curse of sin invaded the earth, man and woman were relegated to unfruitful labor: "Cursed is the ground because of you; through painful toil you will eat of it all the days of your life" (Gen. 3:17). Creative work is part of the blessing of God; meaningless toil or idleness is the result of the curse.

The implication for CCD is that we have to ensure that people are given the opportunity to be engaged in productive work. This certainly speaks to the effort to deal with the high rate of unemployment in the inner city. In our neighborhood in west Jackson, Mississippi, a staggering 58 percent of men did not work *at all* in 1989. Men and women cannot fully experience their created nature in this type of setting. Those involved in CCD will have to make job procurement, and if necessary, job creation, a part of their overall strategy.

However, more is involved than just filling up people's time or helping them find a job simply to make money. This is the failure of the current "workfare" efforts. Although working for a support check is desirable, this is not the ultimate goal. Our main effort should be to develop people to the point that they are using their God-given skills and abilities in satisfying work that is also benefiting the community. As Mary Nelson points out in her chapter on "redistribution," the CCD movement is just beginning to address this issue.

Besides the picture in Paradise, a key concept in Scripture of the blessing of God is found in the Hebrew concept of *shalom*. *Shalom* is usually translated "peace." However, shalom entails a peace that is more than merely cessation of hostilities or peace as opposed to war. Shalom envisions a state of general well-being, wherein one experiences the fullness of all the blessings God has for his people. It is akin to Jesus' promise in John 10:10: "I have come that they may have life, and have it to the full." God's shalom is a thread that runs through the prophets, especially as God looks forward to the restoration of a people who have experienced the ravages of sin.

One good example is found in Isaiah 61. This one is particularly useful since Jesus appropriates these very words to sum up his ministry in Luke 4. In Isaiah 61:1–4 the servant of the Lord has been divinely anointed to preach good news to the poor, bind up the brokenhearted, proclaim freedom to the captives, release prisoners from darkness, and proclaim the year of the Lord's favor. He comforts the mournful and redresses the "spirit of despair" (vv. 2–4).

However, in verse 5, there is a shift in the action. In verses 1–4, the Messiah speaks of what he will do: I will preach the good news, I will bind up the brokenhearted, and so on. In verse 5, the prophetic message says: "They will rebuild the ancient ruins and restore the places long devastated; they will renew the ruined cities that have been devastated for generations." Who are the "they"? Precisely those who inhabit those ruined and devastated places who have received the "good news" (gospel). In other words, the mission of the Messiah—and our mission—is not complete until we have empowered those living in the devastated places, the ruined cities, to restore and rebuild their own community.

The principle of indigenous leadership development sets Christian community development apart from social service efforts. John Perkins has said that indigenous leadership development is simply helping those in the community solve their own problems. The measure of success for CCD is not how many people have moved into the community from other places, but rather how many of those from the community have stayed and are being empowered and equipped to assume positions of leadership.

The Three Rs

The three Rs of Christian community development are reconciliation, redistribution, and relocation. One cannot talk about Christian community development without them. It is important for us to be clear on one point: these three Rs are not man-made principles. We must agree that they are rather man-given labels for clear biblical principles. Unless we can find them grounded in the Bible, they should rightly be dismissed by serious Christians as fine social theory but not very good theology. There will be additional scriptural foundation given in the separate chapters on reconciliation, redistribution, and relocation in part 2 of this book. My goal here is to provide a general biblical foundation.

Reconciliation

In Ephesians, Paul uses the first three chapters to lay the groundwork for the principle of reconciliation. In chapter 1, Paul tells the Ephesian believers that they are called to bring glory to God. Toward that end, God put into place a divine plan—a "mystery" Paul calls it—to bring all things in heaven and earth under one head, even Christ. In chapter 2, Paul talks about how God has brought those who were formerly alienated together into one body. Again, it is presented as a major, long-term plan by God: "His purpose was to create in himself one new man out of the two, thus making peace, and in this one body to reconcile both of them to God through the cross, by which he put to death their hostility" (vv. 15–16). Then in chapter 3, Paul brings up the "mystery" again, this eternal plan to sum up all creation under one head: "This mystery is that through the gospel the Gentiles are heirs together with Israel, members together of one body, and sharers together in the promise in Christ Jesus" (v. 6).

There was no room in Paul's gospel for theological or racial division. In Galatians, Paul relates how he had to confront the apostle Peter after Peter had been hypocritical in his dealings with the Gentiles in Antioch. It seems that Peter was fine interacting with them as long as his "Jewish homeboys" weren't around. When they showed up, Peter withdrew. Paul says he confronted Peter because "they were not acting in line with the truth of the gospel" (Gal. 2:14).

It is clear that the message of reconciliation between Jew and Gentile was a central part of the gospel Paul preached. A gospel that could not reconcile humans across the most difficult barrier of the day was no gospel at all. So it is with us. If the gospel is not concerned with reconciling us across the most stubborn ethnic and racial, indeed all man-made, barriers, then it is no gospel at all. Reconciliation is not optional, it is not a specialized calling for a few, it is not a trivial concern, it is central to the heart of the gospel.

Redistribution

Mention the word *redistribution* and the level of the debate over how best to help the poor increases several decibels. On one end of the spectrum, there are many people of compassion who have a Robin Hood understanding of redistribution, whereby we take from the rich and give to the poor. Such people would say that those who are rich have benefited from an unjust economic structure, and it is time to even things out. The reason the poor are poor, they maintain, is systemic oppression.

At the other end of the spectrum are those who believe that the government has already picked their pockets enough. Money is not the problem. We have spent billions of dollars on programs to help the underprivileged and have created a gigantic welfare structure. The result is an increase in the number of poor and the destruction of initiative in millions of welfare-dependent people. The problem is personal responsibility. The argument from these voices is, "You are not going to take any more of my money and give it to people who won't work. If you want to redistribute something, redistribute moral values and the work ethic."

The biblical principles on which redistribution is based speak to both of these concerns. First of all, we need to be clear on who owns what. Psalm 24:1 says: "The earth is the LORD's, and everything in it, the world, and all who live in it." Say it out loud ten times: "All the resources in the world belong to God! I belong to God!" Once we have that clear, then we can go to the Bible and discover how God wants us to use his time, his money, his education, and his skills, which he has merely entrusted to us to invest for him. It's not a matter of picking *my* pockets, or giving away more of *my money* out of the goodness of my heart.

Second, we need to understand an economic system as God presented it. When God gave the law to his people in the Old Testament, he set up a system so that, if handled properly, "There should be no poor among you, for in the land the LORD your God is giving you to possess as your inheritance, he will richly bless you, if only you fully obey the LORD your God and are careful to follow all these commands" (Deut. 15:4–5). Then God outlined several ways that a person could work his/her way out of poverty: all debts were to be canceled at the end of seven years within the people of God (Deut. 15:1–3), fields were not to be harvested to the corners, nor were reapers allowed to go back through the fields a second time to get what they left the first time, instead these gleanings were to be left for the poor (Lev. 19:9–10). If a person fell into poverty and had to sell his property, then his nearest relative was to redeem it for him, and, finally, there was the year of Jubilee, wherein every fifty years all property reverted back to the original owner's family (Lev. 25).

The assumption behind these laws speaks to both sides of the debate on how to help the poor. They acknowledged that some people will fall into poverty, perhaps through personal mismanagement, but also because some will use the economic system unjustly to oppress others. Thus God built in safeguards. The people of God should have a deep concern for giving a helping hand to those who are poor. Scripture also acknowledges that personal initiative must be taken by those in poverty to take advantage of the opportunities God provides in his system.

Redistribution means providing opportunities to the poor to obtain the skills and economic resources to be able to work their way out of poverty, whatever the cause for their situation. Redistribution means putting our lives, our skills, our education, and our resources to work to empower people in a community of need. As Mary Nelson points out in chapter 7, redistribution is not complete until the community has its own economic base.

The story of Ruth is an excellent case study in how the economic system established by God comes together with personal initiative. Ruth and Naomi were two widows living in Bethlehem. Ruth, with Naomi's encouragement, utilized the right of gleaning in order to provide food for herself and Naomi. As God would have it, she happened to glean in a field owned by Boaz. Boaz, touched by her commitment to Naomi, and her personal initiative, assisted her by ordering his servants to leave an extra amount for her to gather. Through her desire to work, using the system established by God and with the help of a gracious man named Boaz, Ruth is not only economically empowered, but God uses her in the ancestry of Jesus himself.

A third principle of redistribution is found in understanding why God gives wealth. In 2 Corinthians 9, Paul says that "Whoever sows sparingly will also reap sparingly, and whoever sows generously will also reap generously" (v. 6). The church often interprets this as the "10 percent keep-the-pump-primed principle." That is, as long as I keep giving my tithe (10 percent) to God, then he will keep the blessings flowing my way because I have kept the divine pump primed by "returning a portion to God." The other 90 percent is mine to do with as I please. However, if we read on, it says: "And God is able to make all grace abound to you, so that in all things at all times, having all that you need, you will abound in every good work. . . . You will be made rich in every way so that you can be generous on every occasion, and through us your generosity will result in thanksgiving to God" (vv. 8, 11). Notice the promise to us is that we will have all that we *need*, while the abundance is to enable us to "abound in every good work" and to "be generous on every occasion." God makes us wealthy so that we can invest it in his kingdom and in accordance with his economic principles.

In all of these Scriptures on redistribution, we want to make it clear that we are not talking about the seizing of someone's property. Redistribution is not socialism or communism. We are making the case that when God is working in the hearts of his people they will want to use his resources in accordance with his principles. One of the clear principles in Scripture is God's concern for economic development of the poor.

Relocation

The last of the three Rs is relocation. By relocation, we mean the people of God bringing the resources of God into the community of need in a personal way. Relocation is the method by which we accomplish reconciliation and redistribution. Neither reconciliation nor redistribution can be done effectively long distance. Relocation, the need to live and work among those to whom we are attempting to bring the hope of the gospel, is the least popular of the three Rs. Relocation is personal. It involves putting ourselves in threatening situations, coming into areas that others have long since abandoned, or merely planting our feet in neighborhoods that "smart" people are leaving. It is fortunate, therefore, that the biblical basis for relocation is perhaps one of the clearest in Scripture.

Jesus gave his disciples a job assignment and a method in Matthew 28:18–20, in what we refer to today in evangelical Christianity as the Great Commission. "Then Jesus came to them and said, 'All authority in heaven and on earth has been given to me. Therefore go and make disciples of all nations, baptizing them in the name of the Father and of the Son and of the Holy Spirit, and teaching them to obey everything I have commanded you. And surely I am with you always, to the very end of the age.'"

Many commentators have remarked on the Greek sentence structure behind this command. There is only one active verb, "make disciples." This is our task, as Christians, and more particularly as those involved in Christian community development. There are three participles, which tell us what our *methods* are to be: going, baptizing, and teaching. Going is as much an essential part of making disciples as baptizing and teaching.

Throughout the Scriptures, God's chosen way of reaching the unbelieving world is to put his people into strategic contact with the unbelievers. God chose a man named Abram in Genesis 12 and told him to leave the place he was living, and "go to the land I will show you" (v. 1). There God promised to prosper him so that "all peoples on earth will be blessed through you" (v. 3). God took Moses from the palace of Pharaoh, into the land of Midian, where at the age of eighty, God told him to go back to Egypt and tell Pharaoh to let his people go (Exod. 3:10).

Is it sometimes difficult? Of course! God told a man named Ananias to go to a street called Straight and help a man there named Saul receive his sight again. When Ananias resisted the assignment because this man was only recently killing members of the Christian church, God reiterated his command: "Go!" (Acts 9:11, 15). When he got there, he was to tell this Saul that God was going to send him far away to the Gentiles. "I will show him how much he must suffer for my name" (v. 16).

The ultimate example of relocation is found in the example of our Lord Jesus. John tells us that "The Word became flesh and made his dwelling among us" (John 1:14). Philippians 2 contains what many accept as the clearest summary "Christological" passage in all of Scripture:

> Your attitude should be the same as that of Christ Jesus: Who, being in very nature God, did not consider equality with God something to be grasped, but made himself nothing, taking the very nature of a servant, being made in human likeness. And being found in appearance as a man, he humbled himself and became obedient to death—even death on a cross! Therefore God exalted him to the highest place and gave him the name that is above every name, that at the name of Jesus every knee should bow, in heaven and on earth and under the earth, and every tongue confess that Jesus Christ is Lord, to the glory of God the Father.
>
> Philippians 2:5–11

Christ's act of love for us was to leave heaven and come to earth (relocation), and there to give his life, even to the point of death on the cross. So, Paul says, our attitude should be the same as that of Christ. We should be so committed to reaching the lost for Christ, especially the poor and oppressed, that we are willing to suffer if necessary.

The "Wheel of Ministry"

If the church is going to adequately address the needs of the poor, then it will need to recover the biblical concept of salvation. In the Old Testament the concept of salvation meant primarily deliverance from one's enemies or from danger. "The LORD is my light and my salvation—whom shall I fear? The LORD is the stronghold of my life—of whom shall I be afraid?" (Ps. 27:1).

Salvation was often a community event. The major event in the life of Israel, which contained God's salvation for his people, was the deliverance of the people from Egypt. After the Exodus, Moses and the people of Israel sang this song: "The LORD is my strength and my song; he has become my salvation. He is my God, and I will praise him" (Exod. 15:2). In the prophets, salvation of God's people after the exile meant restoration of the ruined and devastated cities (Amos 9:13–15).

In the New Testament, the concept of salvation took on a wider meaning, which included first and foremost the forgiveness of sins through Jesus Christ, but which also included the concepts of salvation from poverty and destruction included in the Old Testament. This can be seen clearly in the song of Zechariah: "He has raised up a horn of salvation for us in the house of his servant David, . . . salvation from our enemies and from the hand of all who hate us. . . . And you, my child, will be called a prophet of the Most High; for you will go on before the Lord to prepare the way for him, to give his people the knowledge of salvation through the forgiveness of their sins" (Luke 1:69, 71, 76–77).

The gospel message in Scripture is a message of salvation that speaks to the needs of the individual as well as a message of transformation of society. In his book, *A Quiet Revolution*, John Perkins developed a concept of the proclamation of the gospel known as the "wheel of ministry."[3] The wheel of ministry, as the diagram on page 39 indicates, illustrates that effective communication of the message of salvation consists of five parts: call, evangelism, social action, economic development, and justice, all grounded in the church.

The Call

Rightly understanding the message of salvation for the inner city begins with the call that Jesus has given to his church in the Great Commission: "All authority in heaven and on earth has been given to me. Therefore go and make disciples of all nations, baptizing them in the name of the Father and of the Son and of the Holy Spirit, and

The Wheel of Ministry

Justice

The Call

The Church

Economic
Development

Evangelism

Social
Action

teaching them to obey everything I have commanded you" (Matt. 28:18–20).

The word that Jesus uses in the marching orders for his church is the Greek word *ethnos,* from which we get "ethnic." He is telling us to reach those groups of unbelievers among us—as well as across the ocean—and make disciples of them. Dr. Ray Bakke, professor of ministry at Northern Baptist Theological Seminary, describes the inner city neighborhood in Chicago where he lives: "There are 233 nations in the world, and in my one-mile-square block in the middle of Chicago, 60 of those nations (25 percent) are represented. In May 1982 the *New York Times* survey of Chinatown found refugees from every province of mainland China—four blocks in the middle of New York City."[4]

It is possible to go to one-fourth of all the nations in the world without leaving Chicago! These statistics are repeated all over the country, yet Dr. Bakke goes on to say that we do not consider ministry to the inner city the same as going to the mission field in a foreign land:

> I described earlier how Corean and I and our two sons, Woody (four) and Brian (two) moved into a multi-racial, gang-turfed section of Chicago in 1965. Many Christians have reproached us for endangering the education, morals or even lives of our children and have regarded us as foolish . . . I have a missionary cousin who lives in Africa with three children, and they have puff-adders and cobras in the garden. Somehow that is heroic. We have cobras and pythons in Chicago, too, but they are youth gangs! They took no less getting used to, but the suburban church wasn't as willing to give us encouragement or emotional support.[5]

Bill Pannell, associate professor of evangelism at Fuller Theological Seminary, agrees that the church has not taken mission to the nations in the inner cities of America as seriously as those across the sea: "A Vietnamese would have a greater chance to meet an evangelical had he stayed home than he does by moving to the north side of Chicago."[6]

The first part of bringing the message of salvation to the inner city is to see the neighborhoods comprised of many nations as a legitimate mission field and heed God's call to go to those places and make disciples. Apply mission theory and praxis to the "hood."

We must recognize that a call to serve the poor is not the call God gives us. Rather, God's call will come in the form of a call to serve in a defined way, in a particular community. Dietrich Bonhoeffer was a German pastor in Nazi Germany. In his book, *The Cost of Discipleship*, he explains the soul searching he went through in making his decision to return to Germany in 1939 to certain death: "The road to faith passes through obedience to the call of Jesus. Unless a definite step is demanded, the call vanishes into thin air, and if men imagine that they can follow Jesus without taking this step, they are deluding themselves like fanatics."[7]

Evangelism

Jesus' ministry emphasized dealing with sin and the inner person. In Mark 2:1–5, a paralytic is brought to Jesus by four men. Being unable to wade through the crowd with their pallet, they went up to the top of the house, removed part of the roof, and lowered the bedridden man in front of Jesus. In spite of the fact that here was a man obviously in need of physical healing, Jesus' first words to him were: "Your sins are forgiven." Jesus saw beyond the visible infirmities and addressed the deeper need of forgiveness and spiritual healing.

Evangelism is at the heart of Christian community development:

> What separates Christian community development from other forms of social change is that we believe that changing a life or changing a community is ultimately a spiritual issue . . . I want to be clear that a ministry of Christian community development without evangelism is like a body without a soul. To be Christian, by definition, is to live and speak in such a way that our lives continually point to the wonderful person of Jesus Christ.[8]

Evangelism is proclaiming the good news of the gospel through Jesus Christ. The Holy Spirit alone can restore hope in the lives of people who have none. "May the God of hope fill you with all joy and peace as you trust in him, so that you may overflow with hope by the power of the Holy Spirit" (Rom. 15:13). We have agreed that poverty is in many instances a result of sinful or dysfunctional lifestyles. If we are going to bring about change in the inner city, there must be change in the hearts of people. Personal sin and immorality must be challenged and changed.

Social Action

When Jesus inaugurated his earthly ministry in Luke 4:18–19, he quoted from Isaiah 61. He defined his life-calling to preach the good news to the poor, the prisoners, the blind, the oppressed. This is evangelism from the bottom up:

> In a world where misery is the prevailing reality—especially among urban populations—our task is clear: to ask the Bible to speak to us from a vantage below, from the bottom up. *We must recover a biblical view of salvation from the bottom up rather than from the top down, as is now the prevailing model.* The task should not be all that diffi-

cult. The Bible was written in many situations of misery, deprivation and need.[9]

John Stott says that the truly Christian understanding of evangelism and social action is to view social action as "a partner of evangelism. As partners the two belong together and yet are independent of each other. Each stands on its own feet in its own right alongside the other."[10] Furthermore, the basis of the call to social action as part of the mission of the church is found not in the Great Commission, but rather in the Great Commandment.

> Here then are two instructions of Jesus—a great commandment "love your neighbor" and a great commission "go and make disciples." What is the relation between the two? Some of us behave as if we thought them identical, so that if we share the gospel with somebody, we consider we have completed our responsibility to love him. But no . . . God created man, who is my neighbor, a body-soul-in-community. Therefore, if we love our neighbor as God made him, we must inevitably be concerned for his total welfare, the good of his soul, his body and community.[11]

Evangelism brings us face to face with the physical needs of people as well as the spiritual needs. Social action means that we must be willing to use our resources to meet the people's need for food, clothing, housing, education, and so on.

Economic Development

The late Dr. Tom Skinner often said that if all of the money that passed through the hands of African Americans in the United States were considered as the gross national product of a country, the amount of money represented would make it one of the richest nations in the world in terms of financial resources. Economic development means simply helping those in the inner city manage their wealth so that the economic power remains in the community to build up the community. The dollar circulates one time in the inner city: from the hands of the residents, into the hands of the store owners who live outside the community. Many of those businesses do not even hire anyone from the community, thereby extracting the financial power from the community with no benefit to the community except providing goods for consumption.

As John Perkins says: "Economic development then becomes asset management. Asset management finally grows into developing an enterprise that you own. The challenge for Christian community-based economic development, then, is to enable the people of the community to start local enterprises that meet local needs and employ indigenous people."[12]

The strength of most CCD organizations is the development of people: spiritually, educationally, physically, providing housing, and so on. Our weakness is our lack of expertise in the area of economic development. If we are going to meet the needs of the inner city and reverse the decline that is all too evident across the country, then we have to come to grips with the need to provide an economic base. One place we can begin is through the partnership of Christian businessmen working alongside churches in the neighborhood, finding Christian businessmen and women to mentor those who have the potential for being business owners.

Justice

God is concerned about the structures that keep a person oppressed. We live in a society that has been given a political structure through authorities instituted by God, according to Romans 13. Speaking up for justice is the prophetic role of the church in calling those structures to account like the prophets of old.

John Stott says that dealing with the political structures is an indispensable part of following the Great Commandment:

Moreover, it is this vision of man as a social being, as well as a psychosomatic being, which obliges us to add a *political* dimension to our social concern. We should be concerned with preventive medicine or community health as well, which means the quest for better social structures in which peace, dignity, freedom, and justice are secured for all men. And there is no reason why, in pursuing this quest, we should not join hands with all men of good will, even if they are not Christians.[13]

Contrary to what some are currently saying, the government does have a biblical mandate to care for the poor and weak among its citizens, and world governments will be accountable for how well they have done this:

> God presides in the great assembly; he gives judgment among the "gods": "How long will you defend the unjust and show partiality to the wicked? Defend the cause of the weak and fatherless; maintain the rights of the poor and oppressed. Rescue the weak and needy; deliver them from the hand of the wicked . . ." Rise up, O God, judge the earth, for all the nations are your inheritance.
>
> Psalm 82:1–4, 8

It is important that the voice of believers be heard in those places of power where decisions are being made that will affect the life chances of those in the inner city. Many decisions are made everyday in city halls, governors' mansions, state legislatures, and the United States Congress that will have tremendous impact on the ministry we are called to do in the neighborhood. We need Christians there to be the voice of those who cannot speak for themselves. As John Stott says, this job is so big that we will need to join with whoever has a genuine concern for justice for the poor.

The Church

In the center of the wheel, stands the church. In Matthew 16, Jesus asked his disciples to fill him in on who people in the street were saying that he was. Then he asked them, "Who do you say that I am?" Peter answered "You are the Christ, the Son of the Living God." Jesus went on to give to Peter what I believe is the mark of whether or not we really believe that Jesus is the Christ, the Son of the Living God: "I will build my church, and the gates of hell shall not prevail against it." In this imagery, the church is on the move, and Satan is busy throwing up gates to keep his people in and the church out of his territory. All the while the marauding army of the church of Jesus Christ is trampling down every stronghold of Satan.

In too many cities in this nation, it appears to the casual observer that it is Satan who is on the move, and the church is throwing up gates, and fences, and burglar bars to keep their property safe and Satan out. When all else fails, the church abandons the inner city and gives it over to Satan. If we believe that we are part of this same church to whom Jesus gave the power to bind on earth whatsoever we desire, then we have to believe that as the church heeds the call of the Great Commission and the Great Commandment, those substantial strongholds already set up by Satan will have to fall. Maybe not today, maybe not this year; but fall they must!

In conclusion, it should be said that these principles of CCD are not the only way to bring the hope of the gospel to the poor in our inner cities. One does not *have* to relocate in order to help the poor, for example. We are saying that they are biblically based principles and that they are "time-tested" as John Perkins says in chapter 1. We are further saying that the question is not "Do I *have* to do it this way?" rather "How effective do you want to be?" That is, if an alternate method of involvement is chosen, it should be pursued because it is more effective than the three Rs, and not as a matter of personal comfort or individual preference. If the wheel of ministry does not adequately illustrate the concept of salvation, develop a better model.

Remember what Jesus says in Matthew 16:24–25: "If anyone would come after me, he must deny himself and take up his cross and follow me. For whoever wants to save his life will lose it, but whoever loses his life for me will find it." If you want to have "the good life," invest it in doing the hard work of the kingdom of God.

The Key Elements in a Theology of Christian Community Development

- The Christian community development approach to the problem of community development is based on "time-tested" biblical principles.
- Mankind's deepest needs are for a spiritual relationship with God. In Christian community development the local church is the most effective agent in bringing about that relationship.
- The biblical vision for Christian community development is for people to be in loving fellowship with God and with one

another as they toil in fruitful labor, which benefits their community of need. The family as a unit must be reinforced. Leadership for their needed common efforts comes from within their own community.

- The methodology of Christian community development—relocation, reconciliation, and redistribution—is merely a restatement, in man-made terms, of clear biblical principles.
- God's master plan of reconciliation is to bring all things in heaven and earth under one head. If the gospel is not concerned with reconciling us across the most stubborn ethnic and racial barriers, then it is no gospel at all.
- When viewed from the Bible, the Christian community development principle of redistribution has three parts to it: everything belongs to God; God said "there should be no poor among you," and provided law, which allowed the poor to reclaim their portion of his wealth; and God makes us wealthy so that we can reinvest in his work.
- The clearest example of the principle of relocation in the Bible is that of Christ's act of love for us in leaving heaven to come to earth and, once here, giving his life for us.
- The wheel of ministry provides a helpful model for understanding the biblical concept of salvation. The wheel's components are call, evangelism, social action, economic development, and justice, with the church at the center.

3

Understanding Poverty

Lowell Noble and Ronald Potter

Exploring Why the Poor Are Poor

Theories of poverty might helpfully be divided into two basic groups. One theory emphasizes the personal responsibility of those who are poor. Personal dysfunctions are blamed: lack of motivation, laziness, little education, poor family structure, or cultural values that no longer contain a sense of morality. The second theory blames society for poverty—the rich and powerful who control the political and economic institutions discriminate against or exploit the poor; the poor are created by and damaged by oppression.

Theory A: Society at fault	Theory B: Poor at fault
political and economic institutions	problem to society
↓	↑
discriminate and exploit	unqualified workers
↓	↑
culture of poverty	culture of poverty
↓	↑
damaged individuals	defective individuals

Much of the public dialogue is being controlled by persons staunchly in one camp or the other. Liberals and conservatives not only adhere to their preferred theory, but they also revile those in the opposite camp. Liberals would strongly support theory A, that society makes its own poor through systemic oppression. They label those in the other camp as mean-spirited and lacking compassion for the poor and oppressed. Any attempt by conservatives to speak of personal responsibility is dismissed as "blaming the victim" or an effort to try to force their personal values on others. Conservatives would be in favor of theory B, that the poor shape their own life situation. They would say that theory A is an ideological cover to avoid dealing with personal responsibility. Any discussion of justice and oppression is dismissed as socialism. If they refer at all to social dynamics, it is usually in a negative reference to the way that the welfare system has damaged individuals and families.

Yet out of the glare of TV cameras and away from the sound bites of the media, there seems to be a growing consensus at the grassroots level that our situation with regard to the poor in America is the result of personal and societal anomic conditions. While there would still be significant disagreement concerning *the extent* to which each comes into play in the ever growing problems in our inner cities, many agree that we must take a look at both the individual and his/her family, as well as the systemic pressures. Certainly those involved in Christian community development have experienced both sides of the issue.

Do those involved in CCD recognize that we have a crisis of individual and family values in our communities? Of course! Who has not been heartbroken at seeing girls as young as eleven and twelve years old having babies? Who has not wanted to grab these young women and the young men involved to wake them up to the damage they are causing? Haven't we worked hard renovating houses only to find that those we put in those houses won't pay their mortgage on time, if at all? Haven't we been asked to provide crisis assistance for rent, food, or utilities to poor women who have able-bodied adults living in the house who are not working and have no plans to be employed? You will surely encounter children for whom you develop a tutoring program only to discover that they are involved in a culture that actually believes that if you make good grades in school you are not cool. In some cases, they may even suffer personal injury for trying to "act White." You will likely experience the disappointment of investing months and even years into people only to find they cannot keep their commitments because of a drug or alcohol addiction.

We know that, especially in the Book of Proverbs, the Bible has much to say about how these kinds of personal choices and qualities will lead to poverty.

> Go to the ant, you sluggard; consider its ways and be wise! It has no commander, no overseer or ruler, yet it stores its provisions in summer and gathers its food at harvest. How long will you lie there, you sluggard? When will you get up from your sleep? A little sleep, a little slumber, a little folding of the hands to rest—and poverty will come on you like a bandit and scarcity like an armed man.

> Proverbs 6:6–11

> Lazy hands make a man poor, but diligent hands bring wealth.

> Proverbs 10:4

Paul makes it very clear in 2 Thessalonians 3:10: "For even when we were with you, we gave you this rule: 'If a man will not work, he shall not eat.'" Within the body of Christ, we should not reinforce laziness. We also know as Christians that when one violates the laws of God as they relate to personal holiness and purity, there will be consequences for the individual and society.

Since there is a crisis of individual responsibility, one has to ask the question: How did these people get this way? Were they born genetically inferior, or were they shaped this way through socialization? Most would agree that socialization shapes our character. Then we need to ask: Are there societal forces that conspire to shape certain people in certain ways, or that tend to limit their life opportunities? This same Book of Proverbs, which speaks so clearly about individual responsibility, also speaks to systemic causes of poverty: "A poor man's field may produce abundant food, but injustice sweeps it away" (Prov. 13:23). Throughout both the Old and New Testaments, Scripture has much to say about the rich and the poor and oppression.

Lawrence Richards brilliantly presents the two Old Testament perspectives on wealth. On the one hand, wealth is portrayed as a blessing from God. The person or the nation that obeys God and keeps the covenant relationship with God will be blessed by God. God says in Psalm 112 for example: "Wealth and riches are in his house, and his righteousness endures forever" (v. 3). Richards asserts that by "Jesus' time this theme had been interpreted to imply that riches were a clear sign of God's favor. A person who was rich was ipso facto righteous, one of God's blessed ones."[1]

When riches become a means of oppression, God's wrath is revealed. The Old Testament warns again and again against oppressing the poor in order to gain wealth. Amos, for example, thunders against the misuse of riches: "They sell the righteous for silver, and the needy for a pair of sandals. They trample on the heads of the poor . . . and deny justice to the oppressed" (Amos 2:6–7).

Not only will God destroy idolatrous altars, but also the idolatrous houses of the rich: "I will tear down the winter house along with the summer house; the houses adorned with ivory will be destroyed and the mansions will be demolished" (Amos 3:15).

Judgment will fall on the rich "women who oppress the poor and crush the needy . . ." (Amos 4:1). "You trample on the poor. . . . You oppress the righteous and take bribes and you deprive the poor of justice in the courts" (Amos 5:11–12).

The question then remains: What are some of the societal dynamics that may lead to systemic oppression and thereby aggravate, or, depending on your theoretical viewpoint, cause individual irresponsibility?

Consider the following statistics (based on 1980s data and the 1990 census):

1. In 1989, 12.8 percent of the United States population or 31.5 million persons lived in poverty according to the Social Security Administration's official poverty line. For a nonfarm family of four the poverty line was $12,675.
2. In 1989, 30 percent of African Americans, 26.2 of Latinos, and 10.1 percent of Whites were poor. The median family income for African Americans was $18,083, for Whites, $30,406.
3. Two out of three impoverished adults are women.

4. Of those in poverty, 40 percent are children. Of children under six, 17 percent of White children, 45 percent of Latino, and 50 percent of African American children are poor.
5. Poor-poor are defined as those who live at one half of the poverty line. Twelve million persons are poor-poor; 41 percent are children. Since 1979 that category of poor-poor has increased by 45 percent.

It seems clear from the above that minorities, especially the African American communities, are disproportionately represented in the categories of poverty and underrepresented in the wealth categories. We all know that racism has been a fact of American life, and few would argue that it has not had a historical effect on the Black community economically. Many would hasten to add, that although the more overt forms of racism have been addressed, the effects have been ingrained in the system.

For example, John Perkins relates an early encounter with a family caught in a cycle of poverty in his book *A Quiet Revolution*. John met Hester Evans and her ten children who were barely surviving. They were tearing wood off the outside of their house to cook with, even though that would obviously make the house colder in the winter. John and a church tried to help Miss Hester with some charity, but it didn't seem to change anything. Finally, "many of the people in the community quit trying to be charitable. They began to blame Miss Hester for her own problems."

How devastating; how damaging was Miss Hester's situation. Dr. Perkins elaborates: "For Miss Hester and many folks like her, poverty had moved beyond her physical condition to claim her whole mind. For the real poor, poverty means thinking for the moment. It is the inability to think about the future because of the total demand to think about survival in the present. . . . A little money can't help much."

Dr. Perkins explains that often poverty is passed on from one generation to the next. Miss Hester's daughter lived in a two-room shack with her six children who showed signs of malnutrition. There were rats in the house; in the winter a fire in the garbage can provided heat. He recalls:

I remember that when we used to try to make houses out of playing cards, stacking and balancing just right, the least wrong movement or puff of wind or a cough and they'd fall. And for the masses of black people in Mississippi, life is being lived in a house of cards. All the things that give structure to life—education, employment, income, health, housing, leadership, transportation, and nutrition—are for the most part flimsy excuses for survival, built upon and against each other, so that when one falls they all fall, and are rebuilt only to fall again. . . . We began to see that poverty surrounded them, reached into every structure of their lives, and affected the complete psychology of a whole community.[2]

Many people would stop their analysis of poverty here at the community cycle of poverty level. But Dr. Perkins asserts that we must probe further, push our analysis of the causes of poverty to another level—the societal level of cultural values and social institutions. Why has this human disaster occurred? Sin, social evil, and social oppression pervade our cultural values and social institutions. Perkins states:

First, I began to see plainly how sin had organized itself into structures and institutions of inequality and oppression. Seeing the people and looking at the statistics, the terrible poverty of my people had to be something more than happenstance. To have a victim there must be a victimizer. To have someone who is oppressed, there must be an oppressor.

I became acutely aware . . . that the roots of poverty were in the system itself, growing out of the very culture and traditions and history of the South and America. Paul's words came alive to me: "We are not contending against flesh and blood, but against the principalities, against the powers, against the world rulers of this present darkness, against the spiritual hosts of wickedness in the heavenly places" (Eph. 6:12).

I could see how racism and violence in individuals with power could work their way through the basic institutions of society, and then how self-interest, especially economic self-interest, had led white people in Mississippi to develop structures to control the system and then to justify the enslavement of black people . . . there was such an airtight system of values and traditions reinforcing the system that not only was there no change, there was also no questioning. The effect of the closed society upon black people was to turn them into niggers, a people of dependence and submission.[3]

Twenty years ago when Dr. Perkins wrote these words, to be Black in Mississippi meant by and large to be poor. The life opportunities of a person were limited simply by the color of his or her skin. Racism had been ingrained in the economic system.

In the ensuing years, millions of people have been convicted by the injustice of this scenario, and through the efforts of many compassionate people, the situation has improved in the Black community at large:

- From 1968 to 1987 the number of Black elected officials nationwide increased 600 percent.
- From 1968 to 1985 the percentage of African Americans who graduated from high school doubled, the number who graduated from college increased from 4 to 11 percent.
- Young, educated, married African Americans have nearly reached economic parity with European American couples.

In the 1990s limitations on one's life chances are still affected by the economic system, but the issue is no longer only race, it is also class. One of the more salient features of the urban crisis is class stratification within African American communities. Many Black social theorists and activists either minimize significant class divisions within African American communities or they outright deny the very notion of "social class" as applied to African American reality. These persons contend that White racism has marginalized all Black Americans regardless of socioeconomic standing.

Notwithstanding this conventional interpretation of Black social reality, class stratification within urban Black America is an empirical reality.

Blacks can be divided into three rough groups. One-third are middle and upper class with household incomes above $25,000. One-third of households have incomes ranging from $10,000 to $25,000; this group would include working poor, working class, and lower to medium middle class. One-third have an annual income of less than $10,000, the so-called underclass, a population of about 8 million. The official poverty figure in 1992 was $14,000 for an urban family of four.

While the Black professional class continues to make slow but steady progress, the working poor and the newly emergent "under-class" are on the brink of social death. Indeed, the social plight of the truly disadvantaged appears to be explained less by overt racial discrimination than by the changing shape of current economic trends. Noted African American sociologist William Julius Wilson says we must not fail "to distinguish between the past and present effects of racism on the lives of different segments of the Black population."[4] He goes on to say:

> More specifically, it is not readily apparent how the deepening economic class divisions between the haves and the have-nots in the black community can be accounted for . . . especially when it is argued that this same racism is directed with equal force across class boundaries in the black community. Nor is it apparent how racism can result in a more rapid social and economic deterioration in the inner city in the post-civil rights period than in the period that immediately preceded the notable civil rights victories.[5]

This analysis should not suggest that White racism has somehow ceased. Given the resurgence of right wing "nativist" social movements within this country and in Europe, such a claim would certainly be ludicrous. We are suggesting simply that the impediments to Black social progress within modern America are no longer predicated exclusively upon racism.

Class stratification within the African American community is inextricably tied to a changing economic landscape. As a result of the changes occurring within the society, we have shifted from goods-producing to information-producing industries—that is, industries that are predicated upon theoretical knowledge and technical skills. Much of the American working class today is concentrated in various information occupations. The vast majority of workers involved within this sector are engaged in the creation, processing, and distribution of information. Today, more than 65 percent of the American workforce serve as computer programmers, accountants, bank tellers, insurance people, real estate agents, police dispatchers, etc. All of these occupations are predicated upon the acquisition and utilization of postindustrial skills and knowledge.

Twenty years ago, sociologist Daniel Bell wrote the following regarding postindustrial society: "Differential status and differential income are based on technical skills and higher education. Without those achievements one cannot fulfill the requirements of the new social division of labor which is a feature of that society. And there are few high places open without those skills."[6]

It is important to reiterate that entry into the new white-collar working class, not to mention entry into the new elite professional class (which is comprised primarily of scientists, systems analysts, doctors, lawyers, engineers, and corporate managers), requires mastery of a new stock of knowledge. Needless to say, large numbers of African Americans lack the theoretical knowledge and technical skills needed to insure their meaningful participation in the emerging social order. Black American young adults in particular are increasingly vulnerable to the onslaughts of postindustrial society. The public school system, for example, has ill-equipped many urban youth to survive in the modern world. Social forecaster John Naisbitt states in this regard: "Just when offices are demanding more highly skilled workers—to operate a word processing machine, for example—what they are getting is graduates who would have a hard time qualifying for jobs that are already technologically obsolete."[7]

Pastor and social critic Eugene Rivers is even more emphatic when he states: "As entry into labor markets is increasingly dependent on education and high skills, we will see, perhaps for the first time in the history of the United States, a generation of economically obsolete Americans . . . a 'new jack' generation, ill-equipped to secure gainful employment even as productive slaves."[8]

The African American underclass, a substratum of the Black lower class, is undoubtedly the most disadvantaged segment of the Black populace. This section is affected by intergenerational social deprivation. This social malady is characterized by substandard education, chronic unemployment, inadequate housing and health care, and almost total political powerlessness.

One of the particularly ominous features of underclass existence is social isolation. With few exceptions, African American communities, until quite recently, were heterogeneous in nature. That is, white- and blue-collar middle-class families as well as the working poor lived in the same neighborhoods. These Black social classes shopped in the same stores, attended the same schools, and worshiped in the same churches. Over the last fifteen to twenty years, however, middle-class Black professionals, as well as stable working-class families, have left the inner cities in droves. This exodus from the inner cities by upwardly mobile Black social classes has resulted in a state of social isolation for the underclass. In such a situation, Black youth in particular are deprived of positive role models. To be sure, without the stabilizing presence of middle-class professionals and skilled working-class families, African American inner cities become increasingly vulnerable to debilitating socioeconomic conditions.

Usually accompanying the structural manifestations of intergenerational deprivation are various social pathologies. Violent crime, illegal drug trafficking and addiction, juvenile out-of-wedlock births, and destructive street corner lifestyles all typify a condition of social alienation, resulting in social instability as a consequence of the breakdown of ethical norms and moral values.

Not only is the underclass being socially isolated, they are also being concentrated in ever increasing numbers in the poorest areas of the nation's cities. Wilson reveals, for example, that in the five largest cities in the United States:

> Although the total population in these five largest cities decreased by 9 percent between 1970 and 1980, the poverty population increased by 22 percent. Furthermore, the population living in poverty areas grew by 40 percent overall, by 69 percent in high-poverty areas—i.e., areas with a poverty rate of at least 30 percent—and by a staggering 161 percent in extreme-poverty areas—i.e., areas with a poverty rate of at least 40 percent. It should be emphasized that these incredible changes took place within just a 10-year period.[9]

Exodus of positive role models, increased alienation from the norms of society, and growing concentration of the poorest of our citizens in the worst areas of the inner city all add up to an emergent urban ethos that has been described variously as a "crisis of the Black spirit" and "nihilism in Black America."[10] Eugene Rivers elaborates further on this moral quandary within Black urban America. He writes:

Consider this achievement: a generation of poor black women and children may reach the end of this century in an . . . inferior position to their ancestors, who entered the century in the shadow of formal slavery. Unable to see a more rational future through the eyes of faith, they lack the hope that sustained their forbearers. Lacking hope they experience . . . "social death." But unlike the social death of formal slavery, this new social death is fundamentally spiritual, rooted in the destruction of faith and hope. In a world without faith and hope, history and identity are themselves divested of meaning. And so, . . . their future is transformed into a spectacle of nihilism and decay. It is, in the end, this profoundly spiritual nature of the current crisis that gives it its unique historical character.[11]

Hope for the City

The church of Jesus Christ is no stranger to the hopelessness of the inner city. Bill Pannell says:

> The Bible does not simply convey the story of a rural and pastoral life for God's people. Human beings may have begun in a garden, but human history began in a city. . . . The culmination of history is the descent of the city of God from heaven. . . . A prophet may be recruited while plowing, but he most certainly will deliver his message in the capital city. That's where the politicians and princes are. That's where the buttons, the levers, and the strings are that control the destinies of people in rural parts.[12]

The apostle Paul was no stranger to the hope-killing "social death" of the inner city. When he writes a letter to Christians in the leading city of his day, Rome, things are not looking good for the people of God. Politically, Nero, one of the most brutal of the Roman emperors, is on the throne. Christians are being subjected to the cruelest punishments the human mind can imagine. Poverty and crime are rampant: one can hardly walk down the Via Appia without being solicited, propositioned, or mugged. Yet Paul writes of hope: "Against all hope, Abraham in hope believed and so became the father of many nations . . . he did not waver through unbelief regarding the promise of God, but was strengthened in his faith and gave glory to

God, being fully persuaded that God had power to do what he had promised" (Rom. 4:18, 20–21).

We have hope because we know hundreds of churches and organizations that are using the principles in this book to make a difference in inner city neighborhoods all over this country. But our hope rests ultimately on the power of God and his love for those in the city. A generation that has lost faith and hope, that has given in to nihilism and despair, should spur the church on to bring the gospel of hope to the inner city. As John Perkins says in *Beyond Charity:*

> Our nation's cities are in a crisis. But in every crisis there is opportunity. I believe that this crisis is an opportunity for us, the church, to step forward and lead the way in restoring the inner city by bringing the physical presence of God into the city. I believe that the church has the opportunity to pioneer and model a way of life whereby our nation itself can experience a new birth.[13]

The only question is: Will the church take up the challenge?

The Key Elements Regarding Poverty

- There are two seemingly conflicting theories about the causes of poverty. One blames a society that exploits and discriminates against the poor; the other claims that the poor themselves are to blame for their own plight. Those in Christian community development have experienced both sides of the issue. One cannot wholly blame society and completely disregard personal responsibility issues. Nor can one disregard the part society plays in the problem and only fault individual values.

- In a variety of verses and chapters, the Bible supports both viewpoints. Bad personal choices can lead to poverty. However, sometimes injustice sweeps even those who make good personal choices into poverty.

- Examination of United States Census data shows that minorities, especially African Americans, are disproportionately over-represented in most poverty categories and are underrepresented in the wealth categories.

- In the 1990s, limitations on one's life chances are still affected by the economic system, but the issue is no longer only race, it is also class. Class stratification for the urban Black American is an empirical reality.

- Entrance into the new white-collar working class requires mastery of a new stock of knowledge. Unfortunately, youth emerging from urban public schools are ill-equipped even to qualify for jobs that are already obsolete.

- With the move from inner-city neighborhoods by middle-class Blacks and Whites and the corresponding loss of role models, the African American underclass exists in social isolation, which engenders violent crime and other serious social ills.

- The dire situation in the inner city is an opportunity for the church to proclaim the hope of the gospel to stimulate a revival in America.

4

The Character of a Developer

Do You Have What It Takes to Be a Leader?

John M. Perkins

U nderclass."
For those of us who marched, demonstrated, and risked our lives to move up from "second-class," that word, coined by sociologists to describe the most desperate and hopeless urban poor, leaves a bitter taste in the mouth.

Many bad seeds have grown into the bitter fruit that is all too plentiful in our neglected urban areas: government dependency; the legacy of racism; moral and spiritual decay, of which drugs, crime, and violence are symptoms; and, of course, disintegration of the family. All these things have contributed greatly to our urban problems.

But yet another bad seed sprang up from the very success of our struggle for freedom.

The success of the civil rights movement meant we no longer had to ride in the back of the bus. Success meant no longer attending inferior segregated schools. After the Fair Housing Act passed in 1968, success also came to mean we could live in whatever neighborhood we could afford. Some of us had a new option now, and we seized it!

Many of our best-trained minds—our moral, spiritual, and social leaders; the professionals; college and school teachers; and other upwardly mobile people previously forced to live in all-Black neighborhoods, where maids and business owners alike lived on the same street—could now move up and out in search of a better life.

These leaders were the stabilizing glue that held our communities together. The exodus of their families, their skills, and their daily civic and moral leadership hastened the unraveling of the inner city, leaving a vacuum of leadership.

Our task today is to restore that stabilizing glue.

Refilling the leadership vacuum of our urban areas will require committed, quality, unselfish leadership at the grassroots level: individuals who see the problem clearly, nurture a vision for solving it, and willingly make personal sacrifices.

Leadership Qualities

A leader realizes she cannot solve problems alone, and her passion sparks the energy of others. A leader disciplines herself to remain committed and focused over the long haul even when tempted by personal gain or by the inevitable distraction of personal pleasure.

Do you have what it takes to be a leader?

Courage

History is colored with examples of men and women of character who filled the leadership vacuum of their day, and, by their courage and personal sacrifice, sparked the energy and courage of others.

As a young boy, Booker T. Washington realized for the first time that he was a slave when he heard his mother praying on the dirt floor of their shack that her little Booker T. would not grow up a slave. Today, Tuskegee Institute stands as a testament to his intense commitment to lead his people up from slavery.

Leadership is the courage and conviction of an escaped slave named Harriet Tubman. She was not content with her own individual freedom. She took personal responsibility for the freedom of others by going back into the dangerous South many times to lead more than three hundred other slaves to freedom.

Leadership is the righteous indignation of Rosa Parks, who decided she had taken enough and refused to give up her seat to a White man. Her bravery catapulted a young Baptist preacher by the name of Martin Luther King Jr., in Montgomery, Alabama, into the leadership of the greatest nonviolent movement in the history of our country.

Leadership was Abraham Lincoln's determination to keep this country from splitting apart and his passion to rid it of slavery forever. His resolve to do both was burned into our memory forever in a brief two minutes at Gettysburg: ". . . a new nation, conceived in Liberty, dedicated to the proposition that all men are created equal . . . and that government of the people, by the people, for the people shall not perish from the earth."

Today leadership can be seen in Nelson Mandela's remaining in prison for twenty-eight years, refusing to compromise his principles and thus inspiring his people to continue their struggle for freedom against a brutal apartheid government. Leadership is Benito Aquino's resolve to go back to the Philippines even if it cost his life, only to be gunned down when he stepped off the plane; and Aquino's grieving widow, insecure in her own leadership but picking up the mantle of her slain husband and leading her country to democracy.

Each of these leaders saw the essence of his or her historical situation, took personal responsibility, and made the sacrifice necessary for a solution.

Commitment

As we look at our beleaguered urban communities, what actions of bravery and courage are required of us today? Are we willing to go to the problem level and fill the leadership vacuum trapping hopeless youths and broken families in its void? We cannot discount the importance of our physical presence in deteriorating communities.

I returned to rural Mendenhall, Mississippi, from California in 1960 and saw the many problems my neighborhood faced. I said to my wife, Vera Mae, as we watched what was happening to our young people in the community, "If we are going to make a difference in this little town, we must help these young people get a love for God, a love for themselves, and a love for their community—a love that is greater than selfish materialism. We must help them stay in school and go to college to get skills and education with a purpose. Then we must encourage those young people to bring those skills back to the community."

Twelve years later, Dolphus and Rosie Weary, Artis and Carolyn Fletcher, and other young people began to come back to that neighborhood. Their fresh leadership allowed Vera Mae and me to move on to Mississippi's capital city of Jackson. There we continued our work for ten years.

After leadership was raised in Jackson, we moved to Northwest Pasadena, California. We've been here thirteen years and leadership has emerged again, influencers who live and take responsibility where it is needed most.

The Christian Community Development Association is made up of hundreds of brave leaders who see the importance of living and taking leadership at the grassroots level. These leaders understand that the problems we are facing, especially in our urban communities, call us to go above and beyond the call of duty. As we move to take creative action, our sacrifice can spark the rest of society to follow our lead in applying solutions.

If you can see the problem clearly, if that vision creates a passion in you for resolving the problem, and if you are willing to make a personal sacrifice in order to get the job done, then maybe you have what it takes to be a leader.

Nehemiah: A Model Leader

Nehemiah offers us an excellent model of biblical leadership. Nehemiah was a businessman, an administrator, not a prophet or a priest. He was a Christian community developer; with his leadership, his people rebuilt the wall of Jerusalem. I believe Nehemiah is a model of the kind of leaders America needs today to rebuild our broken society, to bring healing to a nation sick with sin and immorality.

Nehemiah was a cupbearer for King Artaxerxes. When a group of Jews visited the capital of Persia, Nehemiah asked them how his people back home were doing. Nehemiah tells his own story:

Now it happened . . . while I was in Susa the capitol, that Hanani, one of my brothers, and some men from Judah came; and I asked them concerning the Jews who had escaped and had survived the captivity, and about Jerusalem. And they said to me, "The remnant there in the province who survived the captivity are in great distress and reproach, and the wall of Jerusalem is broken down and its gates are burned with fire."

Now it came about when I heard these words, I sat down and wept and mourned for days; and I was fasting and praying before the God of heaven. And I said, "I beseech Thee, O LORD God of heaven, the great and awesome God, who preserves the covenant and lovingkindness for those who love Him and keep His commandments, let Thine ear now be attentive and Thine eyes open to hear the prayer of Thy servant which I am praying before Thee now, day and night, on behalf of the sons of Israel Thy servants, confessing the sins of the sons of Israel which we have sinned against Thee . . .

"We have acted very corruptly against Thee and have not kept the commandments, nor the statutes, nor the ordinances which Thou didst command Thy servant Moses, . . . saying, 'If you are unfaithful I will scatter you among the peoples; but if you return to Me and keep My commandments and do them, though those of you who have been scattered were in the most remote part of the heavens, I will gather them from there and will bring them to the place where I have chosen to cause My name to dwell.'

"And they are Thy servants and Thy people whom Thou didst redeem by Thy great power and by Thy strong hand.

"O Lord, I beseech Thee, may Thine ear be attentive to the prayer of Thy servant and the prayer of Thy servants who delight to revere Thy name, and make Thy servant successful today, and grant him compassion before this man."

Nehemiah 1:1–11 NASB

When Nehemiah heard of the plight of his people he wept and mourned for days. But his response didn't end with mourning. He let God dream in him. Then, with the full cooperation of his people, he acted on that vision and it was made reality. The wall was rebuilt.

From this passage we can discern ten principles that guided Nehemiah's response to the need of his people.

1. *Nehemiah prayed before he acted.* It was not until four months after he heard about the condition of Jerusalem that Nehemiah presented his plan of action to the king. During those four months Nehemiah prayed and fasted on behalf of his people. And it was during those four months that God dreamed a dream in him. A God-inspired plan began to take shape. A vision grew.

   The foundation of all that was to follow was laid during those days of prayer. Prayer equips us for action. Many of us tend to eagerly run out to take on the world's needs without first consulting with the one who can meet those needs. We march off to war before we get our orders. We cannot be effective in God's work unless we first get our directions from God.

   Though prayer equips us for action, it is never a substitute for action. Some people respond to needs by praying and praying and praying, then walk off without ever once asking God how he can use them as part of the answer. Prayer, to be effective, must include a readiness to act. Nehemiah's prayer included that readiness. Nehemiah struck a healthy balance between prayer and action.

2. *Nehemiah sensed God's timing.* "And it came about in the month of Nisan, in the twentieth year of King Artaxerxes, that wine was before him, and I took up the wine and gave it to the king. Now I had not been sad in his presence. So the king said to me, 'Why is your face sad though you are not sick? This is nothing but sadness of heart'" (Neh. 2:1–2 NASB).

Remember now, Nehemiah heard about the need four months earlier. During those four months he had many opportunities to talk to the king, but he waited for God to clearly indicate the proper time. When the time finally came, Nehemiah didn't delay; he acted.

3. *Nehemiah counted the cost.* "Then I was very much afraid," Nehemiah said (2:2). Yet he still presented his plan to the king. Why was Nehemiah afraid? Because a servant did not have the right to be sad in the king's presence. The king's attendants were always to be happy and jovial.

About fifty years earlier, Esther needed to make a request of the king on behalf of her people. She determined, "I will go in to the king, which is not according to the law; and if I perish, I perish" (Esther 4:16 NASB). Just as Esther faced a life or death situation, so did Nehemiah. He knew that.

But Nehemiah was afraid for yet another reason. Years before, some people had returned from Persia to Jerusalem to rebuild the temple and the wall, and they had faced opposition. Their opponents had charged that if Jerusalem was rebuilt, the king of Persia would lose control over that territory. So the king had issued a decree: "Make these men stop work, that the city may not be rebuilt until a decree is issued by me" (Ezra 4:21 NASB).

Nehemiah counted the cost. He knew he was not to look sad in the king's presence; that to make his request to the king was to risk his life; and that the king had issued a decree forbidding the very thing he was going to request. But having counted the cost, and in spite of his fear, Nehemiah did what he had to do.

4. *Nehemiah did his homework.* "Let the king live forever," Nehemiah began. "Why should my face not be sad when the city, the place of my fathers' tombs, lies desolate and its gates have been consumed by fire?" (Neh. 2:3 NASB).

Nehemiah knew that it was part of the religious tradition of Persian kings to worship their ancestors. So he made his appeal in the manner that was most likely to win the king's sympathy. Nehemiah never mentioned the name Jerusalem. He never brought up the political situation.

Before Nehemiah ever made his request he planned carefully: he charted his route, he knew what letters of permission he would need for safe passage through other provinces, and he knew what materials he would need to build the wall (see vv. 7–8). Nehemiah did his homework.

5. *Nehemiah recognized God's control.* "Then the king said to me, 'What would you request?' So I prayed to the God of heaven" (v. 4 NASB). After four months of prayer the moment of truth came and Nehemiah shot off a prayer to God. He was depending totally on God.

After Nehemiah made his requests to the king, he reported, "The king granted them to me because the good hand of my God was on me" (v. 8 NASB). He saw the cause and effect relationship. He depended on the God who was in control.

6. *Nehemiah identified with his people.* Nehemiah had worked his way up into the system as high as a Jew could go. He saw the king every day, but he never lost concern for his people.

When his brothers came from Judah he asked, "How are things in Jerusalem?"

They answered, "Things are tough in Jerusalem. The people are in distress. The wall is broken down and its gates are burned."

Nehemiah didn't ask, "What kind of poverty program can I set up?" He didn't ask the king to send a construction crew. He said, "Send me."

In verse 17, Nehemiah said to the people, "You see the bad situation *we* are in." He didn't say you; he said *we*. "Come, let us rebuild the wall of Jerusalem that *we* may no longer be a reproach" (NASB, emphasis mine). Nehemiah identified with his people. He relocated among them to serve them. "I also applied myself to the work on this wall," Nehemiah reported later (5:16). He didn't just supervise. He worked along with all the rest. Nehemiah didn't go to do the work *for* the people. Nor did he go just to give advice or supervision. He went to do it *with* the people.

7. *Nehemiah tested his plan.* Nehemiah went to Jerusalem. After three days he went out at night with a few men to inspect the wall. He circled the city from east to west, picking through the rubble. The rubble got so bad that Nehemiah's donkey couldn't go any further, so he got off and walked (2:11–15).

What was Nehemiah doing? He was rechecking his plans to see if they matched the real situation. He couldn't do this until he relocated. Testing plans against the real situation can only occur *in* the community of need.

8. *Nehemiah sought God's continued direction.* "I arose in the night, I and a few men with me. I did not tell anyone what my God was putting into my mind to do for Jerusalem" (v. 12 NASB).

Though God had been dreaming in Nehemiah for four months, the plan was not yet complete. Nehemiah went ahead and took the first step—he relocated. Once in Jerusalem he sought God's further direction. God was putting a plan into his mind, but it was only as he checked his general plan against reality that the details of God's plan became clear.

We are sometimes tempted to wait until we have a complete road map before we take the first step. However, that is not how God works. It was only after Nehemiah committed himself to the project, only after he was on the scene, that God's plan was fully revealed to him.

9. *Nehemiah inspired a spirit of cooperation.* "You see the bad situation we are in," Nehemiah said. "Come, let us rebuild the wall of Jerusalem that we may no longer be a reproach" (v. 17 NASB). Then Nehemiah told the people how God had enabled him to return and what the king had said. "Then they said, 'Let us arise and build.' So they put their hands to good work" (v. 18 NASB). Nehemiah focused the attention of the people not on himself, not on the king, but on God and on the task at hand. On that basis Nehemiah recruited the cooperation of the people.

Nehemiah 3 lists forty-two groups of people who are building the wall. Priests and Levites, governors and nobles, men and women, young and old, worked shoulder to shoulder, side by side, to complete the task. Men came from Jericho forty miles away to help. Nehemiah's ability to recruit the support of all these people is a powerful example of reconciliation.

10. *Nehemiah refused to let his enemies distract him.* The Jews faced constant and strong opposition throughout the entire project, yet Nehemiah pressed on with the work single-mindedly. "The God of heaven will give us success; therefore we His servants will arise and build," Nehemiah answered his opponents (2:20 NASB).

Though the threats were strong, God had given them a task to do. Nehemiah kept the eyes of the people on the task rather than on the threats of their enemies. And so the wall was completed.

I believe that America's "wall"—particularly in our ghettos, in Appalachia, and in other poor rural areas—lies in ruins today. Our prisons are full and no matter how many new ones we build, they will never be enough unless more of us take personal responsibility, put our lives on the line, and apply creative leadership to the places that need it most.

Where are our Nehemiahs who will let God dream his dreams in them? Who will sense God's timing and act neither too early nor too late? Where are our Nehemiahs who will give up the comforts of the king's court to live among their oppressed brothers and sisters, to share in their sufferings, to work together with them to bring justice to the land? Where are our Nehemiahs who will act though the future is uncertain, who will test their plans against reality in the community of need, and who will let God direct their work even as they proceed?

Where are those Nehemiahs among us who will focus the attention of the people on God's power and promise and thus inspire a spirit of wholehearted cooperation? Who will not let their enemies, however ominous their threats, distract them from the task, because God has called them to do it?

I believe that throughout our nation and around the world there are men and women whom God is calling to just such a task: young lawyers and doctors; experienced nurses and educators; trained secretaries and journalists; students and time-tested retirees—people, whatever their gifts, whatever their skills, who are willing to be servants. "The harvest is plentiful, but the workers are few. Ask the Lord of the harvest, therefore, to send out workers into his harvest field" (Luke 10:2).

I challenge you to join us in praying for workers for the harvest. And as you pray, do not let your prayer be a substitute for action; rather, pray "Lord, what would you have me to do?"

My fondest dream for my country is that God would raise up an army of Nehemiahs who would relocate in every community of need throughout the land, live out the gospel that gives hope to the hopeless, restore the moral fibers to our broken communities, and bring liberty and justice. God can heal our land! But we have to be willing to let him use us. There is a lot of work to do. Let's get busy!

The Key Elements of Leadership

- Leaders are the stabilizing glue that holds communities together.
- Refilling the leadership vacuum of communities of need will require unselfish leadership at the grassroots level.
- Leaders see the essence of their historical situation, take personal responsibility, go to the problem level, and make the sacrifice necessary for a solution.
- Sparked by Nehemiah's leadership, his people rebuilt the broken wall of Jerusalem. Nehemiah exemplifies key qualities needed by a Christian community developer:

  1. Pray before you act. Many leaders eagerly take on the world's needs without first consulting the one who can meet those needs.
  2. Sense God's timing.
  3. Count the cost. You will face many trials and roadblocks to success.

4. Do your homework.
5. Recognize God's control. Depend totally on God.
6. Identify with the people of the community and work along with them; don't just give advice or supervise. Don't work *for* the people; work *with* the people.
7. Test your plan. See if your plan matches the real situation. Be ready to adjust if necessary.
8. Seek God's continued direction. Don't wait until you have a complete road map before taking the first steps. Some steps won't be clear until after you begin to follow where God leads.
9. Inspire a spirit of cooperation. Focus the attention of the people not on yourself, or on the opposition, but on God and the task at hand.
10. Refuse to let enemies distract you.

Part 2
Strategy of Christian Community Development

*T*hree chapters describe in detail each of the "three Rs"— the daily strategies necessary to enable Christian community development. Each strategy is powerful in its own right, but true Christian community development cannot occur without all three.

5

Relocation

Living in the Community

Bob and Peggy Lupton and Gloria Yancy

Bob Lupton

Relocation—A Growing Trend

Of the three Rs that anchor the guiding philosophy of the Christian community development movement, relocation is clearly the
most distinctive and troublesome. The very thought of returning to
a poverty environment, which has taken years of diligent effort to
escape, can stir up deep emotional responses. It challenges our self-
protective instincts to the core. For those who have never lived in a
low-income setting, the fear of the unknown may be great. But for
those who have grown up in this world and managed to escape, the
thought of returning may seem absurd!

And yet, there is a growing consensus among committed urban
practitioners that being a vested member of the community one is
called to serve is an important key to effectiveness. What may seem

to some like a very radical position is in fact proving to be the most practical approach to effective ministry in disadvantaged neighborhoods. Thus, relocation has become one of the "non-negotiables" of the Christian Community Development Association.

Effects of the Urban Exodus

Over the last four decades the cities of our nation have experienced a mass migration to the suburbs. There were many reasons behind this exodus—improved mass transportation, fair housing legislation, and the shopping mall phenomenon, to name a few. As the American dream suburbanized, city neighborhoods that were once close, economically viable communities turned into ghettos almost overnight. As homeowners left, real estate values plummeted and properties quickly deteriorated. As educated families moved out, the quality of education declined. As the spiritual and moral leadership withdrew, the churches soon followed. Thriving business districts eventually boarded up as merchants pursued new opportunities in the "edge cities" that sprouted up on the periphery of the city limits. In the end, nearly everyone who had the capacity moved out of the heart of the city, leaving behind the vulnerable and the desperate to fill the vacuum created by the exodus.

For more than forty years we have been trying to solve this problem of urban blight with very little success. We have employed some of our most creative social policy thinkers and designed a plethora of programs to remedy the ills created by the unraveling. Huge sums of public, private, and religious dollars have been spent. Enormous amounts of time and energy from very committed people have been invested to reverse the devastating trend. While the best of these programs can claim a measure of success, their success is almost always paradoxically measured in the number of individuals they "empowered" to escape the inner city. The net effect, of course, is that these well-intentioned programs have facilitated the hemorrhage of leadership out of the very places it was most needed. Consequently, our urban neighborhoods are in far worse shape than they were four decades ago when the parade of programs began.

Lowell Noble and Ron Potter have documented this decline clearly in chapter 3, "Understanding Poverty."

Missing Theologies

During the decades of unraveling, there was little discussion in the church about the potential downside of out-migration. There was so much excitement (and some fear) about the historic opportunities for fair housing legislation and equal education that little attention was given to the consequences of leaving urban communities. The American dream became the practical theology of the people of faith and upward mobility became the sign of God's blessing upon the faithful.

Little thought was given to a theology of community that provided the framework for Christians to live interdependently rather than independently. Nor was a theology of neighbor part of the Christian dialogue during this period. *Neighbor* became a word so broadly used to describe any and every human relationship that it lost its meaning. And when *neighbor* was neutralized, it no longer specifically included the people who live next door. Thus, loving one's neighbor lost its practical impact in everyday living. Christians could move away from each other to pursue individualistic interests with little concern for those being left behind.

Also lost was a theology of place that raised the issue of the deployment of God's people. Without such a theology, the people of faith begin to drift toward places of personal convenience and comfort with little reflection on the strategic kingdom importance of where godly neighbors are located. I remember when it first dawned on me that something was wrong with this theological picture.

"Bloom where you are planted," the preacher challenged us one Sunday morning.

It was an important sermon emphasizing the need for Christians to be salt and light in their everyday environments—in the home, the workplace, the neighborhood. I had heard similar messages before and had been moved by them.

This time, however, I felt more troubled than motivated. Something the minister was saying—or maybe *not* saying—was making me uneasy. "*. . . where you are planted.*" An assumption was being made that God, fate, heredity, or something other than personal choice had placed us where we were living. Glancing around the congregation, I began to wonder by what coincidence most of my successful friends owned homes where they did—on the affluent north side of the city. Was it God who had decided that physicians and bankers should be planted among the wealthy? Were there not enormous health and economic needs on the south side of the city? I had the sinking feeling that where we were living had been determined by a long series of intentional personal choices that were primarily influenced by our earning power.

These unwanted thoughts continued to nag at me when I left the service. Later I got on the phone with a couple of real estate friends. They would know as well as anyone what priorities really affect a decision to purchase a home. "Location, location, location!" they spouted with well-practiced humor. "But what underlying values give a location positive or negative qualities?" I probed. Good schools, amenities, easy access to shopping, economic status, and image topped the list. Investment and proximity to work were also important considerations. Absent from the "location/desirability quotient" was proximity to church. Nearness to human need was clearly a detriment.

Then it dawned on me what had disturbed me about the sermon. A major question had been omitted. Neither the preacher nor the listeners were asking, "Why are you planted where you are?" We were simply assuming that the American dream is the guiding standard by which God's people should locate themselves. It is expected that competent, connected Christians establish their homes as close as possible to the lush banks of the deep capital streams.

I have heard hundreds of sermons on understanding God's will for my life. After all, I am a preacher's kid and have been active in Christian work most of my adult life. Early on I became convinced of the importance of seeking God's will in selecting the right college, career, church, spouse, and dozens of other important life choices. Try as I may, however, I cannot remember hearing a sermon on God's will regarding the location of my home.

Perhaps there is silence on this matter because location has a neutral value in God's economy. Maybe it just doesn't matter. Or is it because our homes are our sacred cows that no one dare touch? Our careful avoidance of the subject causes me to suspect the latter. Common sense tells us to protect our families and our investments from people of detrimental influence. Yet God's desirability quotient seems weighted toward becoming neighbors to people in need. In fact, Jesus, giving the same weight to loving one's neighbor as to loving God, described for us those who needed neighbors—the ill-clothed, the hungry, the homeless stranger, the wounded, and the broken. Locating our homes in places protected from the sight of these "lesser ones" neither relieves their plight nor relieves us of our responsibility to be neighbors to them. What is more sobering is that our withdrawal from neighbors in need causes schools to decline, real estate to depreciate, crime to spread, hope to dwindle, communities to collapse, and despair to reign. What good is salt, Jesus said, if it doesn't preserve or season? Or light, if it is safely shielded from the darkness it is meant to dispel?

As the disruptive words of our Lord have penetrated my value system, I have become persuaded that location, location, and location are indeed the critical selection criteria for those who desire to bloom where *God* wants to plant them. And the underlying values of those who perceive the kingdom will be disclosed in the kind of questions they ask. What community lacks the talents and treasures that have been entrusted to us? What school is most in need of the educational and moral values that our family brings? What neighborhood will the unique leaven of our lives cause to rise? Location, perhaps more than any other decision, disturbs the delicate balance we have tried to achieve between mammon and spirit. In this issue, the American dream collides with the vision of God's kingdom here on earth, exposing them to be as different from each other as darkness and light. Convenience, security, and status are confronted by self-sacrifice, downward mobility, and obedience. The instinct to save one's own life stares at the cross. It is a dangerous prayer Jesus taught his followers to pray—"Thy Kingdom come, thy will be done on earth as it is in heaven."

What Makes a Healthy Community?

Ask any group of residents, regardless of socioeconomic status, to describe what a healthy community looks like, and there will be far more commonalities than differences in their definitions. There is broad consensus that for neighborhoods to flourish, they must have safe streets, schools that educate, a viable economy, spiritual and ethical leadership, wholesome recreational and social activities, and engaging political life. There is still consensus that moral values, a work ethic, and self-sufficiency are essential strands that hold together the fabric of community. Even though a majority of urban neighborhoods have become blighted, the memories of healthy ones are alive and strong in the minds of our parents and grandparents. The question that stares at us now is: Can unraveled urban neighborhoods be rewoven into healthy places for children to grow up?

Just because the last forty years of social experimentation have yielded few successful models of urban community, we need not be discouraged in our current efforts. At least we know what does *not* work.

A community will not remain healthy if it is not economically viable. To cut through the rhetoric of nonprofit economic development, a community that cannot attract and harness market forces is not economically viable. The best measure of viability is the capacity to attract competing for-profit businesses that provide affordable goods and services (such as national food chains and branch banks). Wherever the earning power of residents is increasing, wherever disposable income results from vigorous economic exchange, market forces gravitate and free enterprise flourishes. We know that a subsidized economy and artificial redistribution systems—which in the short run may be necessary and expedient—serve as disincentives to economic viability and produce dependencies that ultimately weaken communities. The presence of neighbors who make good wages and who spend those wages in the community is the surest means of insuring that economic strength will increase. Relocation, then, becomes a vital ingredient in community development.

A community will not remain healthy if it does not foster, retain, and attract capable indigenous leadership. The departure of resourced, achieving neighbors has left our urban communities weak and emaciated. Even the most vulnerable, who have no choice but to remain, have adopted an "up and out" mentality for their children. The goal of urban education has become "a good job that will get you out of this place." Programs that facilitate the further exodus of the best and brightest from our urban neighborhoods cannot be considered legitimate community development activities. They may assist individuals toward achieving the American dream, but they are not community friendly. The commitment of CCDA to develop indigenous leaders, to "indigenize" new leadership, and to spark new vision for the rebuilding of our communities makes the movement as practical as it is revolutionary.

A community will not remain healthy if it becomes isolated from the larger systems of the city and society. Historically, urban neighborhoods have thrived with socioeconomically diverse populations. Despite inequities, unskilled workers along with professionals have shared the benefits of decent schools, competitively priced goods and services, and safe streets. Not until suburbanization did we separate our people en masse into distinct islands of sameness. This has worked to the detriment of the affluent as well as the poor. The poor have obviously suffered from dependency and neglect, while the rich have become isolated from each other by individualism and materialism. Productive interdependency is the hallmark of healthy community life. By bringing back into relationship those who are connected to the economic and political systems of the city with those who have become disconnected, we not only bring about reconciliation but also promote the health of the community.

Indigenous Leadership

We are finally beginning to realize that programs do not fix communities. Only neighbors can do that. Urban neighborhoods need vested neighbor-leaders who will organize the taking of playgrounds back from the drug dealers. Needed are new homeowners to repair and restore deteriorated homes. Educated neighbors are needed to revive the PTA and turn the schools back into environments of creative learning. Urban renewal, public safety, and public education initiatives funded and operated from outside the community may have their place. But without the leadership of committed, connected, compassionate neighbors who have a stake in the future of the neighborhood, these programs will have little lasting effect. Any effort, secular or religious, that does not actively seek to develop and retain indigenous leadership within the community must be considered community "unfriendly." This subject will be dealt with at length in chapter 9, "Indigenous Leadership Development."

"Indigenizing" Leadership

There has been considerable discussion in educational, social service, and funding circles lately about the need for community involvement in the plans that are being made for that community. There is a growing consensus that those who live in the environment understand it best and are best equipped to prioritize and design solutions. The prevailing wisdom is that outsiders should never impose their views or programs on a community. Most serving agencies (including the church) interpret this to mean that the agency should collaborate with residents, and if mutual agreement is reached, then agency (outside) resources and trained personnel will be brought into the community.

This collaborative approach often leads to community residents becoming members of advisory boards. Less often does it lead to residents being hired to staff programs. Almost never does it lead to agency staff moving into the community to become a vital part of the life of that community—*unless* it happens to be a CCDA ministry!

An important distinctive feature of Christian community development ministries is the guiding philosophy that relocation is essential to effective community rebuilding. This means that ministry leadership and staff are strongly encouraged to move into the neighborhood where they feel called to minister and become "indigenized" neighbors. Instead of commuting in and consulting with the residents of a neighborhood, CCDA leadership becomes part of the neighborhood. Their lives, their children, their resources, their connections—these become sturdy strands that are rewoven into the fabric of the community and become part of its color and strength.

Thus, a "return flight" is initiated and much needed leadership is brought back into the community. Because these new neighbors become vested (buying homes, starting churches, establishing businesses), they establish roots, which gives much needed stability to neighborhoods that are often high turnover rental areas controlled by external slumlords. This often becomes the catalyst for the rebirth of the community.

Perhaps the greatest need of under-resourced communities is for achieving neighbor-leaders. Achieving neighbors can do much to break the isolation of poor neighborhoods and reconnect them with the life-giving systems that are the common grace of the city and larger society. Achieving neighbors bring living, personal models of hope back into a disheartened environment. Achieving neighbors bring resources and skills into a depleted neighborhood, along with fresh energy to deploy them.

This is not to say that low-income communities do not have valuable resources to draw upon. On the contrary, there are often deep spiritual roots, rich history, and strength of character that endure in the midst of great suffering and distress. There is much to learn from those whose faith has been refined by hardship. And there is within every person created in the image of God great potential to develop abilities designed to engage and change our world. The strength and potential of low-income communities must not be minimized.

However, we must be candid enough to acknowledge the fact that when the strongest leadership and brightest minds have been consistently drawn away from the community, a depletion of spirit as well as capacity does occur. The "pull yourself up by your own bootstraps" approach may have a romantic, rugged American sound to it, but it does not take into account the weakening effects that chronic leadership hemorrhage has upon a community. A reweaving strategy that intentionally recruits new neighbors to repopulate and help to rebuild urban communities goes straight to the root cause of urban decline. This is a primary reason why relocation is such an important principle for Christian community development.

Gentrification

Most successful urban renewal efforts in recent years have been accomplished at the expense of the poor. Real estate development in urban areas very often has displaced low-income renters, torn down or restored older buildings, and reestablished the area as an upscale environment. While this may be good for the tax base of the city, it exacerbates the problems of the poor. Revitalization is necessary for our cities, yet revitalization that does not take into account the needs of our more vulnerable citizens becomes a form of injustice.

It is a strange dilemma. The resources of the "gentry" are badly needed in urban communities. Without the capacities of connected residents, isolated neighborhoods languish in need. And yet the investments of these new neighbors push property values up, turn multiapartment homes back into single family residences, and pressure upgrading, which effectively drives the poor from the area. If, on the other hand, the middle class do not return to the city, the poor remain isolated and dependent upon incomes that are insufficient to raise their standard of living above the poverty level. Low-end jobs, poverty programs, and nonprofit enterprises, as important as they may be, do not have sufficient capacity to attract the market forces needed to rebuild a community. Only disposable income within a community can do that. A healthy community needs an economic mix. Herein lies the only legitimate empowerment potential that has staying power.

An essential and achievable goal of Christian community development is to create economically diverse neighborhoods that enhance the lives of low-income residents while attracting new leadership and investments into the community. Admittedly, such a strategy of mixed-income development flies in the face of conventional real estate wisdom, which counsels toward homogeneous separation. A new vision is needed to create a market. In an urbanizing world where pluralism is rapidly becoming a social norm, perhaps the time is right to proclaim a new wisdom (actually a very old wisdom) suitable to the realities of our day. A community development strategy that is just, inclusive of diversity, economically viable, and socially healthy is both practical and achievable. It is complex, perhaps, but achievable nonetheless. And it is right.

We must take great care to insure that our Christian community development philosophy of relocation does not inadvertently encourage the kind of gentrification that will ultimately work to the disadvantage of the poor. In overcrowded, badly deteriorated areas some dislocation is necessary so that renovation can be done and responsible property management can be instituted. There is doubtless a "healthy" level of displacement required to effect a desirable income mix in areas of concentrated poverty. However, intentional care must be given early on in the planning process to create ownership opportunities for qualifiable renters and to secure affordable rental options for those whose apartments will be renovated. Obviously, these issues are more complex than this chapter can adequately address. There is, however, much "acquired intelligence" in these matters accessible through the Christian Community Development Association's consultative network. Perhaps it is sufficient here to say that we must remain vigilant in our concern for justice and seek always to protect the interests of the vulnerable.

Economics and Relocation

The single greatest cause of sustained poverty in our cities is isolation. Public housing projects are perhaps the best example of what happens when people are housed for prolonged periods of time in poverty compounds. We have seen that they become isolated from the major systems that serve the city: political, economic, and religious. Politicians pay little attention to housing project residents. Police see them as problematic. Churches may do outreach in the projects but are often reluctant to involve project youth (or their families) in the life of the church. Unemployment is high in the projects, and the jobs residents do pick up are low skill and minimal wage. In their isolation from free access to and participation in the systems that are the common grace of the city, hope eventually gives way to despair and aspirations seldom rise above a survival level.

The strategy of many ministries has been to assist people to escape low-hope environments rather than to rebuild them. This may certainly be of great benefit to individuals or individual families, but it does no good at all for the community. The Christian community development strategy seeks to empower individuals and families to rebuild their communities. Relocation is an essential ingredient for reconnecting neglected neighborhoods to the vital systems of the city, thus ending the isolation.

Consider this personal example. When Jonathan, our younger child, turned sixteen we encouraged him to get a job. One of the better employers in our part of the city is Zoo Atlanta. They don't pay high wages but the working conditions and benefits are good. So Jonathan went over to the zoo to put in an application. Unbeknown to him, I knew someone in management there and called that person, alerting her that Jonathan would be coming in to apply for employment. Though I didn't ask for any special favors, the fact that someone in authority knew that my son was applying for a job doubtless had some influence. It was no great surprise to me when Jonathan landed a job at the zoo.

In his off hours as he was shooting basketball with his buddies in the neighborhood, Jonathan mentioned job openings that he was aware of at the zoo. "Use me as a reference," he would encourage them. In a few weeks, five of his friends had jobs at Zoo Atlanta.

We did not need a youth employment program on our block. We simply needed a connected neighbor! We did not need external funds to do a job readiness training. We needed an insider who was willing to share important employment information and give a personal recommendation for some disconnected friends. Programs are a poor substitute for what neighbors can do best. The same has happened among adults who live in our neighborhood. When connected neighbors share the influence they have in the marketplace, the church, the educational institutions, and the political systems, the flow of resources begins to spread into places long ago shut off. Relocated neighbors end isolation.

Neighboring and Church Involvement

On our street, the most unneighborly residents are those most involved in their churches. This strikes me as being rather odd.

The Mays (I've changed their name and revealing particulars) are a good example. They are a solid African American family with much to offer a neighborhood. Jim is a hard worker and natural born leader. Betty is a teacher and is great with kids. Their three children are well behaved, neatly groomed, and bright. Their leadership, spiritual values, and strength of character are much needed influences for struggling families and youth in our urban community. But there is a conflict: the Mays are heavily involved in their church. The same talents that are needed in our neighborhood are also needed in their church. And there doesn't seem to be enough time to do both. Jim and Betty never come to a community meeting or work on the playground or support a neighborhood youth activity. About the only time we see them is when they are pulling in and out of their driveway. And the Mays are just one example. There are a number of others in our neighborhood too involved in church to be involved in community life.

I'm not saying that these are bad neighbors. They're more like unneighbors—people who live on our street but contribute nothing to the well-being of our street. With the church as the center around which their busy lives revolve, they become isolated from their neighborhood. Prayer meetings, choir rehearsal, visitation, Bible studies, committees, retreats, and two services on Sunday pretty well consume their non-working hours. But how can you fault them? These are honorable, upright people who take their faith very seriously. They're good Christians, just not good neighbors, that's all.

With our nation's cities rapidly unraveling while church attendance climbs to record highs, I cannot help but wonder if something has gone wrong with the way we are doing church. I am beginning to suspect that a model of church that competes with, rather than promotes, being a good neighbor may be fundamentally flawed. My understanding is that God placed a rather high value on being a good neighbor, elevating it to a level of importance equal to that of loving God. One would have to wonder, then, just how acceptable to him is the substitution of being a good church member in place of being a good neighbor.

Our urbanizing society is coming apart in large measure because of the disintegration of our communities. To oversimplify, healthy families produce healthy communities and healthy communities produce healthy families—these are the fundamental building blocks of society. Families are as vulnerable without stable communities as communities are without stable families. Without interconnected neighbors functioning as living ligatures to hold neighborhoods together, disintegration occurs. We see the results in living color each night in our living rooms on the evening news. If our contemporary model of church encourages—implicitly or explicitly, by its demands or its theology—the withdrawal from active, redemptive community participation, it may unwittingly be promoting this disintegration.

Is there an unavoidable conflict between our community of faith and our community of residence? Do strong loyalties to church necessitate disengagement from those who live next door? If so, I have a misconception of the role of the Christian in this world. I have understood the historic mission of the church to be a proactive force, armed with vulnerable love, infiltrating every stratum of society, transforming fallen people and systems through the power of the Spirit. While it is tempting to allow the local church body to become our enclave of like-minded friends, which provides a protective haven from the daily bombardment of destructive values, engagement—not withdrawal—has always been the operative word of the church militant. And love of one's neighbor remains its fundamental tactic.

I wonder what a church would look like that measured its success by the quality of its members' neighborly love. What impact would such a church have on a troubled society if it undertook intentional training in loving God by loving neighbor? How different—how welcome—would be the model that commissioned its most gifted to the strategic office of neighbor!

Some Practical Suggestions

Don't do it alone. Relocating in a culturally different, sometimes dangerous environment can be a challenge. Having others with you who share your faith, commitment, and culture makes the transition much more of an adventure. Individuals (or couples) can become very isolated and alone if they do not have supportive co-workers to bear each other's burdens and listen to each other's concerns. While we do know a few "lone ranger" types who ride boldly onto the frontier armed with nothing but a Bible, most of us need the support and camaraderie that the body of Christ is designed to provide. Accountability, safety, spiritual and emotional support, and friendship with others who are experiencing the same changes—these are important ingredients in the relocation process.

Consider neighboring vs. fixing. No one likes to be someone's project. But we all like to be considered someone's friend. Treating our neighbors as objects of ministry can define those relationships in unhealthy ways. If we become defined as dispensers of food and rent money, then we are likely to be treated as a resource rather than a neighbor. Like a doctor, whose patients show up only when they are sick, we will see people only when they want something from us. And this is *not* how healthy relationships or healthy communities work. Healthy relationships are reciprocal. Each has something of worth to contribute to the other. Good neighbors keep watch on each other's house. Neighbors borrow from and lend to each other. Neighbors watch each other's kids. Interdependency is the operative word. When we move in as fixers rather than neighbors, we set ourselves up to be used. And that isn't healthy for anyone.

Relocation doesn't always equal reconciliation. Simply moving into an urban neighborhood does not guarantee that community development will spontaneously occur. Suburban isolationism can thrive just as well in the city as it does in the suburbs. The cocooning effect of shutting oneself off from neighbors can separate us just as surely in a city row house as it does in an upscale town home development. High board fences, lack of interaction with next door neighbors, pulling the blinds—these are the messages of individualists who value privacy and control over community and interdependency. Involvement and engagement are the operative words for those committed to community development in their neighborhood. This does not mean that we relinquish all control over our schedules and family lives. It does imply, however, that we go out of our way to be interactive, interested neighbors and accept as normal the unexpected (and often disruptive) intrusions of others into our daily lives.

Peggy Lupton

Relocation: Whose Calling Is It?

As I share my experience of relocation into the inner city, I am aware that my journey is unique, as is that of every other woman who has made a similar decision. For years I compared myself with other relocated women and felt a sense of disappointment with myself if I didn't display the same level of courage or commitment that they seemed to be living out. It was only after entering into dialogue with others that I came to see how personal and individual this journey really is. We bring with us onto this new frontier our unique backgrounds, our own culture and heritage, baggage that we have inherited from our parents and, for many of us, a relationship with a spouse who has an agenda, which we refer to as a call. Also, the particular place where we relocate is in itself very unique. I've had the privilege of visiting a number of urban ministries in other cities. Sometimes I've left saying, "It would be a piece of cake to live there," or "I hope God never calls me to that city." My place of reference is Atlanta. If you have ever visited here you may be able to picture the territory I've called home for the past fourteen years. Perhaps a little personal history will help you to better understand how I have experienced relocating here.

I grew up in a rural setting in Ohio. I lived the first twenty-one years of my life in the house that my grandfather built, the same house in which my mother was raised. I attended a Presbyterian church that my family had attended for generations. The idea of community was a very familiar one to me from an early age. Of course, the kind of community I knew was pretty homogeneous.

Bob and I met when we were twenty-five years old. Our relationship was love at first sight. Within eight months we were married, and within the first year of marriage Bob was sent to Vietnam, and I was pregnant.

Now you have to realize that when I met Bob he was a manager with the J. C. Penney Company. His being drafted and sent to Vietnam was an unwanted intrusion into our lives. In less than a year he was back home again, and we began building our future. In my mind I saw us buying a home in the same area where I grew up, Bob pursuing his career and me staying home to raise our children. These were the traditional roles that were modeled in both our homes. My dreams fit well within the time and culture in which we grew up. I knew nothing about parachurch ministries, so when Bob shared with me that he felt a call to work with delinquent teens through Youth for Christ, I was very surprised, to say the least. This wasn't at all like my dream of what home and family would be. The only missionaries I knew about were those who went overseas. And the concept of raising our own support was a totally new and somewhat embarrassing idea.

As I look back on those years I recall being genuinely excited with Bob about his dream and very supportive. In fact, I've always considered myself to be his partner in ministry. Within six weeks we had left our quiet community in which I had spent my whole life and moved to Detroit for a six-month internship in urban youth work. We then moved to Atlanta to start up a program working with delinquent youth. As Bob started working with boys from the juvenile court, I counseled on a part-time basis with a couple of troubled girls. My primary ministry, however, was as a mother and a wife. My family was my priority. I found it both natural and enjoyable staying at home while Bob was out doing his ministry. His hours were long, but I felt I couldn't complain because, after all, he was doing God's work.

In 1975 Bob got his Ph.D., and I "got" our second son, Jonathan. This was our fourth year of ministry. We were living in the suburbs as we had all of our married life up to this time. Every once in a while the discussion of moving to the city would come up. We'd take a drive downtown and without much thought would say, "No, that's not for us." For a country girl, living in the suburbs was a big enough step.

Three years later we decided to move a few miles farther from the city into a racially mixed neighborhood. It was about half Black and half White. We were delighted because we felt the kids that we were working with, mostly African American, would feel more comfortable coming to our home. We had not yet learned about White flight. Little did we know that an integrated community in Atlanta, Georgia, doesn't stop at half Black, half White; it just keeps transitioning until it becomes an entirely Black community. By the time we were ready to put our youngest son in school there were no White children in the kindergarten. I felt fine about our children being minorities, but I did want them to have some peers of their own race and culture to relate to. So we decided to move still farther out of the city and build a house close to our church. I will say that Bob was doing this for me. I wanted my kids to have the same kind of educational experiences that I had. I wanted schools where they would have the same friends from kindergarten through the next twelve years. We found a builder that was just starting a house, and we entered into a contract with him to build it to our specifications. For me this was a thrill, since I am such a nester. I had fun dreaming of colors and light fixtures, carpets and cabinets.

One night as Bob and I were lying in bed, I told him I wanted to discuss the house. We were about five weeks from completion and there were a lot of decisions that had to be made. He said he didn't think we should talk right now and, of course, that made me even more insistent. So he proceeded to tell me what was on his heart. He said he had been hearing from a lot of different sources that we shouldn't be moving farther away from the city but that we should be moving *into* the city. And he didn't stop there. He said that he felt we should put our children into the public city schools. If he had put a knife into my heart it couldn't have hurt more. I know that sounds strong but then so were my feelings of providing a secure environment for my children. We talked and cried a lot that night. In the morning I asked him if God was calling us to the city or if it was his own idea, because if it was his idea I wasn't going. He said that as well as he understood how God speaks to him, he felt it was a call of God. I told him I wanted it in writing. This now seems humorous, but I'm the type who has to have something tangible to hold on to and refer back to. I need to ponder things over and over. So with a loving spirit Bob wrote me the following letter. Though I have not shared this letter publicly before since it is quite personal, I feel that it does communicate some of the delicate dynamics involved in making this difficult choice.

Dear Peggy,
It seems like all of our married life you have had to shape your schedule and lifestyle around my dreams and schemes. You have had to take my word for it that God was leading here or there— telling me this or that. In some ways I have victimized you and have put you in positions where to do other than agree with me would make you look unspiritual.

And here we are again! But this time it is different. You have caused me to see how manipulative and destructive I have been in the past—that my spiritual leadership was not by service but by power. You have caused me—forced me—to grow in this awareness, and I love you for it. I want very much to avoid doing it again to you. That's why I want to say to you again: If you do not feel peace in your heart about this move, I will lay down this dream and pick up yours and give myself to loving you and the children. And I won't look back, nor will I ever throw it up to you. I want you to have true freedom to choose.

You ask me to put in writing the thoughts I have regarding this whole issue. I'll try to do it as accurately as I can. Several weeks ago I was talking with Marc Hoffman-Beals and Jon Abercrombie about God's will. I articulated for the first time that if I would do what I felt was most consistent with God's will for me (not considering you and the boys) that I would move into the city among the poor and live in the community. That was the first time I ever articulated it in a personal way. Since then, I have been exposed to a series of people and experiences that have not allowed me to escape facing this issue. Ray Bakke, John Perkins, Dale Cross and others spoke to me in ways I could not avoid. I had heard them all before but this time it was different. It was for me.

Your question is a good one: Did God really speak to me and tell me to move to the city? I have felt His strong directing in my life three times that I can remember. Once when I felt called into YFC, once when we started FCS, and now, again, on the issue of our move. I must rank this movement of God in the same intensity and clarity as the two previous calls. God has worked this way before in my life; I must conclude that He is once again directing me in the same manner and will provide for all of our needs as He has done in the past.

It is not merely a blind step of faith into which I believe He leads this time. There is perfect rationale to it. If I am called to serve the poor, leading them to our Lord as well as enabling them in other ways, ten years has proven to me that apart from the nourishment of the Body, they will not grow spiritually. If evangelism and discipleship are to be part of my work, then I must be a part of a Body that provides this for them. The call that I feel is not merely to a geographic place, but to responsible discipleship. I have been given the gifts of leadership and it is clear to me that I am being called to use them in the context of a community of the poor.

It is strange (wonderfully so) that prior to this call God has for months been dealing with me about responsible spiritual leadership in my home. I know you sense the change in attitude that He is beginning to work in me in this regard. I feel like an aroused sense of responsibility for my own family is an essential if we as a family enter into a new environment together. One seems to be a precondition for the other.

I would like for you to ask me any questions that are on your mind. Seek the counsel of those others whom you trust. Pray honestly and earnestly for a sense of God's words for you. Take as much time as you want or need. I'll try to give you plenty of room. Then let's sit down and make a decision. If you are not convinced that this move is God's will for us, then we will move near Crossroads Church. If you are at peace with a move to the city, then we will seek housing in Grant Park.

One thing I want—must have—more than anything else: the oneness and intimacy of our marriage relationship. More than that is what I promise you, honey, regardless of our decision. I do love you deeply and want your joy to be complete.

Lovingly,

Bob

I carried this letter around with me for a couple of weeks. I shared it with trusted friends and with our pastor. But mostly it was for me to read and reread. God worked in my heart during this time of searching. He brought so many of the Old Testament characters alive to me. I thought about Jonah running from what God wanted him to do. The story that really touched my heart was Abraham and Isaac. I was negotiating with God that maybe we could go to the city for the summer and kind of test the water. Just put our toes in. But God reminded me that when he asked Abraham to sacrifice his son, Abraham's answer wasn't, "Can't I just amputate his leg?" God was asking me to give him my children. He reminded me that he had only entrusted them to my care and that he loved them more than I did. That is probably a mother's most difficult work—to let go and trust God with her children. There are so many fears and uncertainties—education, safety, playmates, exposure to harsh urban realities at such a tender age. And yet, at the end of this time I had become convinced that Bob had received a call of God and that there was no real choice for me other than to submit. I would not disobey God.

As I have talked with other wives over the years, I've heard a number of them say that they weren't the ones who felt called to relocate. I think as wives we can find common ground in knowing that in marriage God has designed husbands and wives to be one. And if husband and wife are seeking God's will together, he will not call them in opposing directions. Time may be the key to relocating in marital harmony. At some point both husband and wife must have inner peace about the move. I'm not saying that all the questions have to be answered or that nothing will be hard about the move, but the peace that only God can give must rest in both partners. Then it becomes really OK to relocate even if we are not the one feeling the call.

Once Bob and I made the decision to move to the city, God wrapped his arms around me in the form of saints that he had sent before me. There were three other middle-income, White families who lived in the community we were moving into who had their children in the local elementary school or who were planning to enroll their children there in the fall. That alone helped me know I wasn't crazy. One of our ministry staff persons brought me a red rose, another made me a welcome card—"random acts of kindness" I believe they're called today. Another significant affirmation was that the builder who was building our new suburban home released us from our contract and gave us our money back.

Probably one of the greatest barriers to relocating is the fear/safety issue. The Scripture passage, "Do not store up for yourselves treasures on earth, where moth and rust destroy, and where thieves break in and steal," took on new meaning for me. "Letting go" of the few pieces of silver that I have, my microwave, and other personal things I value, was a discipline at first. Soon, however, they took their familiar places in our new urban home, and the fear of losing them was put to rest. A much harder issue for me was physical safety—especially when it came to my children. Figuring out the acceptable boundaries and influences for my children was difficult. It's hard enough in today's society, but when you add the realities of life in a large city, you have to develop street savvy quickly. I've always thought that raising girls in the city would be harder because they are easier prey. But lately I've come to a different position. An attack on a female seems as likely in the suburbs as in the city. However, because males seem to be so much more aggressive and have a need to display this to other males, the inner city with its gangs, guns, and violence was a frightening place for our sons. Much more so than they ever told us about. Our younger son, Jonathan, was beaten by a gang of youths while attending a parade downtown. No parent would ever choose this to happen to his or her child, but as Romans 8:28 promised, God used it for Jonathan's good. The following account, which Jonathan wrote his freshman year in college, provides some insight into how this traumatic event affected him.

Forever Changed

A day of celebration was in order to congratulate the Atlanta Braves on their worst to first baseball season of 1991. My mom even agreed to let me out of school early on this joyous occasion. Downtown Atlanta was alive with activity. The sidewalks were so filled with people that the overflow had to scale telephone poles, signs, cars, and even billboards. Every window along the parade route was filled with faces anxiously anticipating the coming of the heroes who had kept them up past their bedtimes during the World Series. I joined the multitudes by climbing onto a mailbox to watch the players go by. The crowd cheered as their favorite team members passed by. Kids on their parents' shoulders screamed at the passing parade cars. The amount of energy along the winding street of Atlanta was tremendous.

I had gone downtown to witness this tickertape celebration with two of my friends, Susan and Ashok. Susan was an innocent looking, pale-skinned young woman who rarely came downtown. Her parents gave their permission this time because of my male protection. Ashok was a dark complexioned Indian who stood about six foot three and had the build of a football player. We had joined in the screaming as our favorite players rode past. After the parade passed by, the barricade that held back the crowds came down and people flooded into the street.

On the way back to the car as we rounded a corner, we found ourselves in the midst of a street completely full of what appeared to be high school students like ourselves. I soon became aware that I was the only white male within sight. I'd be lying if I said that I felt no sense of threat because of the color of the people that surrounded me. I'd also be lying if I denied being tempted to turn around and take an alternative route. Another side of me said that I had no right to be scared just because of racial differences. Who was I to assume that I was in danger simply based on the fact that the crowd around me was African-American? I made a conscious decision that day not to judge based on the color of people's skin but to respect people as individuals. So the three of us began to make our way through this sea of faces. Our pale faces were like stormy white caps of tension on the large but smooth waves of activity in the street. It felt like every eye in this surging audience was focused on me. I watched my feet carefully to avoid kicking anyone or stepping on anyone's toes. I still felt guilty for feeling frightened.

Suddenly an elbow jammed the back of my neck and knocked me forward into Susan. The force knocked me to the pavement. I found myself the target of kicks from I don't know how many pairs of legs. Instinctively, I cradled my body into a fetal position to protect my face and vital organs. From this point I had no concept of time. I don't know how long I lay there absorbing this abuse. The mere shock of the incident made me feel like I was in a dream. I felt no pain and was no longer afraid. I felt very distanced from the situation, like a bystander might feel. This couldn't be happening to me.

Then the kicking stopped. I felt a pair of strong arms grasp hold of me. A man feigning possession of a gun was helping me to my feet while fending off my attackers. I scanned the faces of the crowd that pushed for a view of the beating. Susan was in tears, her face filled with terror. Ashok looked at me sympathetically and apologetically, for he had not attempted to rescue me. And the crowd seemed like an excited circus audience with me playing the part of the clown. I could not understand the excitement, even pleasure that I saw in their faces. I looked down at the blood stains on the knees of my jeans. I felt my face and discovered that it was also bleeding. Was this some sort of an outrageous joke? I didn't get it. Several of the attackers tried to jump in for encore performances but the stranger shielded me from their reach. With the help of this unknown rescuer, we were hurriedly escorted to the safety of a police car.

I was comforted by the repeated questions from my friends, "Are you OK? Do you want to go to the hospital?" But the only question that remained in my mind that day was "How will I feel when I get back home and my black friends and neighbors greet me?" Despite the fact that the man who rescued me was black, I wondered if this experience had forever turned me into a racist. I was scared again.

When I got home, I was still feeling in shock. I recounted the episode to my mom like I was telling the story about someone else. Her worst nightmare about living in the city had come true. I told her that I just needed a nap and went into my bedroom to sleep. I was awakened first by my dad who attempted to console me by explaining what I was going through psychologically. This didn't answer my greatest concern of whether I had become a racist. My big brother was the next to call. I had to hold the phone away from my ear as he expressed his anger at the event. He told me that he had a Louisville Slugger in his trunk and that if I ever saw these guys again, I should just give him a call. This wasn't the answer either. Later, my black friends from two doors down, having heard the news, came into my bedroom and embraced me. At this moment I knew that I no longer saw the color of these guys who I grew up with. They were not my black friends anymore. Carnell and Darnell were my friends.

The next morning on the bus on the way to school, I sat in the back as usual drifting in and out of sleep. I noticed that there seemed to be an extra sense of excitement that carried over from the festivities of the day before. On this bus of friends and acquaintances, I was liked and respected, and again I was the only white face present. As I listened to the conversations of the morning, one story had a familiar sound. A couple of seats ahead of me someone was telling the humorous story to a couple of giggling friends of some white guy that got the crap beat out of him downtown yesterday. I leaned forward to inquire of the location and time of this beating. Their report confirmed my suspicion. I calmly said to them amidst their laughter, "That was me." They laughed louder at what they thought was another one of my jokes. Their expressions slowly sobered as they realized how serious I really was. Suddenly they put a real person, even a friend, in the place of a punch line and suddenly the joke was no longer funny. A few made attempts to apologize but most, including me, just sat there silent, forever changed.

Culture shock. That's what I experienced when we moved into the city. Bob and the kids just jumped right into their new surroundings. But I was the one who felt like I didn't fit. I'd go to the bank, grocery store, or post office and I might be the only White person there. I felt out of place. I'd walk to our church down the street to the informal service and meal on Wednesday and come home weeping from seeing such brokenness. A lot of the White women who had lived in the community for a while were what I called "city women." They were counter-culture types (didn't shave their legs, wore clothes made from only natural fibers, and ate health food). What I missed greatly were peers. I tried to stay connected to my suburban friends but the contrast in our worlds was so great that I felt like they didn't understand. I confess that I was also jealous of the benefits my suburban friends' kids had just because of where they lived, like organized sports and schools with all the extras. That further separated us. I felt very alone and culturally displaced.

The two middle-class White mothers whose children were in Jonathan's class at school seemed to handle things without a problem. Why was it so difficult for me? Recently I talked with both of them to see if I could understand how they dealt so naturally with life in this culturally foreign environment. One of these friends is a Mennonite and has missionaries in her family. She and her husband came to Atlanta and lived in the community with others doing like work. They bought their house before they had children. She was in a sewing club with neighborhood women, joined a baby-sitting co-op, put her kids in a cooperative preschool, and volunteered at the local elementary school, even before her children went there. In other words, she was fully "enculturated" to the community years before her children arrived. The other mother said she was aware of deep feelings about justice issues at a very young age. She and her husband also bought a home in the neighborhood largely because of their involvement with the Mennonite group already established here. This was before they had children. She had five plus years to consider education options before she was actually faced with that choice. I had one month. This was all a dramatic change for me, and though I worked hard at adapting to my new environment, it took years before it felt like home.

Bob and I both felt it was important to put our children in the local public school. We knew that if our children were there then we would be involved. We would insure that our children were getting a decent education and in the process hopefully increase the educational opportunities for everyone. For me, this was the hardest part of our relocation. You only have one chance at raising your kids. There is no going back and doing it over. But I have to say here that the educational values perpetuated by the suburban church and society are quite different from the values of the kingdom. As hard as it was for me (though not our kids), raising and educating them in the city has been a powerful developmental force that has shaped and formed them in positive ways. What a rich experience to grow up cross-culturally! They know the world isn't all White and middle-class. They are sensitive to color, class, and culture in ways that can't be learned in books. But as I mentioned earlier, I couldn't have done it without friends who made the same choice to put their kids in the public school. And when it came to middle school where the standardized test scores were abysmal and where there were no other children of their color, we made the decision to have them bussed out of the neighborhood to a better public school. This was certainly a compromise, but we did what we thought was best for our boys. The truth is, we all have to seek God's will and realize that we won't all come out in the same place on this issue. There are many choices for parents today. Our decisions must be guided by prayer and careful consideration of our children's unique strengths, talents, and needs. Our decision making must find a balance between our responsibilities as parents to provide our children with a beneficial peer influence and a suitable learning environment and our commitment to be active salt and light in the community where God has sent us.

Perhaps the most prolonged struggle for me was over the death of my dreams. As a little girl I had fantasies of how I would raise my children and the kind of home I would have. I am by nature a home-maker. The joy of my life is being a mother and wife. The home of my dreams was always filled with warmth and stability, surrounded by familiar friends and extended family. Bob's call to the city changed all that. I think I was willing to yield my dreams to the will of God, but I never consciously let them go. I followed Bob's dreams and tried as best I could to adapt mine to fit his. I felt a recurring sadness but kept telling myself to get over it. It wasn't until years later that I recognized that my sadness was actually grief over the loss of my dreams. When I was able to recognize and affirm the legitimacy of those dreams and my grief over their loss, I eventually became able to enjoy my urban home more fully. We built another house of my design on the street where we raised our boys. We live among very diverse neighbors whom I have come to love dearly. Today I cannot imagine living anywhere else. I am truly at home in the city.

Gloria Yancy

Relocation: Coming Back

My parents came to California from New Orleans when I was two years old. Many of the African Americans who relocated from the South to the West during the 1940s found employment in the Richmond shipyards. That's where my mother and father both found work. We lived in the government projects called "War Housing Projects."

The youngest of four children, I was three years old when my parents separated. By my twelfth birthday Mother remarried and our family immediately grew by six new children. We moved to a larger project apartment and later were able to rent a house in north Richmond.

I was reared in a God-fearing home and attended church all of my childhood years. My mother used to say, "You will either go to church or Sunday school." I always chose Sunday school so that I could go to the movie theater early. In spite of my religious upbringing, I chose to live in the fast lane during my teenage years. Because I liked parties, dancing, drinking, and riding in cars and on motorcycles, I found myself involved in delinquent behavior. When I was old enough, I went to work so I'd have my own money. By the age of nineteen I was married. My husband and I stayed in the Richmond area and began our family—three sons and a daughter. By this time the War Housing Projects were gone and my husband and I bought our first house in the same area. It was a neighborhood that had once been White but as colored moved in, Whites moved out. My husband and I separated shortly after our fourth child was born and I found myself single and carrying the parenting responsibilities alone.

One day a neighbor of mine who worked with Child Evangelism asked if she could start Sunday school with my children. Even though I wasn't following the Lord and didn't understand Christ's death and sacrifice for my sins, I was eager to have this woman teaching my children. I began to work with her, driving my station wagon to take my children along with other neighborhood kids to the church. One day while I was in Sunday school with my kids, the teacher spoke about Christ's death and his sacrifice being for us all. For the first time I understood Jesus died for me. I accepted him as my Savior that day.

Not long after this I moved away from the old neighborhood. I had gotten a better job working at the hospital and had a much more positive outlook on life. I wanted my children to have a healthier place to grow up so I purchased a bigger home in a predominately White section of suburban San Pablo. I continued attending the Sunday school classes in the old neighborhood, still picking up children from there to hear the good news of the gospel. As my own children grew up they continued to help with the classes. William, my oldest, was good in music. Vincent, my second son, was a great storyteller. Using visuals was his specialty. The two youngest, Mark and Linda, would assist me in both songs of worship and storytelling.

One year for my birthday my children gave me a CB radio for my car. When I asked them what CB stood for, they responded like I should have known. "Mom, it's Citizen Band!" As I prayed asking the Lord how he wanted me to use this gift, he brought to my mind the Scripture 1 Corinthians 15:3–4, which speaks of what true belief in Christ is about. Then it dawned on me what CB could also mean—Christian Believer! That's what I would name the ministry I felt God calling me toward.

Christian Believers began as a ministry with children that hung around on the street corners near our home. My children and I started helping in the neighborhood, providing donated clothes, food, and transportation to those in need. My home was always open to community children and their parents. Eventually we were able to rent a storefront building in San Pablo where the ministry continued to grow. We weren't a church but rather a ministry that offered help and emergency relief to anyone who needed it. The number of dedicated volunteers increased and soon we were ministering to so many people that we were filled to capacity.

My desire was to purchase the rented building we were in and develop it as our permanent ministry site. But even though the owner had it listed for sale, he was unwilling to sell it to us. Not knowing what to do, I made a trip to visit John and Vera Mae Perkins in Pasadena. We prayed and talked and believed God would make a way. I decided the only way to get through this Red Sea was to fast and pray.

While driving through my old neighborhood in Richmond where I grew up, I saw an old building on 4th Street with a "For Sale" sign in the window. Immediately I knew that this was where God was leading me. Drugs, prostitutes, shootings, fighting, loitering, traffic all day and all night—these were the realities that we would be facing daily if I moved my family back into this neighborhood. Yet I knew God would see us through whatever trials we faced. No one could understand why we would consider leaving our nice, safe, suburban home to relocate in an area of Richmond that had 25 percent of all the crime in the city. I must admit that I had my own misgivings to deal with as well. But I knew that Christ sacrificed it all for me, even before I knew him, and I needed to be willing to sacrifice for this community that was in such dire need. So I bought the building, and my children and I moved in.

God had obviously been preparing my children for this move. They were very supportive and jumped right into the cleaning and fixing up. Soon the Christian Believers ministry was going strong and providing assistance for many broken people in the community. We were eventually able to purchase an old apartment building across the street, which a drug addict had previously owned and lost. With the help of ex-offenders, prostitutes, drug abusers, and alcoholics, we fixed up the building, established decent housing there, and went to work cleaning up the rest of the neighborhood. When I gave up my beautiful, secure home where I had raised my children for twenty-one years and moved into a violent, crime-infested neighborhood, many of my old friends thought I had lost my mind. However, I knew that God had placed his vision within my spirit, and I could do no less than follow him.

God has continued to prosper the ministry. Even in the midst of much brokenness, he is using the outcasts of this world to do the work of his kingdom. In an environment of danger he gives a spirit of power over fear. He proves to us daily that what is impossible with man is possible with God. I have not looked back with regret. God made this decision for me. He uses ordinary people like you and me to accomplish his purposes. I have had the joy of seeing my children grow into fine adults who are committed to doing Christian community development work in a wide variety of ways in our neighborhood. I am indeed blessed.

The Key Elements of Relocation

- We can most clearly understand the real problems facing the poor if we relocate into the community of need. Then their problems become *our* real problems.
- Relocation is a biblically based principle. Where we live frequently reflects our economic desires rather than God's will.
- The single greatest cause of sustained poverty in our inner cities is that they are isolated from the major service systems of the city. Relocation provides connected neighbors who can share the influence that they have in the marketplace, church, the educational institutions, and the political system. The flow of resources can begin to end the isolation.
- Leadership in a community of need must be indigenous—i.e., persons who are living in the community and are therefore aware of the true needs of the community. Relocation is a means of indigenizing those who are led to poverty areas through God's Word. Leadership development is a means to

foster the latent leadership abilities of those persons already in the community.

- Some practical suggestions when considering relocation: don't do it alone; the basic idea should be one of "neighboring" rather than "fixing"; and remember that relocation doesn't necessarily mean reconciliation.
- Relocation is a family affair. The call to ministry must be a shared call. With prayer, God will lead you in the right direction. The entire family will grow with the experience. The positive effects on family outweigh the negative ones.
- Probably the toughest form of relocation is for the person who once lived in the community of need to move back after they have finally "made it" and moved out. This relocation of indigenous leaders is greatly needed if Christian community development is to be as effective as it can be.

6

Reconciliation

Loving God and Loving People

Spencer Perkins and Chris Rice

One sign and wonder, biblically speaking, that alone can prove the power of the gospel is that of reconciliation.

Vinay Samuel, Indian theologian

Chris Rice

In 1906, the Holy Spirit took hostage a little Black storefront church in the heart of Los Angeles. A movement was sparked bringing hundreds of Blacks, Whites, Mexican Americans, and Asians together into exuberant worship. For twenty years, the traditional walls of race lay crumbled in newborn Pentecostal churches.

But even though the walls were torn down, people never learned how to step over the rubble. Fragile seedlings sown by the Spirit on Azusa Street were eventually choked by long-established habits of separation and distrust. Because relationships did not go beneath the surface, Sunday worship in itself was powerless to keep the walls from being re-erected in the 1920s.

Even good intentions can't rush a deep relationship into existence. Unless the habits of trust, partnership, and mutual respect are formed, eventually the romance of the early years fades into a shallow, distant, and sometimes bitter memory.

The story of Azusa Street has a familiar ring to the call of Christian community development. Two basic callings that are often at odds in Christianity came together in a powerful and unusual way at the grass roots: reconciling people to God, and reconciling people across the toughest human barriers. The work of reconciliation is at the heart of Christian community development. Surely one of the greatest signs of the truth of the gospel is racial reconciliation.

The joy of Azusa's early years also resounds with the experience of Christian community development, because it is truly remarkable when walls come down in America's most segregated institution. What Dr. Martin Luther King Jr. called "the beloved community" is a living reality in many inner city neighborhoods where the sons and daughters of diverse racial experiences live, worship, and work side by side. Churches of Latinos and Anglos put salsa on their spaghetti, and Black/White congregations sing "Lift Every Voice and Sing" and "My Country 'Tis of Thee" in the same service. The members of these churches have indeed tasted "How good and pleasant it is when brothers [and sisters] live together in unity!" (Ps. 133:1).

But those in racial trench warfare also identify with the struggle of Azusa. It is one thing to be "integrated," but quite another to be "reconciled." Reconciliation brings great rewards, but it involves denying yourself and sometimes carrying a rugged cross.

The church from which Spencer and I come is a joyful, intense environment where Blacks and Whites have attempted to work toward a true down-to-earth unity of spirit and purpose. While it is far from perfect, this laboratory for reconciliation is an inner city neighborhood in Jackson, Mississippi, home of Voice of Calvary Fellowship Church. Members of our primarily Black and White church have wrestled with race through two decades of social twists and turns, from the James Brown "I'm Black and I'm Proud" era, to Michael Jackson's 1990s "It Doesn't Matter If You're Black or White."

For Spencer, it has been a thirty-year struggle in the trenches—from the political picket lines of the struggle for racial justice in Mendenhall, Mississippi, to the spiritual front lines of the dream of racial harmony in Voice of Calvary's multiracial community.

My odyssey is as different from Spencer's as for any White who doesn't have to deal with race until it hits you in the face. I grew up as a missionary kid and relocated to a Black community as a college student in 1981. Building relationships didn't come easy, and I have fought off the urge to put the racial mess behind me and get on with life.

The principles we offer are forged on the anvil of a long and continuing give-and-take between Black and White Christians, a dialogue based on a firm determination to hang in there through tough times together, "in sickness and in health."

While Spencer's and my context is Black and White, we have learned that many of the dynamics are the same in other multiracial settings. Dealing with racial reconciliation from the perspective of Latinos and Asians is relatively unexplored territory for Christian community development. As churches and ministries pioneer into this territory—such as La Villita Community Church in Chicago, Discipleship Chapel in New York, and First Church of the Nazarene in Los Angeles—they will offer new flavors to the call to racial reconciliation.

Competing Models

Mix the cross-cultural ingredients of Christian community development together and it might seem like a recipe for racial disaster. For the very first time in their lives, many volunteers and staff, indigenous and transplants, find themselves on racially mixed turf. Down the street, brothers from the Nation of Islam push their newspapers bearing the message of Black nationalism to our neighbors. Congregations all around, at the next corner and up the interstate, are rarely racially mixed—and content to stay that way.

The biblical call to reconciliation is constantly contending with competing ideologies. Three fierce competitors vie for hearts and minds in our communities and hinder our attempts at creating models of racial reconciliation.

Homogeneous church models—with two extremes being White homogeneity and Black Afrocentric—promote same race congregations as a comfortable, fast-growth strategy. They preach a gospel that saves but is too weak to reconcile.

A close cousin is the *multicultural* model, which is winning the day with minorities who fear they will have to give up their culture to join the integrated group. This model is driving minority churches and Christians on college campuses to separate along the same lines as the rest of society—in the interest of cultural self-preservation. They fear that racial harmony means assimilate and become White. Let's all respect each other, they say—but from a distance.

The *integrated* church model, featuring Whites with a sprinkling of minorities, embodies the most popular concept of race relations. But integration has been a one-way street that in the final analysis costs Whites very little. As demonstrated by Azusa Street, an integrated church is not necessarily a reconciled church.

The reconciliation model requires a decisive paradigm shift—one evidenced by friendships of trust, common mission, and mutual submission that go beyond Sunday morning.

The shift to the reconciliation model begins with a shift in theology. Obviously, Christians once together at Azusa Street found a way to justify why they could part ways and still be OK with God. Action follows thinking. And for Christians, our thinking should flow out of our theology.

Spencer Perkins

The Greatest Commandment

One of the oldest known strategies of warfare is to divide and conquer. By isolating your enemy you rob him of his strength. Then you can do just about whatever you please with him. Christians have used a strategy similar to this in our attempts to deal with the hard teachings of Jesus. We have separated basic principles of Scripture that God never intended to be separated, consequently robbing them of their intended power.

Our inability as Christians to reconcile loving God to loving our neighbor has done great harm to our claims that Jesus is the answer.

It would be very easy to sum up our entire gospel in the word *reconciliation*. Second Corinthians 5:18–19 says, "All this is from God, who reconciled us to himself through Christ and gave us the ministry of reconciliation: that God was reconciling the world to himself in Christ, not counting men's sins against them. And he has committed to us the message of reconciliation."

It is important for us to understand that this reconciliation that Paul speaks of here has two parts: people and their relationship to God, and people and their relationship to other people. Everything in Scripture falls under these broad categories.

In the third chapter of Genesis, man and woman broke their relationship with God by disobeying him and eating the forbidden fruit. In Genesis chapter 4, we broke with each other when Cain killed his brother Abel. The rest of the Bible is a record of God attempting to reconcile the human race back to himself and reconciling us to each other. And these categories should not be separated.

Once Jesus was approached by a religious lawyer who wanted to try to make him separate the two basic thrusts of the gospel (Matt. 22:36–40). He challenged Jesus, "Which is the great commandment in the law?" This was an opportunity for Jesus to say definitively what the point of Jewish religion was. The first part of Jesus' response was expected: "[You shall] love the Lord your God with all your heart and with all your soul and with all your mind. This is the first and greatest commandment."

We have a tendency to stop here. We hear many sermons that concentrate on this one commandment. But Jesus did not stop here. Jesus says, before you can reduce the gospel to just you and God, before you can make it into a spiritual exercise, there is a second commandment and it is like the first, "[You shall] love your neighbor as yourself."

Then Jesus goes on to make what must be one of the most overlooked statements in Scripture. "On these two commandments depend all the law and the prophets." Under these two categories falls everything that was taught by Moses and the prophets and by Jesus and his disciples. Boiling it all down to its raw essence, what God wants is for us to love him and love our neighbor.

Who Is My Neighbor?

To many Christians, the idea of racial reconciliation may sound extrabiblical. Given all the other problems facing our nation, we put it pretty low on the priority list. "But why must we deal with this?" people ask. "Is racial reconciliation that important?" The answer might surprise you, once you realize who your neighbor really is.

When Jesus was asked, "How do I inherit eternal life?" and he answered "Love God, and love your neighbor as yourself," the follow-up question was "Who is my neighbor?" Jesus' reply came in the form of the Good Samaritan story. For all practical purposes, Jesus turned the question into a racial issue.

It is no coincidence that Jesus picked a Samaritan and a Jew in telling the story. Jews didn't see the Samaritans as their neighbors. Samaritans were the half-breeds, the scum of the earth, the outcasts.

Jesus said our neighbors are particularly those people who ignore us, who separate themselves from us, who are afraid of us, whom we have the most difficulty loving, and who we feel don't love us. *These* are our neighbors.

In Matthew 5:46 Jesus asks if you love only those who love you, what reward will you get? Anybody can do that.

Christianity doesn't require any power when its only challenge is doing something that already comes naturally. On the other hand, it will take a powerful gospel—a gospel with guts—to enable us to love across all the barriers we erect to edify our own kind and protect us from our insecurities.

Jesus said our witness, our credibility to the world, is demonstrated by our love for each other. There is no greater witness to the genuineness of our gospel. Think about it. If, because of Christ, people of different races could live out a model of reconciliation that has not been attained by any other force, the world would have to ask, "Why?"

Remember that the "who is my neighbor?" question was clarifying how we make sure we go to heaven when we die. Therefore, living out the answer has potentially eternal significance.

It is time to seize the opportunity in this race relations crisis to demonstrate to the unbelieving world a Christianity more powerful than any other religion. At the Lausanne II Conference on World Evangelism, Indian church leader Vinay Samuel voiced the following concern:

The most serious thing is the image around the world that evangelicals are soft on racial injustice . . . One sign and wonder, biblically speaking, that alone can prove the power of the gospel is that of reconciliation . . . Hindus can produce as many miracles as any Christian miracle worker. Islamic saints in India can produce and duplicate every miracle that has been produced by Christians. But they cannot duplicate the miracle of black and white together, of racial injustice being swept away by the power of the gospel . . . Our credibility is at stake . . . If we are not able to establish our credibility in this area we have not got the whole gospel. In fact we have not got a proper gospel at all ("Evangelicals and Racism: The Lausanne II Press Conference" in *Transformation,* January 1990, 29).

Chris Rice

We can't just spiritually snap our fingers and presto! *We're one in Christ!* Spencer and I view the task of making a theology of reconciliation a practical reality in our lives and ministries as comprising three steps.

First, we have to *admit* that racial separation exists, that our relationships are uneasy, and that they misrepresent what God intended for his people. Second, we must *submit.* We must hand ourselves over to God by falling on our faces before him and asking for help, recognizing that we can't be healed apart from him. We must also submit to one another by building loving relationships across racial barriers. Finally, we have to *commit.* Deep and lasting reconciliation will be realized only as we commit our lives, our ministries, and our churches to an intentional lifestyle of loving our racially diverse neighbors as ourselves.

The First Step: Admit

It is a painful surprise to plunge with excitement across the dividing line of race only to find treacherous territory hidden beneath the surface. Voice of Calvary has always been ahead of its time in race relations, and in 1981 I was just one of hundreds of visitors and volunteers who trekked from across the nation and even the world to witness the unusual site of Black/White partnership in Jackson, Mississippi—the heart of what was once dubbed "The Closed Society."

Black and White families lived side by side in a small fifteen-block area. There was an interracial gospel choir, where White boys like me learned how to sing, rock, and clap at the same time. There were creative ministry programs in everything from housing and health care, to economic development and youth ministry. On Sunday morning, a White senior pastor shouted out his sermons like a Black country preacher. There was intense discussion about reclaiming our evangelical heritage but among people compassionate for the poor and committed to social justice.

When I arrived in 1981, I fancied myself as the solution to racism and poverty. Growing up as a missionary kid in South Korea was my cross-cultural badge of honor. I had been discipled and educated by the best in church, parachurch, and academia, so I thought I had the skills and resources that poor people really needed. It was exciting to use my gifts and talents to serve, and I jumped into the middle of Voice of Calvary's ministry free-for-all.

But in 1983, in a series of heated exchanges that came to be known as the "reconciliation meetings," Blacks charged me and other Whites in our church with the dreaded R word—*racism.*

The topic of one meeting was why so many ambitious Whites had come to Voice of Calvary and moved into leadership positions. The Blacks argued that VOC's goal was not to develop Whites, but Blacks. Whites could go anywhere and find no doors closed. They needed to step aside so Blacks could step forward.

After the meeting that night, as I walked alone the few blocks to my house, my insides churned. If Blacks lead, what role do Whites have? How will I ever fulfill my God-given potential? Doesn't reconciliation mean not looking at Black and White? How can Blacks be so angry? Don't they know I came here to help?

As confused as I was by their anger, I could no longer claim that race wasn't my problem. This was personal—they didn't trust me and I didn't trust them. I realized that in spite of all my good intentions, I didn't really know or trust these Black brothers and sisters. Mentally I began to pack my bags. I was ready to join the trickle of members, both Black and White, who began to leave our church. I didn't need angry Black folks telling me what was wrong with my lifestyle.

Somehow, by God's grace, I and other Whites and Blacks hung on to each other in spite of our exposed weaknesses. In a small Bible study group that we formed after the meetings, I got to know Spencer and to see that he and I, like most Blacks and Whites in our church at the time, had experienced the reconciliation meetings totally differently. In the secure and safe environment that began to form in our small group, all of us began to become more like-minded. Through these friendships, God slowly knit a safe place of acceptance where I could assess my racial baggage more objectively. These secure relationships provided the context in which I could face the truth of the reconciliation meetings.

When Blacks had said, "Step to the side," I'd heard, "Step back." When they said "mutual submission," I'd heard "Black domination." When they mentioned the importance of Black leadership, I'd heard "No room for White leadership." In the final analysis, those meetings had not been a purge, or a coup that would elevate Black over White. We were partners, moving ahead side by side. It has been said that when you are used to being in charge, true partnerships will feel to you like you are being dominated.

Voice of Calvary's understanding of racial reconciliation had reached a turning point in 1983. The challenges we faced were the stuff that church and denominational splits are made of. We learned the valuable lessons that individuals, leaders, churches, and ministries must face up to in beginning the transition from being integrated to being reconciled.

Racial Residue

Germs left over from the disease of forced segregation, discrimination, and social separation lie deep within us all. For Blacks, the residue is anger, bitterness, inferiority, and blame. For Whites, the residue that years of social and spiritual disease have left behind includes denial, fear, guilt, superiority, and racial blinders. This residue will inevitably surface and have to be contended with in a multiracial setting.

Hardly ever do Christians discuss their true feelings about race—the issues are explosive: mistrust between the races; Whites' tendency to dominate the leadership of an interracial group; unresolved residue from growing up in an unequal society. Relationships between Blacks and Whites have been so strained that the trust needed to begin and sustain a relationship does not always come easily. Some Blacks, whether consciously or unconsciously, will throw up a defensive obstacle course for Whites to overcome before they will open up and begin to trust.

We learned that in an interracial environment, nearly every conflict will be perceived as a racial issue—especially by Blacks. Those conflicts will only get worse as Blacks talk to Blacks and Whites to Whites. Little molehills can become nearly immovable mountains. Major issues, such as the role of Whites in a development effort focused on a Black inner city neighborhood, were not being openly talked through either. Racial residue cannot be ignored. If there is not a safe atmosphere to openly discuss racial issues, you may pay the price with an explosion down the line.

There is a basic psychological principle that people cannot move beyond that which they cannot express and own as a feeling. Often, White participants feel very uncomfortable during the reconciliation section of VOC's training workshops. After spending three hours on Black history and racism someone will usually comment, "Can't they just forgive and get beyond all this?" A Black friend once told me, "I don't know if I can trust a White person who isn't willing to feel a little uncomfortable with the reality of racism."

White Blinders

Spencer's and my working definition of racism is: One group of people thinking they are better than another group of people, and then acting on that belief by separating, discriminating, and sometimes eliminating the other group. Before those meetings I would have said I knew who racists were—they wore hoods, burned crosses, threw Black people out of their churches, and used the word *nigger.* And I hadn't done any of those things.

But a new twist on the definition was introduced at VOC in those years. Though four hundred years of the old, overt racism is gradually disappearing, a subtle but lethal strain of the disease remains. While its effects are still separation and distrust, its symptoms are not as obvious as lynchings, forced segregation, or telling ethnic jokes. We call it passive racism. And we need to learn how to detect it in ourselves and our institutions.

Passive racism is a way of looking at the world that is much like wearing racial blinders—not bothering to see and understand the effects of race because we don't have to in order to survive.

Blinders are ingenious. By limiting a horse's peripheral vision, the horse forges forward in the only direction it can see. It is undistracted by the world going on around it. But even if the horse cannot see this other world, it still exists—full of dangers, difficulties, opportunities. The horse is just unconscious of it.

Probably the most glaring example of White blinders is the fact that as the majority culture, we don't have to deal with race. We say "I don't see color," but the reality is we don't have to see color. I can walk away from VOC and Black people and the whole mess of race anytime I like. I can cross town tomorrow and enter the White world and know I will be treated well and not be denied opportunities because of my color. But my Black friends don't have that option. Like it or not, they will always have to deal with racism.

Another subtle result of White blinders is that we tend to have lower expectations for Black people than we have for ourselves. One well-intending college professor once asked me and Spencer if he should grade his Black students' papers more leniently than his White students' papers. Many White volunteers who come and work with neighborhood children often treat them as "pets" rather than holding them to high standards of excellence and discipline. Often they will allow the neighborhood children to misbehave in ways they would never tolerate from their own children or siblings. If there is anything that we have learned from the past thirty years of race relations, it is that low expectations—whether motivated by guilt or sympathy—do harm to both parties involved.

Dismantling Institutional Blinders

When racial issues and conflict cannot be openly discussed, when leadership does not eventually represent the cultural makeup of the church, if gifts of different racial groups are not being exercised within the body, when Sunday morning smiles do not penetrate our separate worlds—institutional blinders are operating.

Lingering racial superiority and insensitivity can survive very quietly within our structures. After the reconciliation meetings, we realized that most of our church elders were seminary-educated Whites. These were never explicit criteria for being in leadership; it just happened that way. There is a Black brother in our church who doesn't have much formal education, but he is a prayer warrior who has made us more of a praying church. Today he is an elder in our church, something that wouldn't have been the case before our racial crisis.

For many years, VOC staff were required to raise their support from churches and friends. We began to realize that this practice favored those who came from a natural family or church support base, most of whom happened to be White. Our commitment to a majority Black indigenous staff was being compromised by this policy. We committed ourselves as a ministry to raising support for Black staff who didn't come from a strong support base.

Skin-Deep Relationships

For two years I enjoyed the many Blacks with whom I lived, worked, and worshiped. But when they started talking racism in our own church, I was ready to back away. I realized how little I knew my Black "friends." They were fine with me as long as they stayed on the safe topics.

I had lived in a Black neighborhood, worshiped in a mixed church, and worked in ministry with Blacks for two years, but I realized that I couldn't name a single Black peer whom I considered a trusted friend, and who trusted me. I saw new sides to their personalities and perspectives I had never seen before—and it wasn't always very comfortable or pleasant to deal with.

As I made Black friends, I was astonished to see the extent to which they had to battle with racism on a daily basis—whether it was dealing with a local banker's reluctance to do a routine transaction, not finding videos for their children with positive Black characters, or having a Black friend's five-year-old say he wanted to be White because his teacher said God washed us "white as snow." I also discovered that Black people are bilingual and bicultural, that my friends talked and acted differently around Whites than they did with each other.

Often Whites think relationships are further along than they really are. Spencer once told me that trust really isn't developing between Whites and Blacks until racial and cultural differences can be safely discussed. I've found that to be a pretty reliable rule of thumb.

Confronting the Caseworker Mentality

By moving to the inner city, I had fancied myself as the solution to racism. After the reconciliation meetings, I was insecure about my place as a White outsider and questioned whether I even had a role to play. I realized there was another side to my "do-good" motives. My life was all mapped out: I would offer my skills to the inner city for a while and then get on with my "real" life. At a deeper level, I didn't want to stay at Voice of Calvary if my potential for leadership might be limited.

In the years since, I have become convinced that there is a place for transplants in Christian community development and in a minority community. In finding my place, my relationship with the Black community has changed from that of caseworker to convert to comrade. Each of these role changes has called for a deeper commitment, each time in response to God's call.

When transplants come to the community of need, it's usually with the motivation to "help those who can't help themselves." God accepts us where we're at. Motivated by compassion, we want to meet a need, to accomplish a task that will glorify God. We organize a work group, volunteer some time, or decide to give regularly to an inner city ministry. All are much needed services. Others go further than that. We see the need for leadership and providing new services. We step out decisively to initiate a new effort.

The most important commitment a caseworker can make is to truly serve those he or she has come to help. One church group we hosted at VOC had worked hard all week renovating a house for a low-income family. After dinner, each household member gave a brief testimony, then one of our Black members talked for fifteen minutes on God's concern for racial reconciliation. After he finished, there was a long pause before one volunteer spoke up: "Thanks for the food, but I'm tired, and I came here to serve Christ, not for Black and White. So I'm going to leave." Soon other group members joined him in making it clear that they had come to do ministry, not learn about racial reconciliation. For another hour, we tried to point out the contradiction in their commitment but made no headway. As they left the house, we felt devastated.

They had come to do something for the poor. But they weren't willing to listen and learn from the very people they considered themselves serving, only to tell and do.

Our motive for racial reconciliation needs to be for our own sakes—for what God wants to do in us rather than our "do good" motives for others. If you are only willing to serve as far as your private agenda extends, the message is: "I'm better than you, because you need me but I don't need you."

As well intended as their motives might be, caseworkers often want to dictate when, where, and how they will help rather than asking what is needed. They are willing to serve as long as their lifestyles or attitudes aren't confronted. But when the going gets rough (and it always does), when their potential isn't realized, when decisions don't go their way, or when they're required to receive and learn rather than to give and help, caseworkers often retreat from involvement.

Starting out as a caseworker is okay. But when presented with more understanding and the opportunity to grow, we are called to mature beyond being helpers to allowing the community to help us in our walk. Those who begin to embrace and work through difficulty move beyond the role of caseworker to become converts. I will return to this next stage later in the chapter.

Spencer Perkins

Much of the focus on the race issue, as it was in Voice of Calvary's reconciliation meetings, is on White racism. Racism is one of the major obstacles to reconciliation, and whenever it surfaces it must be addressed. Blacks were more than willing to allow Whites to "pay their dues." But if reconciliation is to happen, people of color will have to own up to some things, too.

Minorities Have to Do Their Part

Blacks easily talk about what's wrong with White folks and are understandably concerned about racial discrimination. But we are often reluctant to forgive and begin to trust. Sometimes we even use race as a weapon to keep Whites at bay. But while minorities are very concerned about racial justice, we are not—to the surprise of many White Christians—very interested in being reconciled.

Every Black person has his or her share of bitter encounters with racism. But there comes a time when we can no longer afford to hold on to our anger, when cradling anger only does harm to the one who is holding on to it. It is not uncommon to speak to Black men and women who cling so tightly to our historical oppression that they are immobilized from taking action to improve our future.

Anger and bitterness can be very consuming. The heart attempting to entertain them will have very little room for anything else. When Jesus said that if we do not forgive men their trespasses, neither will God forgive us (Matt. 6:15), he was not just being stubborn. Christian love just won't fit into a heart trying to retain anger and bitterness. Whites who want to begin building interracial relationships will have to be patient with us, as we will have to be with them.

It is next to impossible to be reconciled to someone whom you do not respect or who you feel does not respect you. Attempts at racial reconciliation between two unequal partners will be superficial and result in further damage. The negative reinforcements to the "inferior" partner are more obvious, but the false sense of superiority to the other partner is just as negative. This type of relationship will inevitably produce future conflict. Until both parties accept and internalize this need for equality they will only spin their wheels.

If we assume that our values, our intellect, and our lifestyle (even our worship style) are superior to another's, we will approach the relationship from a paternalistic point of view. Sociologists call this attitude ethnocentrism. It is a very close cousin to racism.

One of the results of the reconciliation meetings was a renewed resolve to develop Black leadership. In an all-Black church setting, Blacks have no problem taking leadership. But we realized that when Blacks and Whites come together for a common cause, the Whites tend to feel more secure taking on the leadership roles—

whether it's volunteering to lead in a church project or being willing to be considered for eldership. So we decided to make an intentional effort to affirm Black culture and encourage Black leadership. This was not an attempt to put Blacks over Whites but only to balance the scales—especially since we lived and worshiped in a Black neighborhood.

After twelve years of intentionally affirming "Blackness," we have been successful in bringing about more Black leadership. However, we have become nearly 70 percent Black. So, in 1995, the church committed to reach out in some intentional ways to win more Whites. It was exciting to see many Blacks voicing the need for this new emphasis—a true sign of reconciliation.

Truth and Love

It has been said that "love without truth lies, and truth without love kills." A shallow relationship that gushes superficial love will not survive the harsh realities of race. And a budding relationship that only focuses on cold hard truth with little concern for the emotional well-being of the other party will not get off the ground. The biblical principle of speaking the truth in love, whether in a group or as individuals, offers us the best foundation on which to build and maintain relationships.

The emphasis of the reconciliation meetings was more on truth than on love. We don't recommend our type of explosion as the way to address racial issues. If we had to do it over again, we would have addressed issues long before they exploded.

Over the long haul, neither love nor truth alone takes us further than the color of our skin. Alone, each is powerless to heal. Brought together, however, they become spiritual dynamite.

In the admitting process, we allow God to humble us, to purify our motives, and to bring us face-to-face with sinfulness—our racial blinders, guilt, anger, bitterness, and unforgiveness. For some, it may take years to come to the point of seeing the depth of our racial residue. Others will conclude that the cost is too high and may want to give only lip service to this necessary step of healing. Christian community development leaders, ministries, and churches that have the courage to embrace these discoveries with openness and humility will find that God does not leave us here.

The Second Step: Submit

Reconciliation, unlike integration, is spiritual. Therefore our strategies must be spiritual. Submitting is acknowledging our weaknesses before God and inviting him to take us where we can't go on our own.

Voice of Calvary's reconciliation meetings forced a showdown between two of the most powerful forces in the universe: God and race. Thirteen years earlier, I had watched intently as my father struggled between these two foes after he was nearly beaten to death by White policemen in the Brandon jail. Until those meetings I had never seen Jesus win over race on a large scale.

Before the meetings I hadn't been secure enough to climb into the same foxhole with the people of the church—especially my White brothers and sisters. After the meetings, I saw many of these people through different eyes. Not only my faith in them but also my faith in Christianity had been strengthened because of their commitment.

I believe the reason we persevered and stayed together is because as weak as we were, we had a motivation deeper than human self-interest. The Blacks did not seek to put Whites under their rule. Even after 1983, Blacks at VOC didn't ask Whites to take a back seat. None of the White church leaders or ministry staff were asked to leave. Our White senior pastor, Phil Reed, offered to step down, but Black members exhorted him to stay put. Chris was even promoted to a position of more responsibility. And Whites didn't stick around just so they could prove they were racially "hip."

I believe we hung on to each other because we knew it was what God required of us. It is for this reason that Chris and I grow weary of attempts to promote racial understanding and healing outside the context of the church. Reconciliation is a profoundly spiritual concept—one that tackles some of our worst human tendencies with some of the best that God has to offer his people.

Without God as architect, our plans for building reconciled relationships will eventually collapse under the weight of our old racial residue. Political motivations will change with the wind, guilt will pass, and anger will eventually subside. But when God turns our guilt into conviction and our anger into passion, then we have some strong tools to cultivate reconciliation for the long haul.

Forgiveness as a Way of Life

Forgiveness is so important that our willingness to forgive each other is the single prerequisite that God imposed on his forgiveness of us. If any relationship is to survive and thrive, it will have to depend on forgiveness. Because race carries so much excess baggage, interracial relationships will need to rely on forgiveness even more.

In 1994 a student at a northeastern college asked Chris and me if he had to be a Christian to be committed to racial reconciliation. "Are you saying that's the only way?" he asked. The answer is simple, I told him. If we weren't Christians, Chris and I would have parted ways long ago. Why would Chris have put up with racial confrontation, painful growth, and the sting of Black anger? If not for my faith in God, how could I be free of bitterness for my father's beating? Why would I bother to forgive—and to seek reconciliation with—Whites unless I believed Jesus required it of me?

Only after we've sincerely admitted that we have fallen short of God's call to reconciliation, and after we have submitted the problem before the only Physician who can heal us, are we ready to make the commitments that will lead us to personal lifestyle changes as well as new structural approaches.

Chris Rice

The Third Step: Commit

Racial reconciliation is a marathon, not a one-hundred-yard dash. Personal courage and all our institutional resources will be needed to help us develop the stamina, vision, and unity of purpose necessary to surmount the "heartbreak hills" that inevitably come. A commitment to reconciliation will surely add a whole new dimension to already complicated decisions such as selecting leaders, planting churches, hiring staff, building networks, and choosing priorities. But it is crucial to our witness to the unbelieving world that we be willing to go out of our way to give our gospel this added credibility.

From Caseworkers to Comrades

As my blinders slowly came off, and I saw how God wanted to deal with my own character, I felt like God was moving me through something like a conversion process—taking away the old and replacing it with the new.

As relocated transplants make this shift, they move from being caseworkers to what I call converts. If the motivation of a caseworker is "helping the helpless," the convert says, "I'm here for my own spiritual growth and development."

Some at Voice of Calvary were not able to make that shift. When faced with the prospect of accepting limited leadership options, transplants (especially Whites) often begin packing their bags. Many people are more concerned with their own rights and personal development than they are with the development of others and are sometimes unwilling to make any personal sacrifices for the sake of reconciliation. The cost of giving up some individual ambition for the sake of the entire body's growth is too high a price to pay.

For Whites, it's hard to accept that being "color-blind" is not what reconciliation is about. It's hard to listen to the anger of Blacks. But I learned that if I as a White person could take the initiative to be patient, seek to understand, and persevere, the bonds of trust that resulted between myself and Black people were worth the wait.

When I wondered about whether I was going to achieve my potential as a transplant to the inner city, I was buying into a value of upward mobility that our culture takes for granted.

Philippians 2:5–7 expresses the Christian counter-ideal: "Your attitude should be the same as that of Christ Jesus: Who, being in very nature God, did not consider equality with God something to be grasped, but made himself nothing, taking the very nature of a servant, being made in human likeness."

The process of becoming a convert is a painful kind of "rite of passage" that prepares ours hearts for God to do greater work through us. That "something greater," for those who are called, is to put your life into the same boat as those in the community you're serving.

In each difficult moment that tested my commitment, I had two choices: get as far away as I could from dealing with this stuff, or work through it. Each hardship bonded me closer to the community and to the other committed Blacks and Whites. I had more of a personal stake in seeing change not just for others, but for myself.

This stake is carved out through down-to-earth commitments. As different races live as neighbors, worship side by side, share our most personal experiences, and submit our lives to one another, we move to the highest expressions of our unity in Christ. We have more and more of a personal stake in bringing justice to our communities: we want to see things change not just for the benefit of others, but for ourselves and our own families. A great paradox of servanthood is that while we are called to die to our selfish interests, it is not until we put our own interests at stake that we can become full partners in ministry.

Those who make these commitments become comrades with the community. There comes a time when trust is earned, when dues are paid, and when the rites of passage are complete: you have become a leader in reconciliation. This is the time to stop worrying about what others might think and take the responsibilities that go with leadership. Becoming comrades is a step toward mutual submission between White and Black: "Submit to one another out of reverence for Christ" (Eph. 5:21). Reshaped through the purifying and refining process of becoming a convert, White people's gifts make a positive and vital contribution.

For Blacks, becoming comrades with Whites means moving beyond anger to forgiveness and trust. For Whites it means moving beyond racism and guilt to embrace a lifestyle that witnesses reconciliation in our choices. For both it will mean encouraging and confronting and dealing with each other not on the basis of race but character.

Spencer Perkins

Kingdom Choices and Intentionality

We can't change the past. You can't change that you weren't exposed to other races where you grew up—that you were raised in an all-White suburb with churches where everybody looked like you. You can't rub away what adults taught and demonstrated to you as a child.

But you can decide to forge a different path for the future. You might have been raised isolated from people different from you, but your children don't have to be. There are life choices we can make in our attempt to pursue reconciliation that will put us at God's disposal as his personal agents for racial healing.

These "kingdom choices" set an example and create a legacy for our children. Because Chris's parents took a risk and went to Korea as missionaries, it wasn't difficult for him to go to a Black community in Mississippi. My parents were pioneers in reaching out to Whites. They made a conscious choice to invite Whites to join them in their ministry in Mississippi and California. Because of that, I am freer to venture out into the waters of race relations navigated first by my parents.

Our parents' kingdom choices were among the greatest gifts they could have given Chris and me. Our choices make it easier, or more difficult, for our children to dare to invest their lives in the risky principles of reconciliation. Each choice we make for the sake of the kingdom gives them something more to build on.

Sometimes visitors come to VOC and see Blacks and Whites worshiping, singing in a gospel choir, and relating easily together and remark, "What a wonderful place!" They want to jump right in without realizing the cost that's involved. They don't know the many years of blood, sweat, and tears that are behind the joy. They think it's a miracle—and it is, by God's grace. But as Elisabeth Elliot once wrote, "Personal sacrifice paves the way for God's miracles."

Churches and ministries that are effective at reconciliation have made cross-cultural unity a priority in corporate life. For some churches, an intentional commitment to reconciliation has led them to set up co-pastors of different races. This makes the church's priorities crystal clear. Other ministries make a point of forming inter-racial teams in every area of ministry, thereby creating a safe environment for airing racial concerns and issues. At Voice of Calvary our racial crisis was the price we paid for not being proactive in dealing with racial conflict. Leaders must not be afraid to create an open atmosphere for working out differences.

Those in Christian community development have found creative ways to make reconciliation happen in their churches and ministries. Rock of Our Salvation Church in Chicago is proactive about dealing with racial issues through "Fudge-Ripple" meetings. One Sunday each quarter, the Black members meet with pastor Raleigh Washington and discuss their questions and concerns together (the "chocolate" meeting). Then the White members do the same (the "vanilla" meeting). Finally, all the members gather together and are led in discussion by Pastor Washington through the most significant issues that surfaced in both groups. The goal is unity, not racial dumping. Afterward, Black and White members eat fudge-ripple ice cream together to celebrate their unity in Christ. Pastor Washington says these meetings more than anything have helped hold Rock Church together.

Peter Anderson and Gary Ham formed an intentional friendship across racial lines. Peter is a White medical doctor living in the suburbs. Gary is Black and directs an inner city ministry in Newport News, Virginia. Every Thursday morning at 8:15 sharp, they meet for breakfast at a Shoney's restaurant. It is a sacred hour in their lives—an appointment that is not lightly broken. Peter and Gary talk about everything: how to love their wives better, how to be better dads, how they live out their sometimes differing political perspectives. Their lives are open books to each other. Peter is a key board member and volunteer in Gary's ministry, so their relationship is making an impact on the inner city. Peter and Gary will forever have a passion to improve race relations, because their own relationship is at stake. Sure, they have to go out of their way a little, but the rewards are worth the effort.

Reconciling Different Cultures into One Body

God himself often goes out of his way to highlight ethnicity. Take Acts 13, where Luke mentions the ethnicity of each of the leaders at the church at Antioch. His point is powerful: to prove the power of this new religion, which could even break down walls of culture and class. Even in God's ultimate plan we do not lose our ethnicity. Just look at Revelation 7:9, a picture of heaven, where a multitude "from every nation, tribe, people and language" worships together before God.

But surely we are Christians first, not Blacks, or Whites, Latinos, Asians, or Native Americans. So how do we reconcile these two biblical truths—the gift of ethnicity and the ideals of Christianity—into a single vision in our churches and ministries?

A vision of a melting pot is one option, but it's boring; what's attractive about a single monocultural blob? And too often, melting pot really means "become White." Another vision is the "salad bowl." All together, but each part separate and unchanged by the other ingredients. At VOC we prefer a "stew pot" vision—where each ingredient, simmering in one church, at the same time retains its distinct taste, takes on the flavor of the other ingredients, and corporately becomes a new and different creation.

But this vision only works when each ingredient—each race and culture—sees a need for each of the others, when they see the unit as something much better than they can ever be apart. Sometimes there is a need to highlight certain ingredients because their value has gone unrecognized, their flavor unappreciated, their unique role unaffirmed by others or even downplayed by itself. One thing we really highlight at our church is Black History month.

Whether highlighting ethnicity helps or hurts depends on the motivations of those involved. Things like Black history are important not just for Black kids, but for White children, too. When ethnicity becomes an end in itself, when being true to your ethnic identity is the highest ideal, it becomes harmful. There have been times at Voice of Calvary when people have had to be confronted about putting their culture higher than Christ.

Christians should have a higher standard, eagerly going out of our way to appreciate and "mix it up" with the many ingredients God has put into his church. At our church, our White pastor teaches the annual Black History lesson. That's racial reconciliation at its best.

Rather than be points of conflict, our cultural differences should become opportunities to learn from and enrich one another. In our church, the White members have learned to enjoy singing songs from Black culture. Then there are the "in-between" songs—beautiful melodies written and recorded by Whites and sung with a special Black gospel flavor. One of our church's favorite choir songs is Handel's "Hallelujah Chorus"—sung with the soul, flair, and strength of the Black church tradition. Now that's the best of both worlds!

Stepping out of your culture can be risky. Blacks have plenty of labels for those who dare to embrace Whites as brothers and sisters—"sell out," "wanna-be," "Oreo," and "Uncle Tom" are among the favorites. White evangelicals have their own favorite name for voices of racial justice. Just call them "do-gooder-social-gospel-guilt-manipulated liberals" and then you don't have to enter the debate. Just remember that being a reconciler means being willing to be a bridge. And you know what they say about bridges—they get walked on from both sides.

Black people need to receive truth from Whites, too. They need to be able to listen and not label Whites racist as soon as they ask an honest question with a sincere heart. We should be able to take the best of each culture and exhort one another in areas of spiritual and cultural weakness. It's kingdom culture we're after, not Blackness or Whiteness.

Friends and Yokefellows

Nothing will give reconciliation a surer foothold in the church than one-to-one friendships of genuine trust formed across racial lines, especially between leaders. Why should children, students, and congregations take risks and sacrifices that their parents, teachers, and pastors aren't willing to take? Leaders will only be able to guide their constituencies as they experience this one-to-one trust in their own lives.

Raleigh Washington and Glen Kehrein of Rock of Our Salvation Church and Circle Urban Ministries of Chicago are two leaders who have been pioneers in the cause of racial reconciliation. In their book, *Breaking Down Walls*,[1] they lay out eight principles that are essential if reconciliation is to be taken seriously.

1. *Commitment to Relationship.* Racial reconciliation is built upon the foundation of committed relationships. (Ruth 1:16)

2. *Intentionality.* Intentionality is the purposeful, positive, and planned activity that facilitates reconciliation. (Eph. 2:14–15)
3. *Sincerity.* Sincerity is the willingness to be vulnerable, including the self-disclosure of feelings, attitudes, differences, and perceptions, with the goal of resolution and building trust. (John 15:15)
4. *Sensitivity.* Sensitivity is the intentional acquisition of knowledge in order to relate empathetically to a person of a different race and culture. (Eph. 4:15–16)
5. *Interdependence.* Interdependence recognizes our differences but realizes that we each offer something that the other person needs, resulting in equality in the relationship. (2 Cor. 8:12–14)
6. *Sacrifice.* Sacrifice is the willingness to relinquish an established status or position to genuinely adopt a lesser position in order to facilitate a cross-cultural relationship. (Phil. 2:3–4)
7. *Empowerment.* Empowerment is the use of repentance and forgiveness to create complete freedom in a cross-cultural relationship. (2 Cor. 8:9)
8. *Call.* We are all called to be involved in the ministry of reconciliation, but some are gifted with a special call to be racial reconcilers. (2 Cor. 5:17–21)

For the past twelve years, Glen and Raleigh have not only been friends, they have also been yokefellows—partners together in a dynamic ministry in inner city Chicago.

Chris and I have also made a commitment to each other that goes beyond our own comfort zone. Biracial friendships are wonderful, but we need more than just our usual fickle friendships, which turn sour when feelings get hurt. Cultivating any relationship takes effort. Throw race into that pot and the stakes are immediately raised. But, like in any game, when the stakes are higher, though the agony of defeat is more intense, the thrill of victory is much more meaningful.

However, when you have a mission that must be accomplished, a mission too large for one individual, then a relationship that would normally not have a basis for existence must be formed in order to accomplish the task. Those differences in personality, interests, and life experiences then become gifts or assets making the team more formidable. Compatibility with each other is not as crucial as ability to accomplish the task. Wars and sports produce excellent examples of this type of camaraderie. Lifelong relationships are formed in the preparation and execution of the battle plan together. Ex-athletes speak more of missing this camaraderie than they do of the games.

This type of relationship exists between what Chris and I call "yokefellows." In the Book of Philippians, Paul speaks to brothers and sisters with whom he has shed blood, sweat, and tears. In chapter 4, verse 3, he addresses one of those dear friends as "yokefellow." The idea of a yoke is powerful: two creatures yoked together for the sake of a common mission.

There are several distinctions between friendships and yokefellows:

- Friendships can happen with very little effort; yokefellows are intentional.
- Friendships are built for the benefit of the friends; yokefellows come together for the benefit of the kingdom.
- Friends are drawn together by their common interests; yokefellows are drawn together by a common mission.
- Friends like each other; yokefellows respect each other.
- Friendships are based on compatible personalities; the yokefellow bond is based on gifts that are needed to realize the goal.
- Friendships are fueled by emotion; yokefellows are linked by commitment.
- Friends separated by a fight may never speak to each other again; yokefellows will cheer each other on until their goal is reached.

The cause of racial reconciliation needs yokefellows, not for the good feelings that might follow, even though they will; not for the adventure, even though it is an exciting trip; not because it is a good thing to do, even though it is good; not solely for the sake of racial harmony, even though it will lead to that; but for the witness of the gospel.

The cause of the gospel needs biracial teams yoked together who are willing to take the dangerous point position into the gray, unknown territories that have traditionally separated White and Black Christians. They must be willing to face the spears and arrows that will surely fly from the hands and mouths of threatened people of all races insecure about leaving the comfort of the familiar. These teams of yokefellows, male and female, must be willing to face the uncertainty of the unfamiliar as scouts preparing the way for the army of God to follow.

The cause of the gospel also needs bodies of believers who are yoked together. Congregations must go out of their way to reach out to each other, confronting together the ills of their towns and cities, a cause too big for either to tackle alone. Congregations must come together, offering their different gifts to the cause, giving witness to the power of the gospel, and giving opportunity for racial healing to take place among their members.

Be warned: Any relationship that is significant to the kingdom will be attacked. At those moments you will be tempted to break the yoke. And be assured that the powers of darkness will seek to find any crack in the yoke and marshall all forces against that weak point. There will be the whispers in the ear: *He's getting more credit than you; She's not carrying as much weight as you; Why does it seem like he always wants to be in charge? Who needs this hardship anyway?* At times you will begin to distrust each other. You may even begin to question why the Plowman ever put you together.

But remember that if a yoke is broken, each partner loses one-half of his or her strength, one-half of the gifts needed to realize the goal. Breaking yokes doesn't just affect you; it affects all those who look to you for leadership. Your mission will be compromised. Sure you may be able to pull the plow alone for a while. But the rows you till and the terrain you cover will inevitably be much shallower and less challenging.

Like Chris and me, others who are in yokefellow relationships—among them Glen Kehrein and Raleigh Washington, Julie Ragland and Priscilla Perkins, Wayne Gordon and Carey Casey—describe their partnerships as similar to a marriage. The basic commitments of "in sickness and in health" and "for richer or poorer" enable us to endure for the long haul.

Azusa Street offers us a valuable and bittersweet lesson. God can tear down the walls of separation, but unless we do our part to step over the rubble and create some new personal and corporate habits, our witness of unity will only last until the thrill of our new cross-cultural fellowship is gone and the first major disagreement surfaces. Going the distance, moving from integration to reconciliation, requires making major shifts in our theology, relationships, and use of our resources.

As the world, and especially our cities, becomes more and more ethnically diverse, racial reconciliation becomes more important. If we as Christians are to take our gospel into the tough places, then we will need to be able to minister and to relate across racial and cultural barriers. Our ability to be reconciled with our racially different neighbors will be a key factor in our future success or failure.

Every Sunday millions of Christians sit in church and proclaim in song that "Jesus is the answer for the world today." I often wonder if we should add to the end of the song, "except for the race problem."

My next-door neighbor used to have a little dog named Scottie. Every day when I would walk past Scottie's house he would bark ferociously, jumping up against the fence that separated us as if to say, "If I had the opportunity, I would rip you to shreds." One morning as Scottie and I went through our regular routine, he pounced against an unlatched fence and to his surprise and mine, the gate swung open—presenting Scottie with the opportunity of a lifetime. To my surprise and relief, Scottie did not and would not come through that open gate. From that day on, I had no more respect for Scottie.

The tattered relationships between the races in this country offer Christians a historic opportunity. For centuries we have barked loudly and intensely that we, alone, had the answers to the world's problems. If that claim has not been all bark and no bite, then it is time for us to move through this open gate of opportunity—or stop our barking. Those committed to Christian community development have an incredible opportunity to lead the way through the gate.

The Key Elements of Making Racial Reconciliation a Practical Reality

- The biblical model of racial reconciliation contends with three competing ideologies: the homogeneous church model, multiculturalism, and integration. Remember that an "integrated" church is not necessarily a "reconciled" church.
- The raw essence of Scripture is that we are to love God and to love our neighbor. Jesus is clear about our "neighbors" being those we have the most difficulty loving.

Reconciliation is a three-step journey in our lives, ministries, and churches: admit, submit, and commit.

- First, we have to ADMIT that racial separation exists, that our relationships are uneasy, and that they misrepresent what God intends for his people.

  1. Racial residue will eventually surface and have to be contended with in a multiracial setting. In a Black/White context, White residue includes racism, guilt, superiority, and fear. Black residue includes anger, blame, inferiority, and bitterness. Often Blacks and other minorities are passionate about racial justice but not reconciliation.
  2. Unintended racial blinders prevent Whites from recognizing subtle forms of racism. Signs of institutional blinders include leadership not eventually representing the cultural makeup of a church or ministry or gifts of different racial groups not being affirmed and exercised.
  3. Don't assume that relationships are as far along as they appear. This is especially true for Whites.
  4. Volunteers, transplants, and supporters should be challenged to mature beyond being "caseworkers." The most important commitment is to truly serve those you desire to help. A deeper role requires greater sacrifice and commitment.

5. Be aware that on interracial turf, corporate culture tends to "drift White."
6. "Love without truth lies, and truth without love kills." The biblical principle of speaking the truth in love offers the best foundation on which to build and maintain interracial relationships.

- Second, we must SUBMIT ourselves to God—recognizing that we can't be healed apart from him—and we must submit to one another, by building loving relationships across racial barriers.

   1. Dependence on God is the only way to persevere through racial hardships.
   2. Forgiveness must become a way of life in an interracial setting. It's the MVP when it comes to sticking together.

- Finally, we have to COMMIT. Lasting trust and partnership grows out of intentional personal and corporate lifestyles of reconciliation.

   1. The roles of volunteers and transplants deepen as they move from being caseworkers, to converts, to comrades. The convert says, "I'm here for my own spiritual growth and development." Comrades join their lives and families with those of the community of need. Each role requires a deeper commitment in response to God's call.
   2. Recognize the kingdom choices that are available both individually and corporately. Leaders and ministries who are effective at reconciliation make cross-cultural unity a priority in family and corporate life.
   3. Ministries and churches must learn how to reconcile both the gift of ethnicity and the high ideals of kingdom culture. The best vision is a "stew pot" where each cultural ingredient, simmering in one church, at the same time retains its distinct taste, takes on the flavor of the other ingredients, and corporately becomes a new and different creation. But be prepared to take the heat from those who put culture over Christ.

4. Nothing gives reconciliation a surer foothold than one-to-one friendships of trust formed across racial lines, especially between leaders. Eight principles are essential in order for these relationships to mature: commitment, intentionality, sincerity, sensitivity, interdependence, sacrifice, empowerment, and call.

5. Seek to build "yokefellow" relationships and partnerships. Two or more leaders, churches, or ministries who have yoked themselves together for the sake of a common mission are the most powerful units for reconciliation.

7

Redistribution

Empowering the Community

Mary Nelson

I went up to the lookout of a drug pusher, who had flashed the "dope for sale" signal to our car as we came to the office, and said, "We're trying to make it better for your mother and children and the whole neighborhood. Please move." His response was that he was just trying to make a living, even if it wasn't an honest one. "At least," he said, "I'm not bopping you on the side of the head or robbing you. I'm just trying to provide for my children."

Christian community developers see unemployed people standing on the corners and know the pain this causes them and their families; we sense the hopelessness and lack of future our youth feel when looking at what's open to them in the job market; we want to do something about it. Some people seem to have too much of everything; other people don't seem to have enough of anything. Economic development or job creation is the new buzzword.

In *Beyond Charity*,[1] John Perkins describes the evolution in thinking regarding redistribution. In the 1960s the motto of community development was "Give people a fish, and they'll eat for a day." In the 1970s it was "Teach people to fish, and they'll eat for a lifetime." In the 1990s the focus has turned to "Who owns the pond?" Perkins goes on to say, "The challenge for Christian community-based economic development is to enable the people of the community to start local enterprises that meet local needs and employ indigenous people." He goes on to describe Thriftco, an enterprise of Jackson, Mississippi-based Voice of Calvary Ministries. Jobs are created in this business when manufacturers and major retailers donate extras and slightly damaged new clothing overruns, which are then sold at reduced rates. First efforts to operate this enterprise as a co-op with no profit and no dividends had to be modified because five years and nine managers after opening, the operation was $250,000 in debt. But strong management was brought in, and persistent leadership evolved, so that in its fourteenth year it is now a strong enterprise with thirty-six employees and gross sales of $350,000 per year.

Bethel New Life, a church-based community development corporation (CDC) in Chicago, started in its low income urban community with a commitment to provide affordable home ownership and community development without displacement of people. After the first several housing projects, with massive efforts to bring down the costs, Bethel soon found out that even the most affordable housing isn't affordable if one doesn't have a job. So, job creation in the community became the important focus. The two-pronged effort was both on establishing employment services to help people get into livable-wage jobs and on creating jobs in the neighborhood utilizing the assets of the community. These efforts led to the creation of an enterprise that provides home care services for the elderly, a business that now employs over four hundred people. It also led to industrial development around recycling and reprocessing. The latter effort directly provided jobs and led into linkages with industrial operators who could supply future jobs. Thus, for Bethel New Life, the journey into redistribution began in an evolutionary way, with associated ups and downs in terms of profitable bottom lines.

In *Return Flight*, Bob Lupton describes the cycle of a dollar as it recycles its way through their community-based enterprises in his Atlanta community. A young man enters the Family Store and buys a wool shirt for a dollar. The store deposits the dollar in the bank and issues a paycheck to Betty, a management trainee in the store. Betty takes her paycheck and buys a crib for her grandson at the Home Resource Center, and the dollar is recycled again as a paycheck to Lonnie who is learning retail operations at the Center. He goes to Park Pointe Community Grocery, a nonprofit food store, and buys groceries. The dollar turns over again—another paycheck. Untrell takes his money and helps his mother make her payment on an interest-free loan for their home. And so it goes. Community ownership and local jobs keep that dollar in the community and recycling to the benefit of many, helping to lead to the economic viability of the neighborhood. "Economic viability can be simply defined as the capacity of a community, through productive, interdependent relationships, to sustain itself," says Lupton.[2] He goes on to say that the key to restoring our communities is in attracting and retaining capable neighbor-leaders.[3]

In the context of Christian community development (CCD), redistribution is about people, community, economics, and justice. One of the seven principles of Kwanza, an African American cultural celebration, is *Ujamaa*, which offers us another definition of redistribution: "To build and maintain our own stores, shops and other businesses and profit from them together." More specifically for Christian community development, redistribution is about developing people. In *With Justice for All*, John Perkins says, "The most important thing we have to redistribute is ourselves. Justice cannot be achieved by long distance."[4] Redistribution results when people reconciled to God and each other, share whatever resources they have to work together for the good of the total community.

Biblical Basis

We don't have to dig too deeply into the Bible to find references to redistribution:

Our desire is not that others might be relieved while you are hard pressed, but that there might be equality. At the present time your plenty will supply what they need, so that in turn their plenty will supply what you need. Then there will be equality (2 Cor. 8:13–14).

All the believers were one in heart and mind. No one claimed that any of his possessions was his own, but they shared everything they had. With great power the apostles continued to testify to the resurrection of the Lord Jesus, and much grace was upon them all. There were no needy persons among them (Acts 4:32–34).

"They do not need to go away," answered Jesus. "You give them something to eat." "We have here only five loaves of bread and two fish," they answered. "Bring them here to me," he said . . . They all ate and were satisfied (Matt. 14:16–21).

Each of you should look not only to your own interests, but also to the interests of others (Phil. 2:4).

The year of Jubilee, as described in Leviticus 25, is a radical call for redistribution, calling for forgiving debts, giving back land, and not charging interest. It is dismissed by some as never implemented and impractical. Yet this passage and the one in Exodus 22, which says, "If you lend money to one of my people among you who is needy, do not be like a moneylender; charge him no interest" (v. 25), are at the heart of the Habitat for Humanity standards. Habitat founder Millard Fuller says that the poor need "capital not charity, coworkers not caseworkers."

Joe Holland, an African American graduate of Harvard University, took his skills into Harlem and started a number of enterprises, including an ice cream store, a travel agency, and a housing program for homeless men. At a recent CCDA conference, Joe walked us through the story of Elisha helping a poor widow (2 Kings 4:1–7). The widow of a member of a group of prophets went to Elisha and said, "Sir, my husband has died. As you know he was a God-fearing man, but now a man he owed money to has come to take away my two sons as slaves in payment for my husband's debt." "What shall I do for you?" he asked. "Tell me what do you have at home?" "Nothing at all, except a small jar of olive oil," she answered. "Go to your neighbors and borrow as many empty jars as you can," he told her. "Then you and your sons go into the house, close the door and start pouring oil into the jars. Set each one aside as soon as it is full." So the woman went into her house with her sons, closed the door, took the small jar of olive oil, and poured oil into the jars as her sons brought them to her. When they had filled all the jars, she asked if there were any more. "That was the last one," one of her sons answered. And the olive oil stopped flowing. She went back to Elisha, the prophet, who said to her, "Sell the olive oil and pay all your debts, and there will be enough money left over for you and your sons to live on."

There is a lot to think about in this passage. It would be an excellent study for a group to undertake:

- Elisha was nearby and ready to respond with suggestions and help to the widow in need.
- The widow was ready to listen to advice and to help herself, not just depend on charity.
- The widow and her family used what resources they had available to them.
- Neighbors willingly shared their empty jars to help the family
- The enterprise was a lot of hard work for the whole family and involved the entire community .
- The enterprise, through God's intervention, met their needs and provided a cushion for the future.

So, as God's people and as neighbors, we emphasize redistribution—working hard together with our neighbors and creatively using the resources of our community and ourselves to create economic opportunity and dignity for our families and our community.

Economics with Values—Why Do It?

As Christians with a heart for our low-income communities, we bring a special set of values to the economic arena, values that include the *common good*, not just individual interests over the interests of the community. That changes both how and why we are involved in economic development. Ours is a people-focused effort, not just the accumulation of individual wealth and property. The measure of our success is found in improved living conditions, a sense of human dignity, and improved community conditions. We know that without ownership, without opportunity for gainful employment, and without opportunity to build a future for the children, people in our communities will continue to live in despair and frustration.

There are a number of business enterprises that have found that economics with values is also good business. For example, the Parnusus Fund, a mutual fund investment firm, invests only in firms that:

- Produce a quality product (good quality and *constructive* rather than *destructive*)
- Are good to the environment
- Are good to their employees (provide affirmative action, equal pay for equal work, and fringe benefits)
- Are good to their neighbors (become involved in and invest in their communities)

Their rate of return over the longer period is much higher than the Standard and Poor's average.

In another example, a whole series of industrial cooperatives with now over twenty-three thousand worker-owners was started in Mondragon, Spain, by a parish priest concerned about unemployed youth. Mondragon Cooperatives use the concept of *balance* as a measuring tool for their enterprises:

- Balance of interests with needs
- Balance of technological imperatives with social objectives
- Balance of financial needs of the firm with economic needs of members
- Balance of an individual's importance with a sense of community

When we consider what our actions should be, we need to be clear about what our goals are and whether we are compromising any of our values. For example, in Bethel New Life's Home Care for Elderly enterprise, the state rate does not allow enough funds to provide adequate health insurance for the employees. We agonize over that fact. As another example, we could create jobs in the community through an industry that pollutes the environment, but that is an unacceptable compromise. If our goal is to enable jobs, then we need to measure success not only by the number of jobs, but also by whether they are livable-wage jobs, jobs with a future, and jobs that are in a business that is good for the community.

If our goal is to make money to support our people development efforts, then it may be that the best way is to get a successful business owner with a heart for our ministries to earmark a portion of the profits to support our ministries. Lawndale Community Church in Chicago has done that. One of a chain of pizza parlors is now located in Lawndale, employing community residents and committing a percentage of the profits to the work of Lawndale Community Church.

When Bethel New Life, Inc. brokers with an industry to move into and operate a plant in their neighborhood, they ask for three commitments from that industry: (1) first source hiring; i.e., jobs for community residents first along with the related job training; (2) full disclosure and environmental safety for the community; and (3) good neighbor policy; i.e., the company will support community efforts such as a day care center and adopt-a-school programs.

In any case, we need to be clear about our values and our goals. Then we need to stay focused on those things, lest we get so busy doing we miss the mark.

Christian Community Development's Roles in Economic Development

There are a number of ways that Christian community developers can approach redistribution in their communities. A few of the most common ones are explored in the next few pages.

Start up enterprises and operate them, primarily as a way to create jobs in the community. It's easier to start such enterprises than it is to maintain them over the long haul. Some of the kinds of businesses that CCD groups have started are thrift shops, construction companies, window shade manufacturing companies, dry cleaning shops, material processing plants, home care industries, industrial sewing shops, grocery stores, and cleaning business franchises. Carrying our values into the enterprises means that we need to explore such things as worker ownership options and profit sharing. Later in the chapter there is a section on starting up a business. A word of caution is needed here; the track record of success in these efforts is not good. Too often we try to combine training programs with trying to operate profitable businesses. The two things are often counterproductive. That doesn't mean we shouldn't try; it just means we need to be smart about it.

Act as a broker-developer for a site as a place to stimulate businesses in the community. The site could be an industrial corridor or a shopping center. Eastside Community Investments in Indianapolis, a Christian community development organization with a lot of community churches involved on the board and as members, developed an industrial site and brought in both new and expanding industries, creating economic growth and jobs in the community. Community Development Corporation of Kansas City mobilized a group of Baptist churches to develop a shopping center containing a major chain grocery store and other convenience stores. Church-based New Community Corporation in Newark, New Jersey, developed a shopping strip including a major grocery store chain. Also, they became equity partners in some of the businesses, so that they gained profits from the stores.

Train people for existing jobs, micro-enterprises, or self-employment. Church-based community groups seem to do well at this kind of effort. There are some exciting examples of micro-enterprise development and self-employment efforts. The Graemean Bank in India has lending circles where poor peasants lend small sums to each other and support and hold each other accountable. Women's Self Employment Program in Chicago trains welfare women in self-employment, helps them develop business plans, and provides them with a micro-loan program. Some of the enterprises started by them include a hot dog pushcart, a beauty salon, a greeting card design company, a graphics service, typing services, and phone answering services. Bethel New Life in Chicago trained twenty-six welfare mothers as day care home providers and assisted them into lease purchases of homes the mothers them-selves helped build. Now there is a network of self-employed day care home providers providing accessible, affordable day care. Other places operate specific training programs in areas where there is already job demand, sometimes partnering with the indus-tries that need the workers. Some operate computer training pro-grams. Some do pre-employment training or specific job skill train-ing. National Foundation for Teaching Entrepreneurship (NFTE), a youth enterprise development program that some Christian community development groups are using, has a tried and tested curriculum and process for teaching small-business skills to youth. It's operated on a franchise model. Similarly, School to Work Pro-grams in local schools allow for good linkages between schools and CCD groups by arranging for youth employment in areas where the youth can develop their business skills.

Assist in start-up and expansion of local businesses through tech-nical assistance and by providing access to below-market interest rate loan funds. A number of community development corporations have taken on this role. One of the most creative efforts is by Coastal Enter-prises, Inc., in rural Maine, another CDC with strong church involve-ment. They assist a business owner in putting together a business plan, help the owner be prepared for financing requirements, and assist in accessing below-market interest rate loans and in packag-ing a marketing plan. Most recently Coastal Enterprises, Inc., has been dealing with "growing green businesses," a particular sector in the business world. In describing their loan and equity investments they said, "The driving forces behind the criteria are an emerging global economy, the need to develop and nurture a trained and com-petitive work force, the community's interest in improving the gen-eral standard of living by preserving the environment, and ongoing imperatives to provide safe and supportive workplaces, as well as improve the health of citizens." Their criteria for determining which investments to make are:

• What is the financial return on investment?
• What is the social return on investment?

- Are quality income, employment, and ownership opportunities created for residents of the community and people with low incomes?
- Does the business provide products and services that offer public benefits?
- Does the business engage in socially responsible practices?

Participate in a community-wide effort of other churches and/or community development groups. Many of the examples given above illustrate this technique in which the church or Christian community development group has given impetus and leadership but is a participant rather than sole operator of the initiatives.

Invest in a company in order to bring in jobs, income, and services. For example, Bananna Kelly, a CDC in New York City, is bringing a Swedish paper de-inking plant into their community. They were able to access foundation and government funds, which paid for the predevelopment costs for the business. This provided them with equity in the business, which they have leveraged into a commitment of the company to pay for and support a children's day care center in the community. Christian community development groups sometimes use revolving loan or investment funds from other activities to put together the equity investment.

Getting from Here to There

Christian community development includes a value base often described as the "common good." Dealing with the "how-to" presumes that you have already decided "why." Is your goal to create jobs or to try to create profit to help your other efforts? Be clear on the purpose. It is hard for one business to do it all. There are trade-offs. For example, bringing in unskilled workers cuts down on the profit. Have clear priorities!

Starting a Neighborhood Business

You've now clarified why you want to start a business, you're sure of your biblical base, you've looked at a number of ways that your organization might be involved, you're confident of your value base, and your objectives have been defined. Now the real work begins. There are a number of necessary steps:

1. *Identify the opportunities and community resources (assets)*. For example, Bethel New Life looked at its very low income community and found the large number of elderly living in the community an asset to build on. Demographics indicated that providing services to the elderly was a growth field. So Bethel started up a service business caring for the elderly. There are now over 350 employees in that business. You may be near an airport, an expressway, a university, or a hospital that needs a lot of services and supplies. The McKnight-Kretzman book, *Building Communities from the Inside Out,* is a great book to use in leading your group through the process of discovering the assets of your community on which you can build. There is a good section in the book on economic assets too.

2. *Determine feasibility.* Before embarking on a full-blown feasibility study or business plan, one must again check on the purpose of the efforts. The Christian community development principle of redistribution includes creating the opportunity for worker ownership, profit sharing, and community shares, rather than purely individualistic gain.

3. *Develop the business plan.* There are several computer programs that provide an outline, so all you have to do is fill in the assumptions and the blanks. Often one can find colleagues with similar enterprises in other areas and ask them to share their business plan as a prototype. Or, you can always hire someone to put the plan together for you. A business plan should do such things as verify the market, identify capital costs, and identify how long it will take to break even. Visit similar projects to get more insight. This can be a very important step. It's a good idea to take some board members along on your visits.

4. *Consider financing.* It's easier to start businesses that are not capital intensive; that is, have low start-up costs. Consider lease-purchase of equipment to spread the costs over time. It always takes longer than anticipated to break even. Working capital is essential; don't cut it short. Of course there are opportunities for "creative financing" using sweat equity and borrowing below-interest funds as "program related investments." (Bethel got a zero interest loan to start its recycling center and has since paid it back.) Some organizations offer "forgivable loans," and there are such things as recoverable grants, church funds, and intermediaries.

It is important that all the participants in the ownership and development of the business have some tangible resources at risk. That ensures a sense of everyone struggling together to make it work. If you do an employee/management profit-sharing plan, have your manager risk something as well as the employees.

5. *Hire effective people for key leadership roles.* For start-up, hire skilled, experienced people, and work on the future development of leaders. Retired or active business advisors help expand ideas and provide an experience base that leads to a good check and balance system.

6. *Don't stop learning from others.* There is a lot of willingness on the part of the corporate community and individual business persons to assist. You don't know it all; don't be afraid to ask for help and use it. Never stop learning. Smart groups ask questions and ask for help.

In the end, when all the technical work has been done, prayer, hard work, and persistence are the keys to success. It's not easy to make a start-up business work. Be prepared to be problem solvers and hang in there for the long haul.

Collective Wisdom on Redistribution

At the Christian Community Development Association's economic development summit in 1994, members wrestled with varied experiences in economic development. There was unanimous agreement on the three core values of dignity, justice, and stewardship. As capsulized by Bob Lupton in the write-up of the summit, the unique strengths of CCDA include the following:

- *Local intelligence*—we have firsthand knowledge of our communities: what is really needed and what resources there are.
- *Moral authority*—we are grounded in community, both in belief and practice. We live there and, thus, can speak with authority.
- *Ministry motivation*—we care more about developing people than about creating wealth or producing goods. CCDA is much better suited to preparing a workforce than to operating single-minded, bottom line for-profit businesses.

We Are Developers, Not Merchants

The role of community developers, like that of real estate developers, is to prepare the soil of the community for new growth. Economically speaking, this means training a workforce, creating a secure environment, mobilizing community support, securing land and/or facilities, and packaging incentives sufficient to induce businesses in our community. We are visionaries. We believe in community development and can promote it better than anyone. Our instincts are toward marketing our ministries. Thus, Christian Community Development Association is a natural vehicle for economic development. We sell vision, develop indigenous leadership, organize neighborhoods, seize real estate opportunities, broker deals, establish partnerships, identify money sources, and perform quite naturally many other tasks essential to economic development. However, because we are hypersensitive to exploitation, we are uneasy making profits from the labor of our people. We feel more comfortable with cooperatives than with sole proprietorships. This hesitation about profit dulls our competitive edge. Thus, we are better suited for the role of developers than sole business owners.

Housing and Human Services
as Economic Development

More recently, community development people have found that social services can be reorganized as community economic development. This has been spurred on by the trend to "privatize" some formerly government-operated functions, from prisons to schools to care for the elderly to day care. Though most of our affordable housing initiatives, health clinics, day care centers, and training programs are nonprofit, they are nevertheless economic stimulators. Not only are they mechanisms to instill a work ethic and teach marketable skills, they create a permanent source of jobs and income within the community. Also, they may be a catalyst for other income-generating enterprises. For example, renovating a vacant apartment building provides construction jobs and creates permanent property management and maintenance positions when the building becomes occupied. These nonprofit activities, though not sufficient to produce the wealth required to revitalize a disenfranchised community, are necessary to "jump start" the economy. We should consider them to be legitimate economic development activities.

A Word of Caution

As some of the seasoned Christian Community Development Association members and advisors reflected on their varied experiences with economic development and redistribution, it was clear that, in terms of making a profit, there were more failures in CCD-operated profit-making enterprises than there were successes. We care more about developing people than about creating wealth or producing a product. While we don't want to dampen attempts to be creative and start businesses, the collective feeling was that in all such ventures we should concentrate more on our strength—developing people.

The Key Elements of Redistribution

- There are a number of approaches to economic redistribution. These include: starting new enterprises to create jobs; being a broker-developer for a site as a place to stimulate businesses in the community; training people for existing jobs or self-employment; assisting in the start-up and expansion of local businesses; investing in a company in order to bring in jobs, income, and services; and getting an industry to move into and operate a plant in your neighborhood.

- Be careful of conflicting goals. Is your goal to create jobs or to try to create profit to help your other efforts? Be clear on your purpose.

- The goal of redistribution is economic viability, defined as "the capacity of a community, through productive, interdependent relationships, to sustain itself." The keys to this are community ownership and local jobs, which keep dollars recycling in the community to the benefit of many.

- There are many more failures in CCD-operated profit-making enterprises than there are successes. People in Christian community development care more about developing people than about creating wealth or producing a product. Remember, the measure of our success is not accumulation of individual wealth and property, but improved living conditions in the community.

- The most important resource we have to redistribute is ourselves. If people live in the community they serve and all those within that community are reconciled to God and to each other the result is redistribution: sharing resources for the good of the whole community.

For those of you looking for more detailed information, specific models are provided on the next pages.

Hope Plaza
North Philadelphia, Pennsylvania

Fifteen years ago, members of Deliverance Evangelistic Church were primarily interested in evangelizing on the streets and other venues. The church was not involved in community economic development projects. The passages of Nehemiah told of the building of the wall of Jerusalem so that the people would no longer be in disgrace. The congregation's response to the Word of God was to build a neighborhood shopping center for the people of North Philadelphia.

The Deliverance Evangelistic Church, the largest congregation in Philadelphia, purchased approximately eleven acres of inner city land in the heart of North Philadelphia. The congregation wanted to present the community with an establishment that was similar in quality to the downtown and suburban shopping centers. The church administration and its congregation believed that the basic service needs of all Philadelphia citizens must be met. Focus was placed on joining physical revitalization with upgraded human service delivery, job creation, and employment opportunities.

Plans began to revitalize a large section of the land into a 50,000-square-foot shopping center that would yield at least two hundred jobs to the church and surrounding community. This center includes a 26,770-square-foot full-service supermarket (Thriftway), which is one of the largest in the city and houses a delicatessen, a bakery, and an extensive line of products. In addition, the center contains a McDonald's, a Baskin Robbins, and a number of other basic retail shops including a family shoe store, bank, cleaners, laundromat, and a number of other businesses. Tenants of the plaza pay both monthly rent and percentage rent to ensure that the center will be self-sustaining. The Plaza is conveniently located near over fifteen employment centers located within walking distance and employing approximately 9,700 people. The center is also near two major education centers situated within walking distance, containing a combined enrollment of 3,400 and staff of 302. A small police station is located on the premises.

The project was funded by over $1 million in Urban Development Action Grant (UDAG) funds. With these federal funds Hope Plaza Incorporated, a 501(c)(3) Pennsylvania Non-Profit Corporation set up to oversee the project, was able to leverage almost $3 million in bank loans and private financing. The Deliverance Evangelistic Church used $1.33 million of its own money to complete the financial package. A tremendous help in controlling project administrative costs was the wise use of secretaries and other clerical staff.

Hope Plaza opened in September 1986. During the first year of operation, Hope Plaza received almost $100,000 from percentage rents. Thriftway and McDonald's have both signed fifty-year leases.

Linwood Shopping Center
Kansas City, Missouri

The Baptist Ministers Union (BMU) of Kansas City was looking for an opportunity to support economic development in its communities. The conversion of an abandoned hospital into a profitable shopping center was the outcome of its search.

The head of the economic development committee of the Union approached the president of the Kansas City Community Development Corporation (CDC) to inquire about possible BMU participation in development projects. The opportunity that presented itself was the St. Joseph's Hospital renovation. The site had been abandoned in 1975 and was an empty shell attracting drug traffic and prostitution. Their first successful task was lobbying against use of the building as a prison.

The building's owner donated the building to the CDC, and BMU was approached to be a partner in the demolition and development of the site into something that would benefit the community. A joint venture was approved by both groups and a nonprofit corporation was established to provide an organizational framework within which to carry out plans and own the center.

Thirty-five BMU member churches raised $20,000 from members to support the project and the CDC added $30,000. The city also contributed funds. An analysis was conducted for uses of the site with funding from the city, the Ford Foundation, and the Local Initiatives Support Corporation. The report showed that $76 million per year was leaving the neighborhood because of inadequate local shopping facilities.

Funding for the development of the shopping center was garnered from the U.S. Departments of Health and Human Services, and Housing and Urban Development; a local minority development corporation; a local foundation; and the Prudential insurance company. These commitments allowed the nonprofit corporation to leverage a construction loan from a local bank and to raise almost $1 million in project equity to complete the funding.

The Linwood Shopping Center opened for business in 1986. The 80,000-square-foot facility was quickly leased to predominantly African American tenants. Since its opening, the retail space has been generally occupied. The success of the project would not have been possible without the political and social clout of the BMU and the development expertise of the Kansas City CDC. The Linwood Shopping Center, with eleven stores and two hundred employees, continues to be successful as both a service center and a business enterprise.

Women's Self-Employment Project
Chicago, Illinois

The Women's Self-Employment Project (WSEP), a nonprofit city-wide financial services and entrepreneurial training program targeting poor women in Chicago, uses self-employment as a strategy to raise the income and degree of economic self-sufficiency of low- and moderate-income women. With a staff of eighteen, the project receives support from national and local foundations, the city, the federal government, and the United Way of Chicago. Since 1986, WSEP has successfully supported the efforts of low-income women to leave welfare and offered new options for their children. The project has also helped these women to achieve economic empowerment, demonstrate credit-worthiness, and launch their own micro-businesses. One of the key ways WSEP aids women is through its revolving loan fund (RLF). With a dual strategy for business development and peer support, the RLF provides financing to start and expand micro-businesses that banks would not help because of the small loan size, the borrower's credit status, or a lack of assets. RLF loans range from $100 to $10,000 through two different programs: the

Full Circle Fund and the Micro Loan Fund. First-time borrowers are limited to $1,500, but they are encouraged to borrow repeatedly with credit increasing in increments up to $2,000 with each successful loan retirement. Borrowers in both programs are also provided with access to no-cost savings and checking accounts with participating banks throughout the city.

Full Circle Fund. The first program, the Full Circle Fund, operates primarily as a lending program. The project's staff help women create "Circles" of five members, using peer support as a form of collateral. Upon completing an orientation process, the Circle chooses two members to access the loan fund. Once those two members make three timely, bi-weekly payments, the next two members may borrow from the fund. The same rule applies before the fifth Circle member may access funds. The Full Circle Fund Strategy has proven successful. To date, with over thirty circles and nearly $200,000 disbursed, the fund has a 100 percent repayment rate.

Micro Loan Fund. WSEP's customers can also access the Revolving Loan Fund through the more traditional Entrepreneurial Training Program. During twelve weeks of business training and technical assistance, participants work to complete a Self-Employment Action Plan. Those who successfully complete both the plan and training may apply for a loan from the individual loan program, the Micro Loan Fund. Borrowers from the Micro Loan Fund must provide 50 percent collateral, 15 percent equity (which can include sweat equity), and have an acceptable credit history. Nearly $280,000 has been disbursed through this program with a 95 percent repayment rate.

New Programs. Recently, WSEP launched a number of new programs. These include an African Refugee Women's Microenterprise Project, which is a membership program providing discounts to other business and service vendors, networks, and marketing services. Other new initiatives are a three-year self-employment program for welfare recipients; a policy component with research evaluation and policy analysis functions; and a consulting and product sales program. WSEP will also increase its loan amount to $26,000 as part of the Small Business Administration's Micro Loan Demonstration Program.

Additional Resources on Redistribution

National Congress of Community Economic Development (NCCED). An association of community development corporations, working for the enhancement and expansion of community economic development. Contact: NCCED, 1875 Connecticut Avenue, Suite 524, Washington, DC 20009 (202) 234-5009.

Human Services: An Economic Development Opportunity: A Manual for Economic Based Enterprises by Thomas Rhodenbaugh. Available through NCCED.

Rebuilding Our Communities: How Churches Can Provide Support and Finance Quality Housing for Low Income Families. World Vision, 919 W. Huntington Drive, Monrovia, CA 91016. World Vision is also producing a handbook on employment efforts.

Building Communities from the Inside Out: A Path towards Finding and Mobilizing a Community's Assets. Jody Kretzman and John McKnight. ACTA Publications, 4848 N. Clark Street, Chicago, IL 60640.

Working Neighborhoods: Taking Charge of Your Local Economy. Center for Neighborhood Technology, 2125 W. North Avenue, Chicago, IL 60647 (312) 278-4800.

Restoring Broken Places and Rebuilding Communities: A Casebook on African-American Church Involvement in Community Economic Development. Available from NCCED.

Rebuilding the Walls: A Nuts and Bolts Guide to the Community Development Methods of Bethel New Life, Inc. Available for $5.00 from Bethel New Life, Inc., 367 N. Karlov, Chicago, IL 60624 (312) 826-5540.

Religious Institutions as Partners in Community-Based Development: The Lilly Foundation Report. Rainbow Research, Inc., 1406 W. Lake Street, Minneapolis, MN 55408-2653 (612) 824-0724.

Economic Home Cookin': An Action Guide for Congregations on Community Economic Development. Community Workshop on Economic Development (CWED), 100 S. Morgan, Chicago, IL 60607 (312) 243-0249.

The Community Ventures Project: Empowerment through Community-Based Enterprise Development. CWED (see above).

Black Economics: Solutions for Economic and Community Empowerment by Jawanza Kunjufu. African American Images, 1909 W. 95th Street, Chicago, IL 60643 (312) 445-0322.

Neighborhood Economic Revitalization: Problems and Solutions. National Council for Urban Economic Development, 1730 K Street N.W., Washington, DC 20006.

Part 3
Ministry in the Community

F our "how to" chapters comprise a valuable resource for anyone considering the field of Christian community development. Chapters 8, 9, and 10 explore in turn the relationship between the church and Christian community development, the development of leaders from within the community, and the implications on the entire family involved in a Christian community development ministry. Chapter 11 focuses on how to put all these factors together when starting a new Christian community development ministry.

8

The Local Church and Christian Community Development

Glen Kehrein

Whenever there is heated discussion about the necessities of Christian community development, the issue being discussed could very well be the relationship between the local church and the Christian community development ministry. Questions abound!

How important is the local church to successful Christian community development? Can you do it without the church? What role should the church play? How do the church and Christian community development work together?

For over twenty years I've experienced a variety of church/CCD ministry connections. My ministry has been church-based, parachurch, and then church-based again. What makes my experience unique is that this journey has been within the same organization, Circle Urban Ministries, CUM, in Chicago! My experiences have wrought in me a strong conviction that true Christian community development can be done only from a church base.

The Faith Community

The faith community is the foundation of all ministry. In fact, good ministry grows out of good fellowship. As believers commit their lives to each other they provide the "stuff" that is necessary for interpersonal support. Without that support long-term commitment is very rare.

Circle Urban Ministries began from a fellowship base, an intentional community of believers who moved into the inner city. We were a subset of a larger church called Circle Church. Committed fellowship lessened the risks by bringing safety, support, and wisdom in numbers.

Within the first month of our move into the neighborhood, an older man was shot through his temple, severing both optic nerves and rendering him blind. The facts were chilling: it happened three doors away, and the shooter was our neighbor. Within a month there were two murders in the neighborhood and even the most idealistic people began to be concerned.

But the fellowship met together, prayed, and shared. Our common sharing eventually led to a spiritual perspective that said it was Satan's attack, and we would not yield. Some quoted Scripture like, "God did not give us a spirit of timidity, but a spirit of power . . ." (2 Tim. 1:7). It is easier to be brave with friends who are in the same boat. Together we rode out the storm (only the first of many to come), and together we processed our first lesson toward becoming streetwise.

Solid ministry grows from sound relationships and the church provides the opportunity to develop those solid relationships. For most committed Christians the church provides our strongest social setting: our primary friends, children's friends, and, particularly in church/CCD ministries, our colleagues. Together we reinforce the values, such as relocation, that are common to us but are foreign to others, even other believers.

When we chose to relocate into the Austin neighborhood on Chicago's West Side it was a racially changing community. John Perkins was just beginning to articulate the three Rs of Christian community development, and we realized that relocation was a non-negotiable. However, many others outside our fellowship thought we had gone off the deep end; they advanced all the typical objections to moving into the inner city. "Why do you have to live there? What about the dangers, your children, the schools, the property values?" But the church provided the spiritually reflective question, "What is God saying we should do?" Everything else was just opinion, no matter how well meaning. If we had settled for commuting instead of relocating, Circle would have been a blip on the urban ministry radar screen. But without a fellowship that understood the deep implications of this decision, we might not have made the right choice.

All of us who minister in Christian community development receive support from many well-meaning friends from outside the community; for example, a financially supportive suburban church. They look at us as sacrificial heroes because we are doing what they could never dream of doing. We need this group desperately, but if we choose our church fellowship from this group, the integrity of other significant choices can be compromised. They wouldn't question our decisions if we choose to live outside the "hood" or if we hire White staff because they are more "qualified" or are able to more easily raise their own support, or any number of other tough, tough choices that we all face in Christian community development. So they will grant us "permission" to do the easy thing when God would rather have us struggle to do the right thing. But if our fellowship base is a local church, made up of people from the community, they will tend to point out our inconsistencies. They don't see our hero status. In fact, they would confront us if they perceived in us a "great White hope" or "Black savior" complex. We need this accountability to stay grounded.

Our journey through life has many pitfalls, which deepen relationships and ministry. Paul and DuRhonda Grant are deeply loved people in our ministry and church. Paul was our first chaplain and ministered to many, many hurting people. Together Paul and Du suffered the tragic deaths of four sons, each born prematurely. As an infertile couple (we've adopted three times), my wife Lonni and I identified with them. At the last funeral as I passed Paul in the front of the church, we embraced and I broke down uncontrollably. I didn't anticipate it, and it shocked many folks because I am normally a very composed person. Those tears deepened the bond between Paul and me. But it was our relationship, forged as we spent many hours together in church matters, that had created that bond. Tragically, Paul himself died a short while later at thirty-one years of age. His loss affected us all deeply and was the first in a series of tragedies to strike the church. As church members walked through those intensely painful times together, we grew in mutual trust and support. Ministry effectiveness also grows with the trust and support that blossom through common pain and struggle. Trust and support are not easily found in Black/White arenas. A close church fellowship, which bears each other's burdens, helps considerably to build it.

The Reconciled Community

Since we believe that reconciliation is the core value of Circle Urban Ministries and Rock Church, we need to spend some time with that concept here. This deep Christian truth must be applied directly in our culturally and racially fragmented society.

While I firmly believe that the best context to facilitate the ministry of reconciliation is clearly the local church, it must be a local church that has accepted racial reconciliation as its mandate. If not, the church can be part of the problem. Historically, the church in the United States has long been a hotbed of racism both in the North and in the South. And today the Black church seems to put little more effort into reconciliation than the White church. But if the church determines to follow Scripture and be a community of reconciliation, there is no better place to anchor the ministry.

Our first interracial fellowship experience began in 1971 when my wife and I began attending Circle Church, a racially mixed experimental church near the Chicago Loop. It was exciting, vibrant, and provided what we had longed for: meaningful worship, fellowship, and social commitment in a biblical context.

Unlike any other evangelical church of its day, Circle addressed racial and social issues. We were young, idealistic, and committed. An exhilarating interracial pastoral team of a White, Black, and Asian led the church with powerful preaching that challenged us to bridge the social and racial gaps of our culture. From that body a group formed, which would eventually grow into Circle Urban Ministries (CUM).

Those years were rich with growth and opportunity. Circle Church received attention from around the Christian world and was covered in *Time* magazine. But it all came crashing down in late 1976 when the church went through a racial split. Although space will not allow me to address the specific reasons for the break, chapter 6 (Reconciliation: Loving God and Loving People) will provide you with good insight into the reasons behind any such split.

The split left the church forever with a "heart wound" that even today has not healed. Those of us who had moved into the inner city to begin a CCD ministry were grievously wounded. A long journey into the "backside of the desert" began. We had totally underestimated the depth of the racial division in a church that did not fully understand racial reconciliation.

Circle Community Center, as we were called back then, evolved into a parachurch organization. *Parachurch* literally means "alongside the church," but as with most parachurch organizations, the linkage between the Center and Circle Church was weak. Circle Church was now an all-White church; we needed to reconnect with the Black community.

We struggled in trying to bring about racial reconciliation. Intentional hiring of minorities sometimes succeeded and sometimes resulted in bitter and abysmal failure. Clearly, true racial reconciliation was not happening. Just bringing Black and White folks together in the same context—work, school, ministry, or whatever—is not *reconciliation,* but *integration,* and the failures of racial integration are historically evident. Integration does not automatically bring about reconciliation.

After eight years of struggle, I guess God decided we had learned enough about trying to make it on our own without the local church body. He intervened. After years of praying and struggling to build relationships with the local Black churches, God did something none of us expected. He began a church in our midst by sending to us forty-five-year-old, retired Lt. Col. Raleigh Washington. Fresh out of seminary, he brought with him a passion for lost souls and the boundless energy needed to plant a church.

Our first plan was that Rock Church would merely share space until it could stand on its own. Besides, if it grew beyond fifty people, our largest room couldn't contain it anyway. But God was taking a flawed and broken vessel and remolding it into his own creation.

Raleigh and I began to live out the principles of reconciliation and apply them to our ministry. Soon the growing church and Circle Urban Ministries were acting like ministry partners. We saw it as a "faith and works" division of labor. But a truth emerged in that exciting growth time: As the relationship of Raleigh and Glen goes, so go Rock and Circle. We began to see how critical it was to live out racial reconciliation in our personal lives if we wanted it to be a ministry reality. We began to learn that reconciliation is the oil that lubricates the whole ministry machine.

But it was the church as the faith community that provided the natural context. When the faith community gathered for worship, God's Word was unfolded and reconciliation could be preached. A vision of a reconciled community could be held up. As members struggled with interpersonal dynamics, reconciliation could be practiced. Church elders and pastors began to call people into account if reconciliation was not pursued.

Struggles abound when Black and White folks get together! Soon we realized that we must become preventive, dealing with problems before they arose, rather than merely prescriptive, dealing with the problem after it had exploded. Raleigh, in his inimitable style, came up with the plan—chocolate and vanilla meetings. Once each quarter the church has a marathon Sunday. During the Sunday school hour all the Blacks get together—the chocolate meeting—and talk about the church from the Black perspective. After church, the Whites get together—the vanilla meeting—and talk from their perspective. Then both groups get together and open up all the issues. The goal is to get issues out on the table and address them proactively. And it works! Much of racial tension comes from ignorance and assumptions. This forum gives the opportunity to address issues, answers questions (even "dumb" ones), and brings understanding. This one practice (now in operation nearly eight years) does more to instill the values and practice of racial reconciliation than any I have ever seen anywhere.

Circle Church went just eight short years before the ever growing racial pressure finally exploded. As of this writing Rock Church is eleven years old and has not experienced a racial crisis, large or small. I believe this is because our emphasis and energy is fixed on reconciliation.

Without a church this context is very difficult to create. Biblical values are carried out with mature spiritual authority. If a person becomes nonreconciliatory, the problem can be addressed directly as sin. Time can be taken in regular gatherings, something very hard to do in the constant press of CCD ministry. Relationships between church members become the shelter that will weather the storms of racial conflict that always arise. Circle Urban Ministries builds upon the foundation of reconciliation incubated and nurtured in the church.

Evangelism and Discipleship

During Circle Urban Ministries' parachurch days we touched a lot of lives. Most visitors were impressed with the wholistic nature of our work, which included youth programs, legal aid, and medical and family counseling. We could articulate how the programs worked together to deal with the needs of the whole person.

The early leadership of CUM was a product of the 1960s. In many ways we were the evangelical counterparts to the antiestablishment counterculture. We wanted to put "new wine in new wine skins," and the methods of the traditional evangelical church were definitely "old wine in old wine skins." Besides, the church was vacating the city with reckless abandon and was still fighting the social gospel battle. Evangelicals condemned most social action ministries as liberal and cared only for getting people "saved." In their eyes, to feed or house a poor person was like arranging chairs on a sinking ship.

Many movements begin as reactions. Many older CCD organizations reacted to the false separation of spiritual and physical needs. John Perkins led the way toward a wholistic gospel, and CUM took up the charge. We emphasized "Making the love of Christ visible" as Circle's first motto. Instead of the overt evangelistic methods of street preaching and witnessing, we would live the gospel out through acts of love, mercy, and compassion. These acts, done by committed Christians, would compel people to ask about our motive. This would give us the opportunity to share our faith in genuine relationships.

Although we had not thrown the baby out with the bath water, a counterbalance approach is seldom wholistic. In fact, one excess is traded for another. Apart from certain activities in the youth program, the truth was that evangelism was not being practiced. About eight years into our ministry I took stock: What is the measure of success? Is it the clients we serve, the buildings we rehabilitate, or the size of the staff? While these numbers could impress a visitor, I knew the real measure of success was in terms of people whose lives had changed. An accurate, honest appraisal of how many of the lives we touched stood as testimonials to the power of the gospel, which could change a sinner into saint, brought shameful results. It was very few.

CCD ministries must be clear on this point. We can write grants, create programs, and touch many lives but see very little spiritual fruit. Pre-evangelism rationalization is fine, if, that is, we ever get to evangelism and discipleship. In my experience and observation of many ministries, unless a local church drives this train it does not happen. The exception is often raised by parachurch youth programs that have evangelistic outreach programs.

But more often than not, it seems, when those youth are not directly tied to a local church, they drift from the Lord in their later years. Occasionally a slightly familiar face warmly greets me on the street. It turns out to be a person from my youth program years ago. Spiritual curriculum was a part of all we did, yet few of those adults have any spiritual life today.

Circle's journey took a unique path in 1983. It was a path that led us back to a church base. In fact, we may be the only ministry whose journey began church-based, became parachurch-based, and moved back to become church-based. The move "back to the future" began when Raleigh Washington came to plant a church at Circle.

Raleigh and his wife Paulette brought the gift of evangelism to our ministry. They had a passion for souls and a deep commitment to plant a church. Urban ministry is like plowing concrete. Our community, like many inner city communities, has storefront churches galore. Not far away there is one intersection with a church on all four corners and two mid-block. Few, however, reach out to the community and still fewer seem to preach true Christian discipleship.

Planting a church in a crowded field is not an easy task. But Raleigh and Paulette's gift did not go unreciprocated; Circle Urban Ministries offered them something, too. Circle could house the new church and provide it with a base of ministry with proven credibility. Door to door visits began with, "Hi, I'm Raleigh Washington. I pastor the new church down at Circle. You know of Circle Urban Ministries, don't you? Well, we have a church there now."

So a "faith (Rock Church) and works (CUM)" partnership grew. It is a partnership that has produced life-changing results.

Evangelism, an emphasis at the church, has become a central motif for Circle Urban Ministries. People's human needs are never neglected but neither are the spiritual. The church has modeled and led in methods of evangelism, and CUM has responded. Eight years ago we began a chaplaincy department. Serving both the spiritual and physical needs presents practical problems. Should a doctor make other patients wait while he shares Christ and counsels a patient? Bringing a chaplain on board (we now have four) provides a better solution.

Today evangelism is happening every day of the week, not just Sunday. Families in our homeless shelter as well as young people in the youth program have come to Christ. The poor have the gospel preached to them.

But the end is discipleship; and that is the task of the church:

> Then Jesus came to them and said, "All authority in heaven and on earth has been given to me. Therefore go and make disciples of all nations, baptizing them in the name of the Father and of the Son and of the Holy Spirit, and teaching them to obey everything I have commanded you. And surely I am with you always, to the very end of the age."
>
> Matthew 28:18–20

As new Christians are fed into the church and become part of the family and the spiritual development process, their lives begin to change. The programs of CUM can do pre-evangelism and evangelism. We can even operate new believers classes, but the long-term nurturing and real spiritual growth and accountability that all Christians need can only be provided in the local church.

If CCD ministries maintain an all-too-typical parachurch stance that is apart from the church, we can spiritually cripple new converts, giving the impression that participation in the church is optional. If my organization does not take seriously its relationship to the church, how can I expect babes in Christ to join a church? While exceptions can be found, if a new convert does not become part of a local church, his or her spiritual life will remain stunted.

Wholistic Partnerships: Faith and Works

Commitment to the Poor and the Parish Concept

All local churches are not created equal. Many are not prepared to partner with Christian community development ministries. Curiously, urban and inner city churches are seldom more interested in reaching the poor for Christ than are suburban churches.

Just north of the Chicago Loop lies an interesting community. The Gold Coast of the rich and famous sits a few short blocks from Cabrini Green, a notorious public housing project. Between and around both communities sit a number of churches, including a Catholic cathedral and several nationally famous Protestant ones. Each Sunday morning commuters can be seen filling their parking lots. Reaching the poor is not a high priority for those commuting to be at church for an hour or two.

But neighborhood churches, even in the poor areas of town, don't fare much better. Some small storefront churches attract a few local folks, but the mark of "success" is the ability to attract the middle class. The pastor of a large church in our community brags that most of his people now own their own homes and live in the suburbs.

On Sunday morning fancy cars double park for several blocks in front of those big churches, and the parade of parishioners makes one wonder if a fashion show is scheduled. Wayne Gordon, pastor of Lawndale Community Church, shares how his church began because the poor kids that he was reaching didn't have the fancy clothes necessary to attend the other local churches. When there are such "fashion parades," a message is broadcast, intentional or not, that this is not a place for the poor.

Because CCD ministries are, by design, outreaches to the poor, it is not difficult to understand why most local churches have no desire to enter a partnership with us; we don't offer too many middle-class membership prospects. So we must be clear that a church willing to partner with a CCD ministry must have a commitment to reach the poor.

Rebuilding community is our focus and can only be done if the local church has a parish mentality. There may be a place for the commuter church in God's kingdom, but the inner city is not it. Hundreds or even thousands of visitors coming into the community do little to enhance the life of a distressed neighborhood. In fact, a commuter church can build resentment as cars block the streets and homes are bought up for expansion to accommodate more "outsiders."

Growing up Protestant I had little appreciation for a parish commitment. The church "happened" to be located in a community that we visited each Sunday and Wednesday. The lower income section of town was nearby but represented a safety concern, not a ministry challenge. But when I moved to the Austin Community on Chicago's West Side I saw the impact of a mentality like mine.

The Austin Community is one of seventy-six such communities defined by the city of Chicago. We are the largest, nine square miles, and the most heavily populated. In the late sixties, fueled by the riots that followed Dr. Martin Luther King Jr.'s death, racial panic spread across Austin. Whites left at a rate of 20,000 to 25,000 a year, until most of the original 138,000 White residents were gone. Soon businesses, institutions, and churches followed. But not all churches abandoned the community. Those churches with a parish concept of ministry, most notably the Catholics, remained. Once a thriving Irish Catholic community, parishes consolidated and downsized because the new Black residents were not Catholic, but their presence remained. Most of their schools remain and provide a quality education to the new residents.

Many of the Protestant churches, most notably the twenty-seven evangelical churches, left the community. They had no commitment to a geographical community. Their community was the body of members who moved out; when they left, the church closed or relocated. I find it hypocritical for the evangelical church, whose churches and seminaries have, for the most part, vacated the city, to now condemn the deterioration of the city. Instead of condemnation we need to take appropriate responsibility.

Our communities will not be reached unless we recapture a parish concept. We must reclaim the inner city by staking our claim and recapturing turf yielded to our enemy. Rock Church regularly prays for our surrounding streets; the leadership visits people in the community and has identified the immediate neighborhood as our mission field. Circle Urban Ministries has focused its community development activities on a small target area of forty square blocks. Once this area was owned by gang-bangers and drug dealers, but we are rebuilding the vacant buildings one by one (twelve to date) and restoring hope that things can change. In the middle sits our five-building, two-hundred-thousand-square-foot complex, which testifies to concern for the community through service and worship.

Commitment to Partnership

A true CCD local ministry strategy must be either a partnership of a parachurch and a local church or a local church with community development ministries. Rock Church and Circle Urban Ministries represent a partnership of the first type. Circle and Rock are both free-standing organizations with independent, interlocking boards. Two examples of the second strategy are Lawndale Community Church in Chicago and the Church of the Messiah in Detroit.

Even for the church with development ministries, partnership is important. These ministries must, for legal and practical purposes, form separate 501(c)(3) not-for-profit organizations. For example, both Lawndale and Messiah operate housing development corporations. Circle's family of ministries has four other separate corporations. As these separate boards form and programs develop, the spirit of partnership is critical to maintain the Christian community development vision. I have watched ministries fracture, even those growing within, but being apart from, the local church. In essence the parachurch said, "I don't need the church." Other times the church pushes an emerging ministry out because the programs don't fit the narrow church mold.

Why is partnership critical? Because the CCD ministry and the church body need each other to fulfill their mission. Christian community development, by nature, is outreach oriented. It is task and program oriented: start the program, rehab the building, drive the bus to camp. By nature, the local church is inward in focus: preach the sermon, teach the Bible study, lead the small group. Which is right—the inward or the outward focus? Both of course. But it is hard for either the church or the ministry to focus equitably on both. That is why each needs the other.

Until Circle Urban Ministries partnered with Rock Church we could not hold on to the people we reached out to. CUM was a place from which to receive service, not a fellowship to join. Regular youth activities formed some group identity, but everyone grows up eventually! Even if a person accepted Christ, which was rare in the early days, there was nothing to nurture spiritual growth. Today we direct, encourage, cajole, and take our clients to Rock Church. Those who embrace the church grow, not only spiritually but in all the areas of their life where they struggle.

But Rock Church needs CUM too. We bring credibility to the church in a community where most churches are seen as blind to the needs surrounding them. Circle Urban Ministries is seen by the community as the outreaching arm of the church. As we reach out beyond the walls of the church, we touch the lives of people who would never darken most church steps. In the front row of the church each Sunday sit seven or eight Black men. Some of their faces betray the hard life that has led them to be residents of Circle's Transformation Home. They need to rub shoulders with non-street people, and the church needs their testimony that God can transform lives, because there are others like them for whom we still have hope. It is the partnership at work.

The most visible expression of this partnership is seen each July at our Harvest Festival. Rural country sees harvest in the fall, but the "Harvest of Souls" comes in midsummer at Rock and Circle. This partnership labor of love combines the efforts and resources of both ministries and many volunteers. Luncheons are given during the week, daily old-fashioned tent meetings with choir and preacher are held each evening, and Saturday climaxes with a carnival and community barbecue. Thousands of people come, and hundreds give their lives to Christ. Follow-up is done by Circle's chaplaincy corps and church volunteers. New believers are integrated into the Rock Church body. From beginning to end, facilities to staffing, this event provides a perfect example of a partnership in action. Neither CUM nor Rock could pull it off individually.

Like any partnership, from a doubles team in tennis to a law partnership, it will work well only if each party brings something to the table that the other needs; together the two are stronger than either would be independently. Without interdependence partnerships are short lived. And if there is an imbalance of contribution, the partnership will not succeed in the long run.

A poetic description of interdependent partnering is found in the Old Testament:

> Two are better than one, because they have a good return for their work: If one falls down, his friend can help him up. But pity the man who falls and has no one to help him up! Also, if two lie down together, they will keep warm. But how can one keep warm alone? Though one may be overpowered, two can defend themselves. A cord of three strands is not quickly broken.
>
> Ecclesiastes 4:9–12

However, a necessary reminder: Organizations partner only as well as the individuals within them, particularly the leaders, partner. No contract or official agreement will bring a partnership into being unless the people bring the relationship to life. Raleigh and I must continually build our relationship to meet the new challenges of a growing ministry. Years ago we recognized the partnership between Rock and Circle was as strong as our relationship; it follows on through the staff and congregation. As relationships build between the people of the two organizations the combined ministry builds.

The Church as Rudder

My maritime knowledge would not fill a paragraph, but I do know this: Each ship or boat, no matter the size, is controlled by its rudder. Should a rudder break free or fail to operate, the ship would not be able to navigate its course. A rudderless ship would easily go astray. The local church acts like a spiritual rudder for a CCD ministry.

To the task-oriented, project-based, program-operating CCD staff, theological concerns are not tantamount. Pressures mount upon us to get things done, respond to the emergency, or meet the deadline. The weightier spiritual issues, while we might acknowledge their importance, just don't get our attention.

One of the strengths that the church brings to the partnership is the theological foundation. Circle grew up as a ministry family with the first generation of peer leaders operating with mutual understanding and trust. Much was just understood because of common background, life, and church experience. But as time passed, some people moved on, and some who stayed, changed. What it meant to be a Christian organization began to be a source of debate. Secular funding began to exert pressure toward separating and distancing ourselves from "this religious thing." New staff brought new interpretation, and we began moving into a subjective, spiritually relative era. We began to lose our way. The journey toward secularization is a well-worn path.

Raleigh appeared on the scene straight from the ivory towers of seminary academia. A pastor/theologian, he began to ask the questions that theologians ask. "Well, what do you believe about . . . ?" "What does your doctrinal statement say regarding . . . ?" Raleigh was calling us to shore up our foundations, knowing that without a solid foundational belief system, the values, once held in common, would dissipate with time.

Because of the strong partnership with the church, Circle Urban Ministries has strengthened its commitment to evangelism, Christian identity, and mission philosophy. Without the church playing this role I believe we would have compromised and moved away from our evangelical Christian foundation.

Conservative Christians, commonly from nonurban settings, have been extremely critical toward "social ministries" on this point of spiritual compromise. It is a historically correct assessment, but responsibility for the decline of Christian social ministries must be shared. When the evangelical church vacated the cities across this land they took their interest and financial support with them. In fact, there exists a kind of disdain for the inner city. Conservative Christians have distanced themselves from the inner city and its problems. While recently some in the church are beginning to admit our inner cities are a mission field, only a very small portion of resources are committed to reaching the city inhabitants and even less to the inner city poor. It is hypocritical then to decry the secularization of urban ministries for which Christian support is almost nonexistent.

It is only logical that organizations seek money where it can be found, because very real dilemmas are faced each and every day. For example, should we close down our medical clinic because we cannot get churches to support it, or should we seek government funds? Is no medical care better than medical care with government restrictions?

A suburban conservative Christian might quickly say, "You must stand your ground or you will lose your soul." But tonight, when his four-year-old wakes with a 107-degree fever, he will call his family physician. He will not have to get on the bus and travel to the public hospital an hour away, only to wait four hours to be seen by a resident in training. He is, in effect, promoting a double standard by saying a clinic should refuse government funding, if he is not compelling his church to support that clinic.

Because of our exposure, Circle Urban Ministries has received considerable financial support from conservative churches. But we are an exception. We have been a leader in challenging other ministries to resist the secular funding traps that entice like the sirens of Greek mythology—seductive and destructive. More than a partnership between a local church and a CCD ministry is needed; we must partner between urban ministries and churches of resource. With this kind of support comes accountability. One of Circle's hedges of protection against secularization is that those who contribute to the ministry keep us biblically sound.

What Is Best for Me?

There is no one-size-fits-all model for Christian community development. This chapter has heavily borrowed from our experience and has been extrapolated to conclusions. But as we travel this country I am reminded of the diversity of communities and situations. There are many models of church/CCD partnerships out there and many more yet to be fully developed.

Models help us because they put meat on the bones and illustrate principles. As we develop CCD ministries they will not be cookie-cutter franchises of any particular model, but the Christian community development movement offers such distinctive principles that they cannot be overlooked.

The Key Elements of a Church/Christian Community Development Partnership

- A local church partnership is the best way for a Christian community development to carry out its work. Without the local church people will not grow into spiritual maturity. Christ is coming back for the church. Christian community development must be a feeder to a local church or churches.
- Relationships are key. Partnership takes intentional effort; it won't happen just because we want it to happen. Staff and leaders must commit time and energy to relationship building. To have integrity and longevity, ministry must grow from our fellowship.
- A Christian community development ministry and the church must hold common values and ministry philosophy. Theological, moral, and ethical values must be defined with mutual commitment. Ministry basics, such as John Perkins's three Rs of Christian community development and wholistic ministry, must be held commonly or the partnership between the CCD ministry and church will erode. The parish concept of service to the local community is essential.
- Reconciliation is one of the core values of CCD. The local church is the place it happens. When God's Word is unfolded reconciliation can be practiced and pastors and elders can call people into account if reconciliation is not pursued. The

church provides a place for healing for those wounded in the daily battles of CCD ministry.

- Evangelism and discipleship must be the primary foci for a CCD ministry. The church acts as a spiritual rudder for the CCD, constantly keeping it directed toward its spiritual focus.

9

Indigenous Leadership Development

Wayne L. Gordon

Twenty years ago when I moved to the North Lawndale Community on the West Side of Chicago, one of the things I noticed immediately was the lack of local leadership. It seemed that most of the community leaders lived elsewhere and commuted. North Lawndale is an African American community, which experienced an exodus of most of its professional and business leaders in the late sixties and early seventies. This trend was repeated across the country. We have lost a generation of leaders in most inner cities. Poverty, racism, desegregation, welfare, and other social and economic variables have contributed to the current plight of our urban areas.

I began my ministry in North Lawndale as a Chicago Public School teacher. The school where I taught was 90 percent Black and 10 percent Hispanic. The teacher breakdown was 60 percent Black and 40 percent White. I noticed that not one of the other teachers lived in the neighborhood. This struck me as quite unusual but seemed to have depicted the philosophy of the community: "If you make it, you move out." When people graduate from college or get a good job, one of the first things they do is move out of neighborhoods like North Lawndale. Undoubtedly this has contributed to the lack of indigenous role models and leaders.

Relocation is a tremendous strategy for leadership development and is one of the basic tenets of the Christian community development philosophy. I doubt that there is anything that I have done that has had greater significance than to live in this community. God has been able to use my sheer presence to make an impact. If we are going to be committed to leadership development, we must be committed to relocation.

My first few years I worked diligently to find leaders to come and join me in our work. I particularly spent time trying to convince African American people to move to North Lawndale and to join our ministry. I was unable to persuade anyone Black or White, other than my wife, Anne, to move to Lawndale with me. This resulted in God working in a providential way. It was during a conversation that I was having with Tom Skinner, telling him about our unsuccessful attempt to attract leaders to come and join us in ministry that Tom gave me some words of revelation. He said, "Wayne, you are looking in the wrong places for your leaders. The leaders are not outside of the community; the leaders are already in the community. . . . What you must do is be committed to raise up a new generation of leaders for this community." It was at that point that I began my life-long journey of learning what it meant to develop and empower leaders from within communities like North Lawndale. I certainly recognize that in the last twenty years of my life, I have only made small strides in this mission of leadership development. In this chapter I hope to encourage you to join me in an effort to raise up indigenous leaders out of the communities we serve.

Establishing Leaders in Our Communities

One thing that hinders leadership development is our lack of commitment to the task as empowered leaders. It is very scary to raise up and empower a young leader who might challenge you or rock the boat. In order for leadership development to take place we must have two very basic commitments.

First, we must commit to believe that the *leaders are already in our communities*. As we look at young people in our neighborhoods, we must not look down upon their usefulness, as Paul tells Timothy, but we must see them with kingdom eyes. We must see the people around us as leaders, people who have insights and intuitions that are far more sensitive to the needs of the community than ours. Our perception of leadership must be different from the world's perception of leadership. Often in our communities the leaders may not be the most articulate or the most polished but have an innate ability to guide and to lead. Therefore, our first commitment must be a strong belief that there are leaders just waiting to be developed.

Our second commitment must be a *commitment to empowerment*. We must be willing to empower the future leaders and help them to be all that God has created them to be. This often takes a great deal of time, effort, money, resources, and stamina. We must never give up. We must relentlessly continue our work of empowering indigenous leaders. Empowering means giving up the power that we have as the existing leaders. As we grow a new generation of leadership, we must be committed to give them responsibility in areas in which they can lead. Often this means that we must take a back seat and allow others to step to the foreground and lead. With this commitment to empower a new generation of leadership from among the very people we serve, our ministry efforts will prove to be successful.

In my estimation it takes at least fifteen years to raise up indigenous leadership from the communities we serve. I often tell people that if they are not committed to staying in their community for at least fifteen years, they will not be successful at bringing up the new generation of leadership. There is no shortcut or fast track to achieve successful leadership development. Therefore I challenge you, as you consider being a developer of leadership, make a commitment to stay put for the next fifteen years. This allows God to use you in a significant way.

Look at Jesus as a model for leadership development. When he walked and talked with people on earth he was a tremendous developer of indigenous leadership. In Matthew we find several strategies of leadership development used by Jesus.

Matthew 4:18–22—Pick Your Leaders

Jesus went and handpicked his leaders, his disciples. As we go about our ministry we must be looking for people with leadership potential. We must then handpick these future leaders to be part of a network of others that we are developing into leaders. While the program may be very loose, it is very intentional. We might invite ten young men to have a Bible study with us on a weekly basis. They may be handpicked with the understanding that they are future community leaders. For years I met with a group of men in Lawndale called the Young Lions. The Young Lions were young men who were already leaders. We would have lunch together every Tuesday with an opportunity to visit, share, and talk about the events of the day. This was not a Bible study. We had a "no agenda" agenda. This was our time to be together. A setting such as this gives an opportunity to build your life into the very people you desire to become leaders.

Matthew 5–7—Teach Them

Ask God who around you will become future leaders in the church and in the kingdom. Then be very committed to spending quality time with them in order to build them up. Matthew 5–7 is known as the "Sermon on the Mount." It is here that Jesus took his disciples with him and taught them kingdom principles. We find Jesus spending special teaching moments with his disciples. He was preparing them for assuming leadership when he was gone. We, too, must spend time teaching those around us to become the leaders of tomorrow. We must pick strategic times to impart the truths we know will make a strong impression on them. We must be teachers if we are going to develop leaders for tomorrow.

Matthew 17:1—Choose a Few from the Many

"After six days Jesus took with him Peter, James and John the brother of James and led them up a high mountain by themselves."
On several occasions Jesus chose three—Peter, James, and John—from among the Twelve to go with him for something very special. He took them to the transfiguration and to the Garden of Gethsemane

with him. We, too, must choose a few out of the larger group for special experiences—for example, accompanying us on speaking engagements, traveling to another city, or just going on a camping trip. Be strategic about whom you pick. Don't base your choices on shallow reasons but give exposure to those with the greatest leadership potential. Do not let accusations of favoritism defeat you. Just pick those persons you plan to develop, and spend some time with them. Then, watch how God, through you, empowers those future leaders.

Matthew 20:26–28—Be a Servant to Them

"[It is] not so with you. Instead, whoever wants to become great among you must be your servant, and whoever wants to be first must be your slave—just as the Son of Man did not come to be served, but to serve, and to give his life as a ransom for many."

Another facet of leadership development is serving the people you are developing. The tendency is to have our young leaders serve us everywhere we go. Of course, sometimes this happens, but we need to work to serve our developing leaders as well.

A great example of how Jesus served is found in John 13. Jesus got down on his knees and washed his disciples' feet. We must under stand that leadership development means being a servant. We must be willing to get down on our knees to serve, get dirty, stay up late, and do the kinds of things that Jesus would have done. We need to be creative and think of ways that we can serve people in a manner that is not demeaning, but so that people are elevated and their dignity affirmed.

Matthew 28:19–20—Make Disciples

The Great Commission of evangelism and discipleship is to go, to teach, to baptize, and to make disciples. The key words here are "to make disciples." Leadership development is discipleship in its truest form. Teaching folks a couple of verses and helping them memorize Scripture during a Bible study is not discipleship. Leadership development is taking the total person, as Jesus did, and teaching him or her as he taught. Discipleship is the process of helping someone to become a true disciple of Jesus Christ.

Over the years I have learned a number of things that have helped me in the development of leaders here in Chicago. While there is no perfect strategy or plan to develop effective leadership, there are some key components that can enhance your leadership development program:

1. *See fifteen years into the future.* As I mentioned earlier, it will take you fifteen years to develop a new generation of leadership for your community. If someone were to ask me: "What should I do to ensure that there will be a new generation of leadership for our community in fifteen years?" I would suggest that he or she take over teaching the kindergarten Sunday school class and stick with that same group of kids all the way through high school, into college, and into the workplace. One thing that helped us here at Lawndale was that I embraced a group of kids when they were freshmen in high school. I supported them through high school, college, adulthood, premarital counseling, and even married them. Now I work with them in postmarital counseling. They have grown up with and are a part of our whole church. Start as young as you can and stay with that same group until they become the leaders that you have envisioned them to be.

2. *Never go anywhere alone.* Leadership development is "Not doing anything alone." No matter where you go, no matter what you do, take someone with you. When you walk out of your office to go to the local drugstore or to the laundromat, take someone with you and spend time together. Often a young grammar school student will hang around your office with nothing to do. Ask if he or she would like to go with you to the basketball game or to the bank. These are experiences that grow and stretch young people in ways that they may not otherwise be exposed to. When you travel, take someone with you. It may be his or her first chance to drive out of town or go on an airplane. It may be a life-changing experience.

3. *Be available/socialize with them.* To develop leaders you must spend time with them. You must be accessible and available to them when they need to talk to you. There is not a week that goes by that someone does not knock on my door while I am home. My home phone number is a listed number, and people know that they can call me at home if they need to talk. It is amazing, but they have respected my privacy. They have not abused my accessibility.

Some of the best conversations can and do take place in the context of just hanging out with people. Go to lunch with some of the kids or others on your staff; just be one of the guys. It is important to have time to laugh, joke, cry, pray, share deep thoughts, and talk about how the Chicago Bears or Bulls are doing. "No agenda" agendas are important in conversations and relationship building.

4. *Expose them to role models.* We must bring role models in front of our young leaders. John Perkins and Tom Skinner preached at our church many times when we were just a storefront church of fifty people. They believed in leadership development. They were willing to develop me as I developed others. We began to bring in many African American role models to speak at our church and to talk with our people. As a young church we made a commitment that every fifth Sunday we would have an African American in the pulpit. Role models from outside the community expose our developing leaders to new people and new ideas.

5. *Have your family be a part of your ministry.* Our families are great assets in leadership development. Often, we have people in our home to eat and spend the night. Even today we still have people who eat at our house on a regular basis. Randy Brown, our gym director, began this process when he was a young man and now continues to eat with us every Wednesday night. Often at dinner we have profound conversations, kick around political thoughts, and discuss what is happening at the church.

On several occasions we have taken others with us on our family trips and vacations. They see the way we discipline our children and they participate in our family devotions. Not only does this help in the leadership development process, but it helps my family feel a part of our whole ministry.

6. *Travel with them.* I have taken young people on trips all over the country—Washington, D.C.; Jackson, Mississippi; Mendenhall, Mississippi; Detroit; and New York City. During a week's visit we talk to as many ministry people and visit as many sites as we possibly can. The cramped sleeping conditions and long van rides encourage the formation of strong interpersonal relationships.

7. *Love! Love! Love!* Jesus told us to love our neighbor. One of the critical keys to leadership development is to love people and let them know it. Love them in every way you know how. Ask God to teach you ways to love. Often young people growing up in our communities have not felt love. I will never forget when Robert Holt, now a college graduate working for UPS, told me that I was the first person to tell him that I loved him. He did not know how to take it at first. But, as the years went by and the words were translated into actions, he began to understand. It is important that we let people know that we love them.

8. *Be positive and affirm them.* It is so important that you tell the people that you are developing as leaders that they are doing a good job. The old pat on the back goes an awful long way. Be sure to praise them for the things that they have done right. I think it is important that every time we criticize or point out a fault to one of our developing leaders, we should praise them forty times. This may seem out of balance, but it is important that we ignore as much of the negative as we can and accentuate the positive. People need to be built up and affirmed, not torn down.

9. *Give them responsibility and let them fail.* Let people know that they have an area for which they are responsible. Give people a job and allow them to fail. Let people make decisions and take responsibility for those decisions. One of the things that often stifles leadership is that the person developing the new leader continues to interfere after he or she has assigned the job. We have to take a back seat and let the emerging leaders make mistakes on their own.

It is important that each person is in charge of an area of ministry. He or she makes decisions, plans, and is responsible for the outcome.

Assigned responsibility must carry with it some established boundaries. The leader needs to know the exact limits of the responsibility. Boundaries can be established using such things as budgets, time limits, and desired outcome statements. A few years ago a group of our college students were running a summer program with grammar school students. I set very broad boundaries for our college staff: we wanted the children to become better readers, have fun, grow in their walk with God, and obtain one life skill not taught in school. It was amazing to watch the college students set goals and directions for the young people. As I sat back and watched, I realized that they possessed tremendous insight into how to achieve the goals we set.

10. *Make them feel important.* Dr. Jawanza Kunjufu in his book, *Countering the Conspiracy to Destroy Black Boys,* quotes Jeff Fort, a notorious gang leader: "We will always get the youth because we know how to make them feel important."[1] Often in our church and other settings we make children and young people feel like they are not important. We push them aside, we tell them to be quiet when they speak up, and we rarely set aside special programs for them. We must make our young people feel important.

This comes with the things I have mentioned—i.e., spending time, talking, and, especially, *listening* to them. If we as leaders would listen to our future leaders, I think we would begin to see that we have a lot to learn. Often, hearing someone out is a very empowering experience for both parties.

11. *Having an education is not the same as being a leader.* Just because someone has graduated from college does not mean he or she is a leader. Of course the opposite is also true: Many of our leaders have not graduated from college. We have one person in particular on our staff who is a tremendous leader. She now directs a program and has several staff people reporting to her. Not only is she not a college graduate, but she did not even finish high school. If she had been disqualified from leadership because she did not have a college degree, we would have lost an excellent leader.

While having an education does not necessarily translate into being a good leader, many of our future leaders are capable of graduating from college and must be encouraged to do so. At Lawndale we do everything we can to encourage potential college students.

College

When I first moved into Lawndale in 1975, I was coaching football. One day I asked Dave, one of our best football players, what he wanted to do when he grew up. He said, "I want to be a truck driver." Now Dave was someone who had great potential not only with his mind, but also as a college football player. Needless to say, Dave did not have high aspirations for his life. I found that almost no one whom I coached or taught had aspirations of going to college. I began to talk about college frequently with my athletes and those coming to our Bible study. I started taking them to college sporting events and other activities. We made a yearly trip to Wheaton College where we slept in the wrestling room, ate in the cafeteria, and visited classes. The more we did these kinds of things, the more our young people began to consider the possibility of going to college.

None of the first ten young people I helped to go to college graduated. We had missed the key point—it's not enough to merely get into college; you must be successful once you get there. At Lawndale Community Church we now have a program to help our young people *graduate* from college. We feel that the following components are vital to this program:

1. *Back-to-school dinner.* In late summer we take all of our college students out to dinner. We ask the upper classmen to share what they thought was hard for them as freshmen. This sharing helps to prepare the younger students and to start them off on a good note. We also spend some time talking about areas for which they need prayer in the coming year.

2. *Winter retreat.* Our college students go on a winter retreat, normally at a hotel in downtown Chicago. We spend two nights together in sharing, praying, and studying God's Word. The first night we always go around the room and talk about something good that happened during the past year and something that was hard. Each person gains the support of many others as a result of these sharing sessions.

3. *Visit on campus.* We have a commitment to visit every one of our college students on his or her campus at least once a year. That we would come half way across the country to visit them makes an unbelievable impact on the students.

4. *Monthly newsletters.* It is important to send a monthly newsletter describing what is going on back home. These "newsletters" might be in the form of a church newsletter, but they don't have to be. Church bulletins, sermon tapes, and just plain letters with lots of news serve just as well to keep the students current and in touch with the scene back home.

5. *Adopted family.* College students are adopted by families in our church who make a commitment to pray for them, send them birthday cards, write one letter a month, and try to visit with them when they are home on break.

6. *Care packages.* As a church we gather care packages three times a year and send them to our college students.
7. *Collect phone calls.* We let all of our college students know that they may call us collect any time they need to talk. This encourages ongoing communication and lets them know that they are important.
8. *Financial help.* Besides some basic scholarship programs, which we have to help our college students, it is public knowledge that we want to help financially any student who is a part of our ministry. Finances should not stop anyone from graduating from college.

In conclusion, there is no one simple answer to the question of how to develop indigenous community leaders. There are as many different programs as there are CCD ministries. This chapter provides some guidelines that will be helpful to those of you who are just beginning a leadership development program. Be sure to talk with other CCD ministries to get their ideas. The two most important things to remember are that *leaders are already in our communities* and *we need to empower them.* Even though you will likely have some early failures, be willing to stick with the program for the long haul, and God will bless you and your community with those sound leaders you need.

The Key Elements of Developing Indigenous Leaders

* Society's pattern for success is "up and out." When people graduate from college or get a good job, they usually move out of the inner city. As a result, most inner cities suffer from a lack of local leadership.
* We must believe that there is a new generation of leaders just waiting to be developed in inner city communities. It is our goal to develop them!
* We must be willing to help future leaders to be all God has created them to be. This requires humility—allowing them to step to the foreground and assume leadership.

- The Book of Matthew offers practical strategies that Jesus used to develop leaders: Choose a few from the many, teach them, be a servant to them, and make disciples.
- Spend time with your young leaders: socialize informally, travel with them, be accessible and available to them.
- Give your young leaders responsibility. Let them make decisions and take responsibility for those decisions, right or wrong.
- Though not a requisite for leadership, encourage and enable them to graduate from college if it is within their capabilities and they desire to do so.

10

Christian Community Development and the Family

Counting the Costs, Counting the Rewards

Vera Mae Perkins

It was December 1969 in small-town Mississippi. Martha burst into the church, her face full of urgency. I froze—in those days, no news was good news, and for Blacks at the height of the civil rights era, it could be a mother's worst fears.

"Mrs. Perkins," Martha shouted, nearly out of breath. "They've got all of those children locked up in jail!"

Among "those children" were several of my friends' and neighbors' children, and my own four oldest: Spencer, 16; Joanie, 14; Phillip, 13; and Derek, 11. I understood the danger. We were all familiar with Southern justice and had seen and heard many times the horrors inflicted on those who tried to challenge the White Southern way of life. But God had called us to this little town; we were doing his work. I had to believe that he would never leave or forsake us. Now it was time for me to stand on that promise.

The anger and suspicion between the races were smoldering beneath the surface, just waiting to blaze into violence. It might have been a good time to get out and come back later when things had calmed down, but there was the Perkins family, right in the thick of it all, organizing, demonstrating, working. We had witnessed scattered racial incidents and been subjected to an ongoing war of nerves and White terrorism—cars following us, people driving by or parking and shining lights into our house at night, telephone threats. But nothing had really touched us so personally before that night . . .

Counting the Costs of Community Development

During the time we lived in Mendenhall, Mississippi, our community was going through the birth pains of the civil rights movement. We all participated as a family. When it became necessary to take a stand, such as in the integration of the formerly all-White public schools, we knew there would be hostility. We expected to see violent opposition, against ourselves, our neighbors, and our children. My husband, John, and I knew there would be costs, but we also knew it was the right thing to do, as parents and as community developers. And we knew that nothing we preached, none of the work we were trying to accomplish in our community, would have any credibility unless we were willing to commit ourselves—even to the point of laying our children on the "altar" of our commitment.

Christian community development, as a ministry, requires that we live a life of submission, accepting the costs as well as the rewards. One thing I have learned after all these years, one thing which I would admonish all other ministers and ministry partners to do before embarking on that long and often difficult journey, is to count the cost—that is, be prepared for what lies ahead for you and your family. Community ministry is no easy road, and even though we make our commitment to that road individually, our loved ones must often travel it with us.

Christ sets a tough standard for us: "Anyone who wants to be my follower must love me far more than he does his own father, mother, wife, children, brothers, or sisters—yes, more than his own life—otherwise he cannot be my disciple. And no one can be my disciple who does not carry his own cross and follow me. But don't begin until you count the cost" (Luke 14:26–28 LB). Christ is not just weeding out the faint of heart. He is telling us to prepare ourselves for the journey ahead so we don't run out of steam or courage before we complete the work we set out to do.

Marriage Partners as Ministry Partners

Now, as I approach retirement, my life is beginning to slow down enough to let me look back over the years and see many things that the Lord has been teaching me about Christian community development and ministry as a family. Life lessons about marriage, motherhood, and ministry have been storing up in my heart, and more and more I feel the need to communicate them to other people who are not yet as far along the path.

Probably the most essential point is this: A wife and husband must become one. In order to stay together and to raise a family under the rigors of ongoing ministry to others, married people must have a strong, Christ-centered relationship. They need a unified vision and a commitment to mutual support of one another. If they neglect their relationship with one another, the family will have a hard time surviving the demands of ministry.

Partners need to affirm each other in their various roles. A wife may stay home and keep the house and children, or she may work alongside her husband; but in either role she must believe in her husband's ministry, pray for it, and, in whatever way possible, be involved in it at the appropriate times. Meanwhile, her husband should acknowledge and affirm the importance of her support, whether in the ministry field or in the home.

When a wife is called into a ministry, she may feel somewhat torn between the responsibilities of home and work. A husband who supports his wife in her calling will be understanding of the extra demands on her time and attention and will help to share domestic burdens as much as possible. He will not lay a guilt trip on his wife or try to force her to choose between the ministry and her home. Husbands who do this are not only hurting their spouses, they are hindering the work of God. In all ways, marriage partners must learn to pull together, for their own good and for the good of those who are blessed by their service.

It's a simple principle: If you have only one ox in the harness, the wagon goes around in circles. It takes a team, with both oxen in the yoke, to go places. For me it has been one of my greatest sources of satisfaction as a woman to know that I have supported my husband in God's call upon his life. I was and still am right by his side, standing with him in all that God has called him to do.

When a wife is committed both to the ministry into which her husband has been called and to her marriage, she can't look back when he is called upon to go down rough roads (after all, looking back might make the difference between being "salt and light" and winding up a "pillar of salt"). A wife has to stand faithful and meek, ready to accept the will of God and the destiny that he has ordained for her.

Sometimes that destiny doesn't seem very glamorous or very significant. The wife of a leader is often cast in the role of silent partner, helpmate, or sidekick. She may work as hard as anyone else for the common goal, but more often than not, she will stand in the shadows while others stand in the limelight, and the glory may sail right over her bowed head.

We silent partners must remember that it is God's glory that matters most, and it is he who will provide the ultimate rewards for a job well done.

Home-Making and Home-Moving

After thirty-five years of moving, ministering, and moving again, I might have thought at the age of sixty-two that I was safely settled and semiretired in my Pasadena home, overseeing the ministry we founded there. But here we were, John and I, discussing our preparations to move yet again, to turn over another ministry to another generation of community servants, our daughter Priscilla and son Derek among them.

So many times in our life of CCD ministry, John, our children, and I have settled in communities of need, made each new place the focus of our love and effort and invested ourselves in its people—all eventually to pull up stakes, settle again, and start over somewhere else. Everywhere we have gone, we have worked to make ourselves at home. But we have always remained conscious of those who would come after us. Everywhere we lived, we set services in motion, purchased buildings and equipment, and tried to leave very little debt, so those who took the reins of ministry after us could succeed without being overburdened.

When I think of the many sleepless nights, hardships, and sacrifices that my family has gone through to build ministries in places like Mendenhall and Jackson, Mississippi, and Pasadena, California, I am reminded of how Jesus said to his disciples, "I sent you to reap where you didn't sow; others did the work, and you received the harvest" (John 4:38 LB).

Many times John has said to me, "You know, Vera Mae, we're like pioneers. We start ministries, lay a foundation, purchase land and materials, make sure the structure is solid, and then turn it all over and move on."

Sometimes it's hard making a home of a place, pouring love, time, and energy into it, and then moving aside to let others build on what you have begun. Building a home and ministry, raising a family, creating relationships with neighbors and friends—these are the stakes we put down, and it can be hard pulling them up from familiar ground to strike out for new territory.

Of course, not everyone is called to move on. Some ministries may require a lifelong commitment in one place. But wherever God calls us to serve, we cannot become so attached to place or possessions that we forget that God is the owner and head of the company. He sends us in to do a job, and he may call us out when he needs us to do work elsewhere. When that call comes, we have to be ready to move.

As a wife and mother I have occasionally had difficulty watching the stresses and strain of ministry take their toll on members of my family. John and I have raised eight children, and probably any parent who has ever relocated has seen how moving young children about can affect their sense of security.

Over the early years of our family life, John and I worked hard to instill in our children a sense of rootedness in God to counteract the sudden changes, the frequent moves, the new schools, new friends, and new situations that were a part of the constant fluctuations of their young lives. We rose early in the morning and prayed and studied the Bible as a family, partly because we wanted the children to understand the basis of the call on their father's life and on our lives as a family, but also because these times bound us together and gave us the strength to overcome the hardships that we often had to endure, even as we moved from place to place.

Making Do with Less

Of course, relocation, in the context of Christian community development, is more than just moving around. It involves giving something of yourself to the community you adopt, and taking on some of the burdens of that community. It means you identify yourself with the needs of those you have come to serve. And sometimes that means making do with less, even while you occasionally rub elbows with people who have far greater material wealth than you possess or a more affluent lifestyle than the one you have chosen to live out.

It may be frustrating sometimes to see other people—some of them Christians—who seem to have so much while others among God's people barely scrape by. But over the years I have seen God provide for me and my family in both material and spiritual resources, far beyond anything I could have asked or imagined.

There were times in the early days of John's ministry when our family's resources were very thin. True ministry to the poor requires us to be "poor in spirit," to identify ourselves with the needs, the pain, and the reality of being poor, but sometimes that identification is all too literal. My oldest children can recall times when we made a game out of opening up the unlabeled cans of food someone had given us, to see what we were going to have for dinner. And then there were days when there was no food in the house at all.

Spencer, my firstborn son, still talks about the times when I sent him to the store to buy a few crackers and some Vienna sausages to feed my family. He is both amazed and proud of how his mother could make a meal of so little. Sometimes I believe the Lord must have taken a hand in stretching the little bit that we had, the way he stretched the loaves and fishes to feed the multitudes.

But one of the great rewards of commitment to ministry is the opportunity that you have to see small miracles happen, to see people rise to the occasion and show Christ's love at just the right time, and to see God's will prevail in situations that seem desperate or hopeless. It seems as if desperate situations encourage and enhance our growth, even as they reveal more to us about ourselves and about God's character.

God brought my family and me through some very tight spaces and, in our latter years, he has blessed us with a certain amount of comfort. Our needs are met continually, and when our wants are not met, we often find that God has worked things out so as to give us something better than what we wanted.

But better than having material possessions is having a constant turnaround of resources, so that we can become the instrument by which God meets the needs of others. People come to the door of the John Perkins Foundation office begging for food and it is good to be able to feed them. It is good to have a roof at the Harambee Christian Family Center, under which many children from broken homes and unhealthy situations can gather to be taught and loved and cared for. It is good to have doors, if for no other purpose than to throw them wide open and invite people in.

Redistribution means thinking of our wealth as the early Christian church did, who "sold their possessions and goods and divided them equally among the people, according to everyone's need." While we must, of course, provide for our own families and give them the best that we can offer, part of the best that we can give our children is to raise them to be givers themselves. If we teach our children how to be abased and how to abound in spite of material circumstances, if we teach them that wealth is meant for serving people, and if we learn how to make redistribution a family way of life, we will be giving our children a legacy richer than anything we can take to the bank or lock up in a safe.

Christian community development takes total submission of yourself, your resources, and your family. This kind of submission is an act that happens on the altar of the heart, where you lay down what you value and dedicate it to God's service. In order to do this you have to be committed to what God is doing, more committed than you are to your own agenda, to your own comfort, or to your own will. If you are committed to a cause, you don't abandon it, even when things get tight. And I must say that the Perkins family has had plenty of tight spots in our thirty-five years of travels.

December, 1969: We were at church, rehearsing for the Christmas program, and some of the kids started talking about some of the recent racially motivated incidents, the most recent being the arrest of a neighbor's son, Garland Wilks. My husband and a White volunteer named Doug had been with him when the police came and hauled him away to jail for supposedly "disturbing the peace."

John suggested that we go up to the jailhouse and try to get Garland out. Immediately nearly everyone hopped into a few vans and cars and drove up to the jailhouse. I stayed behind to close up the house and church building, but before I could get everything secured, Martha, one of our volunteers, came back and told me that the police had John, Doug, and about a dozen of our children locked up in jail!

My husband and children and my friends' children behind bars, being terrorized, possibly mistreated—I didn't know what to do. Nothing like this had ever happened to me before.

I called several people to help, then rushed to the jailhouse. When I got there, all my kids were inside, and I heard them yelling all at once. "Mama, they're beating Daddy up in here! They broke Doug's glasses! They slammed the door on him and broke his glasses!" Even in their own frightening situation, they were more concerned about their father and their friend.

The jailers and police, nervous and unsure how to handle the situation they had created, tried to bargain with them. "We're gonna let you kids out, and you all go home and be quiet."

But the kids replied, "We're not going unless you let Reverend Perkins go!" The police finally had to pull the kids out of their cell, kicking and screaming.

Now, it's one thing to put yourself into dangerous situations or to willingly go through hardship; but it is something else again for a parent to knowingly allow her children to walk into difficulty or danger. Yet community development requires us to invest ourselves wholeheartedly into the place we are serving, and that includes investing our children, laying them down on the altar, and teaching them to lay themselves down for others.

Many of the issues that faced my family and community back in 1969 are not so different from the ones that face community developers today. Back then, it was racial and political turmoil that threatened us. Today we are plagued by drugs, gangs, and violence. But the unity of family is still one of our best defenses against the problems that work to destroy inner city communities. And the family is also one of the best means of demonstrating interdependence and community spirit to the world at large—especially when every member of that family is committed to the same Christian ideals.

Reconciliation: Giving Up the Past

In many ways, racial reconciliation is very much a key to Christian community development because, in order to build community, people must begin to see one another as neighbors. Racial barriers often prevent people from recognizing their mutual need and common goals, and until this happens, there can be no community.

As a Black woman who grew up poor in the very segregated South, it once seemed that for my kind, racial reconciliation was all cost and no reward. It was hard to see what I had to gain by becoming reconciled to the kind of people who had shunned and discriminated against me all my life; the kind of people who unjustly imprisoned, beat, and sometimes killed people of my race without any fear of punishment or reprisal.

I remember how hard it was for me, growing up in the rural South, to get an education. Throughout junior high school, I had to walk nearly two miles to catch my school bus each weekday, then ride the bus for twenty miles to the "colored" school before being able to sit down and learn in a classroom. Had I been White, I could have waited right outside my front door and caught the big yellow school bus to ride to the nearby school in comfort.

That bus used to pass me sometimes as I walked to or from my bus stop, and White children would throw spit-wads at me from the windows. So why would I want to reconcile with them? But my grandmother used to discourage this kind of thinking. She taught me not to be bitter, because "vengeance belongs to God, and he will repay."

Still, rejection hurts. Like a big, hard rock the pain seems impossible to move, so you let it lie there. The rejection didn't end with my childhood either. During my twelve years of living in Mendenhall, not a single local White woman ever held a conversation with me. Reconciliation, I thought—who needed it? But God's answer was . . . "You do!"

At various times in our lives, God pushed my family to the extremes to teach us how much we needed to love our neighbors, whoever they were, whatever our past experience with them might be, for our own sakes. During the civil rights movement, when my husband got unjustly arrested more than once, and nearly beaten to death, and when our whole family was being threatened and terrorized, God used that time to reveal to us just how hurtful racial hatred was, not only to the object of hatred, but to the one doing the hating.

It was a tense, tentative standoff, with White police, state troopers, and jailhouse officials, edgy and hostile, facing the gathered crowd of frightened but determined Black kids, neighbors, and friends of Reverend Perkins. The police wouldn't let me in to see him, and they kept trying to make us disperse, but none of us wanted to leave until we saw that John was all right. We stood out there in the dark, praying and crying, the air thick with the tension between love and hate. The children were still shouting, overcharged with fear. I felt it too.

Suddenly, John appeared at an upper-story window of the jailhouse and started to speak. A hush fell over the crowd as he spoke, and you could hear the pity and sadness in his voice. He said many things, but his words were not angry or rash or fearful. He spoke gently, trying to reach the hearts, not just the ears of the people with a loving message full of self-sacrificing gospel truth. He begged them not to do anything they would regret, not to lose the little they had gained by giving in to anger or violence or hatred, but to pull together and let there be an end to all the suffering.

"I don't know what it's going to take for all this to come to an end," said John. "If somebody has to suffer, I'm willing. And if somebody has to die, I'm ready."

The words John spoke that night mobilized a community and cemented them in a spirit of cooperation. Blacks came together with the strength of unity, not anger. And the message of love and reconciliation planted a seed that would sprout in many hearts and grow into an eventual harvest of healing, brotherhood, hope, and progress.

New Challenges

The healing message of the gospel, applied to racial division and bitterness, may take time to act, but it gets results. It brings about relationships where none seems likely, trust where none seems justified, and cooperation where none seems possible. Today John and I have dear friends who are White and who have committed themselves to us and our ministry in a true spirit of brotherhood. I have White friends with whom I exchange the fellowship, encouragement, and prayer support so essential to sustained joy in our Christian walks.

If you didn't know our history, you would certainly never guess that I had suffered the pain and anger of racist rejection, for myself and for each of my children who had to push their bodies through a line of White opposition to integrate a segregated school. You wouldn't guess that I had been shunned by the White women, even Christian women, in my home community for years. You wouldn't guess that my husband had been unjustly arrested and detained by racist White law enforcement officers; had slept on the cold, hard floor of a bare cell; had more than once had to suffer the terror of imminent death at the hands of Whites in power; and had even been beaten and tortured to the verge of death. You wouldn't know, because God's love has healed those wounds, covered those sins, and built bridges of community where there had once been only walls and fences.

Our family's early trials and sufferings have produced fruits of reconciliation extending far beyond us, even through our children. My oldest son Spencer is co-author of the book *More Than Equals: Racial Healing for the Sake of the Gospel*, with his White ministry partner, Chris Rice. Together they head a ministry focused on racial healing and publish a magazine and newsletter proclaiming the same ideal.

It is as if when we, as divided people, trust God to provide the love necessary to reconcile us, he blesses us by giving back more than we ever had apart from each other. As I search my heart today, I can't find any animosity in it. I don't believe it was ever firmly lodged there. But even if it was, it wouldn't have been the first time God rolled away a stone.

Today, after thirty-five years as a partner with my husband in ministry, I hope that we have labored in such a way that those who follow us will be able to go into the communities where we worked and reap the harvest, taking these ministries to heights that we could never have reached. As we turned over the work and moved on from these places, I felt that we were blazing new trails in Christian community development but leaving behind much clear land for others to build on. Surely there is still much to be done, especially in our inner cities.

Now there are new challenges before men and women who go into communities of need and become instruments of community development there. Besides racism and hostility, these community developers and their families are exposed to the dangers of drugs, crime, and violence. Certainly I understand how parents who are called to serve the inner city must feel when they send their children to schools where drugs and handguns are rampant or when they must bring up their children in neighborhoods where break-ins and gang activity may be out of control. I can see how parents might hesitate to raise their families in a poor community, where education and other public resources may not be top-notch.

These can be difficult decisions to make for those you love. But reconciliation across social and economic barriers, relocation into a community of need, redistribution of your family's resources in order to meet the needs of others—each of these is an education in and of itself. The rewards to the spiritual and emotional life of your family and to the character of your children should weigh heavily against any dangers or deprivations. If we keep his will before us, God's love and grace are sufficient to equip us and our families to rise to the challenges of Christian community development.

Counting the Blessings

As John and I prepared to move on to a new place of ministry, even in the midst of planning and counting costs, I found myself counting my blessings instead. I kept going over the years of trial and triumph, recalling how God has shown us grace upon grace. There is so much satisfaction in a life lived for Christ. Perhaps the chief satisfaction is the joy we receive in having been allowed to see the fruits of our labor as the young men and women we have discipled, mentored, and trained as leaders grow up to take the reins of the ministries we have established or to strike out and establish their own ministries in other communities of need.

We have been sowing seeds for years and God, who gives the growth, has allowed us from time to time to come to rest under the shade of trees we helped to plant and water. It has been wonderful for John and me to watch our children grow to adulthood, maturing in Christ and continuing in ministry. At one time or another, all of our eight children have worked with us in our Christian community development efforts, and most of them have chosen to make it their life's work.

Spencer is in Mississippi, working to promote racial healing through *Urban Family* magazine, *The Reconciler* newsletter, and More Than Equals workshops. Joanie joined him in Jackson this year and is taking a point position in the Christian Community Development Association. Priscilla, Derek, Deborah, and Betty are in Pasadena, taking the reins of the John M. Perkins Foundation, the Harambee Christian Family Center, and the Harambee School. As parents, John and I couldn't be prouder! In a way, raising our children in ministry has been our way of redistributing our richest treasures. God gave them to us, and we have tried to give them back to him.

Remember, Christian community development necessarily focuses on the basic unit of community—the family. It makes sense that entire families should work together as an instrument of restoring and sustaining community. And while there will be costs and casualties in the battle to meet the wholistic needs of our nation's broken communities, poverty-stricken and crime-riddled inner city neighborhoods, and racially divided populations, there is no better tool than the family. As long as we trust God to provide the courage and to meet our needs, the rewards will far outweigh any expense.

The Key Elements of Doing Ministry as a Family

If you have been called to commit your life and the lives of your family to God's work of Christian community development, then yes, there will be costs. Here are some things you should remember:

- When God calls you into Christian community development, he calls you as a family. You cannot separate your ministry from the rest of your life. If you try, those who share your life will suffer and so will your service.
- A husband and wife must have a unified vision and must support each other in their individual roles. The two must keep their relationship solid and affirm each other continually in their mutual contribution to the ministry.
- It's great when both spouses hear God's call together, but many times one may hear the call more clearly than the other. This is when trust and mutual submission become important.
- A home is not a house or a place or anything immovable. Home is a condition of the spirit. We must be able to let go of places and property when the Lord calls us and carry our "home" to the next location.
- It may be a cliché, but it's still true: the family that prays together stays together. Teach your children to love God and to serve him, so that they can grow into the same commitment to people and to ministry that drives their parents.
- Relocation is more than moving into a community. It means taking on the problems and concerns of that community. My

neighbors' needs are my needs, and their struggles are my struggles.

- Suffering for the sake of the gospel is a privilege, and some may be ready and willing to do it. But parents must also be ready to allow their children to suffer for the gospel, especially if it serves the community.

- Christian community development may present challenges to the health, safety, and emotional well-being of the family. But by relying on God, families can overcome these obstacles as a unit and reap miraculous benefits.

- The family is at once a defense and a weapon against the very forces that are seeking to break down our communities.

- As you count the costs of community development, don't forget to count the blessings.

11

How to Start a Christian Community Development Ministry

Mark R. Gornik and Noel Castellanos

Agenuinely healthy movement is always growing, spurred on by God's grace (Acts 1:8; 6:7; 12:24; 1 Cor. 3:9; Eph. 4:15–16). As the twentieth century will soon give way to the twenty-first, we need to be consumed with seeing the work of Christian community development spread and grow in depth and impact!

The profound social and economic challenges facing our most fragile and hurting urban (and rural) communities, the growing "vandalism of shalom"[1]—the diminution of God's intentions for wholeness, justice, and joy—defy easy description. A consensus view is emerging among both ministry practitioners and urban analysts that because of the immense distress in our inner city communities, our shared civic, economic, and spiritual future is at tremendous risk.

Previous chapters have described in detail the Christian community development model, which we believe provides the catalytic ingredients for reviving our cities. The CCD model has emerged as a recognized healing force in many communities across the nation. Our challenge today is to build on these successes and see the CCD model developed in scores of other communities. It is a matter of being stewards of the historic opportunity before us.[2] To that end, this chapter will address how to craft an effective strategy to develop new Christian community development congregations and ministries.

We also strongly believe in the development of new churches because of our experiences in Baltimore (Mark) and Chicago (Noel). In 1990, La Villita Community Church was born in the Latino neighborhood of La Villita (Little Village) in Chicago. And in 1986, New Song Community Church was started in Sandtown-Winchester, an African American neighborhood in West Baltimore. Both congregations were started with deep commitments to the three Rs and have, by God's grace, grown in witness and community impact. We hope that the stories of our churches, both their successes and struggles, will encourage others to embrace the vision of Christian community development.

Joining in God's Reign

Setting the context for CCD is where we must start. Christian community development does not begin with a plan or program to solve a problem, but as a call and responsibility within the drama of God's reign.[3] For it is with the redemptive work of Christ that God's urban promises of rebuilt and flourishing communities (Isa. 61:1–4; 65:17–25) find their fulfillment (Luke 4:16–21; 24:25–27, 44). The Gospels reveal Jesus as the one who has come to the city as the New Nehemiah to restore lives, families, and communities. A well-grounded biblical theology of the city and the kingdom of God is critical.

God's reign has come (Mark 1:15; Luke 10:9; 11:20), but we still anticipate its final completion (Matt. 6:9–10). In other words, it is present "now, but not yet." We know that sorrow, death, exploitation, and weeping will give way to joy and restored relationships, all of which find their center in God in the New Jerusalem (Rev. 21:1–4). But we recognize and grieve that this time has not yet come.

God invites us to joyfully share in his good future in the here and now. The life, death, and resurrection of Jesus Christ provides our sure commitment that the new city—both urban place and community—will become a reality. And so we wait, not with hands folded, but as God's copycats, modeling his love for the city (Luke

10:2). As the community called into being by God's reign, we are to anticipate the shalom of the new city through our corporate life and witness in the present. We are to be "impatient" with brokenness and oppression, because we know the wholeness and mercy in Christ that awaits the cities of our world.

Such a vision of the new city is truly transformational—it is meant to nourish our faith, celebrate new possibilities, and give us a firmly anchored hope. The biblical testimony equips us to be both utterly realistic and truly hopeful at the same time. For while we trust God to do great things here and now, we also hunger and thirst for the fulfillment of his reign (Heb. 1:11).

As our understanding of God's reign grows, we should recognize its claim upon our lives and invitation to take visionary risks in developing new ministries, signs and samples of his reign. We are the manifestation of his community-changing power in the world (Eph. 1:20–21). While starting CCD churches and ministries represents an intense amount of work and potential cost, it can really be the beginning of an abundant life. Where kingdom, city, and calling come together, there is privilege and joy unspeakable!

Hearing the Call

Every church and ministry has its genesis with a deep stirring and burden from God. Similar in internal conviction to a conversion experience, a calling provides a sense of purpose focused on serving God with everything within us.[4] A calling is empowering and sustaining, enabling us to joyfully stick to the task God has called us to through thick and thin.[5] Theologically, a call is the Spirit working with God's Word in terms of our gifts and context (Neh. 2:12; John 16:13–14). What we hear is God's Word about cities, reconciliation, and justice. Our context is a hurting and broken urban world. Practically, we respond to this call out of a vast combination of events, personal gifts and abilities, relationships, and experiences. Later, of course, we can look back and see God's sovereign hand in the smallest details and significant events (Neh. 2:8, 18).

Nehemiah's experience provides a clear example of calling. Having heard of the bleak state of Jerusalem from traveling businessmen, Nehemiah wept, mourned, fasted, and prayed (Neh. 1). Nehemiah's heart was broken by what he heard. He was gripped by a conviction that his city was worth fighting for. As Robert Linthicum observes,

> The starting place for us is with the question, "What makes me weep over my city?" If you answer that question, "Nothing makes me weep over my city," you had better get out of urban ministry because you do not belong there. Only a man or woman who allows his heart to be broken with the pain and the plight of the hurting poor and/or the hurting powerful belongs in ministry there. To be effective in urban ministry, you must have a heart that is as big as the city itself.[6]

And just like Nehemiah, our brokenness must turn to deep and vulnerable prayer.

How God Stirred Us Up

The vision for La Villita Community Church began in October 1989 when I came to visit Chicago after hearing John Perkins talk about the three Rs in San Jose, California. He shared about the start of a new association of community developers working to implement his ideas in poor communities across our nation. I arrived in Chicago for the first CCDA conference hoping to take back some more tools to develop the youth ministry I was directing in San Jose. I left a few days later with a deep sense that God was calling me to relocate from California to Chicago to work in a Mexican barrio (community) I "discovered" while on this trip.

While I can point to this experience in October 1989 as the significant event that began to confirm and shape my family's decision to come to La Villita, the process began much earlier. I would like to share three key factors that God used to move me to embrace the vision of Christian community development.

First, I met Christ through a parachurch organization, then joined the staff of this ministry a few years later. A comment that I heard often was that we existed because the church was not doing its work in reaching our youth. Second, I was deeply concerned that my youth ministry seemed very inadequate to meet the needs of the families these kids were coming from. The little good we did seemed not to last as our kids struggled in families where Christ was not central. Finally, I saw that while families were being ministered to, they continued to live in barrios that did not facilitate growth, health, and opportunity. The barrio had great assets but also lacked the resources and role models with real practical solutions to the issues we faced.

With this as a backdrop, I got off the El train in North Lawndale and walked a few blocks to Lawndale Community Church. When I walked in I was blown away by the sight of a gym with a health center, a learning center, and a full-sized basketball court. I was moved by the incarnational and practical expression of God's love, which was being proclaimed in word and deed. In my heart, I knew that this model was very much what our Latino communities were lacking. I felt very excited about the possibility of seeing a wholistic CCD ministry developed in a Mexican barrio.

I laugh when I think of how God led me to La Villita. The whole neighborhood is filled with Mexican restaurants and bakeries, but the first place I was taken to was a Chinese restaurant!

After seeing this thriving Mexican neighborhood, I went and talked to Wayne Gordon, the pastor of Lawndale Community Church, to ask him about La Villita, which is directly south of his community. Wayne told me he thought it would be great to see a church with a vision for Christian community development established in La Villita and that he would be excited to see this happen. Little did he know I would soon take him up on his offer.

In December of 1989, my wife Marianne and I returned to Chicago to visit with Pastor Gordon and to investigate the possibility of moving to La Villita to establish a church. It all happened so fast and we felt so right about taking this giant step of faith, that we knew God's hand was with us. We felt great peace that God had opened doors for us to move across the country to start this new work. This assurance that it was God who called has helped us persevere through many difficult situations and discouragements.

The first eight months we were in Chicago, my family attended Lawndale Community Church. We were embraced by the staff of

Lawndale and felt encouraged that both the church and leadership were so willing to help us establish a sister work. We also attended staff functions, clinic meetings, and youth events. All the while I was observing and learning what made Christian community development work. I am still amazed at how God opened Pastor Gordon's heart to receive us when we arrived in Chicago in September 1990. As we started to lay the foundations for the ministry of La Villita Community Church, God's clear calling remained central to every step we took.

For me (Mark), I share my call with Allan and Susan Tibbels, who have been two of my closest friends for nearly twenty years. For many years, we wrestled with the obligations of our faith in light of the needs of our city, Baltimore. How could we have grown up in the Baltimore area, yet been so detached from poverty conditions only a few miles away? we wondered. As White Christians, what about our complicity in the structures of racism? How did the parable of the Good Samaritan apply to us today? Influenced by John Perkins and Voice of Calvary in Mississippi, we had a working model in our minds of what a Christian community development church in Baltimore might look like. Our inner call and conviction came together in 1986 as Allan, Susan, and I began a serious discussion about beginning a wholistic work in our city. I was finishing seminary and the Tibbels were serious about deciding to relocate. Soon, our idea became a reality.

Acting on biblical conviction, we moved into the African American community of Sandtown and lived in rental housing. This was particularly challenging for the Tibbels family, who left a spacious ranch-style home in the suburbs accessible for Allan's wheelchair. Row homes were not built quadriplegic-friendly!

The longer you put off the decision to relocate, the more difficult and less likely it will be. For example, many friends told the Tibbels family to at least wait until their young daughters, Jennifer and Jessica, had grown. But Allan and Susan believed their children should not miss out on the blessing and adventure associated with serving the Lord in the city.

Before you start a CCD ministry, be clear on your motivations. Relocate to expend your lives on behalf of those who live there, not to have your own needs met. And remember, relocation must be preceded by radical "surgery" on our hearts. God must first begin healing our hearts of classism and racism ("works righteousness"), sending us forward on the roads of confession and repentance. Don't just "try it out," go resolved to stay. And go based on God's Word, not your feelings.

The opening words of Pastor Carl Ellis's charge to our tiny New Song group as we began our ministry said it all: "Are you guys crazy? Are you serious about this thing? God bless you. We are really glad that you guys are crazy enough to attempt something that is so impossible that, unless the Lord works in it, it would be doomed to failure." In other words, CCD is God's work. As such, it is often counterintuitive to conventional assumptions of what will bring "success" (1 Cor. 1:26–28). It is a way that our "weakness" becomes a display case for the glory and power of Christ (2 Cor. 12:9–10).

A Theology of Place

God's call to relocation involves a conversion of our hearts to a specific community. A broken heart provides the soil for a new vision of community to rise forth. This suggests the need for us to reflect on a theology of place. Where we choose to live, Bob Lupton reminds us, is a theological decision, which turns on our understanding of God's desires and intention for community.[7] The greatest example of this is clearly the incarnation (John 1:14; Phil. 2:6–7).

We find God's concern for all communities throughout the Bible. The psalmist declares that "the earth is the LORD's, and everything in it, the world, and all who live in it" (Ps. 24:1). Every alley, street, and barrio is under Christ's lordship (Col. 1:15–17). Joined to God's concern for his world is the nature of personhood. Created in God's image, there is a sacredness unique to humanity (Gen. 1:26–28; Ps. 8). Thus, to desecrate the image of God through exploitation and oppression is to assault God.[8] Our calling to the struggle for shalom entails recovering a sense of communities of need as "holy ground" because of the people who dwell there. What a contrast the Christian position is to the stereotypically negative view Americans generally hold about our inner urban areas!

The account of the prophet Jeremiah's real estate transaction in Jeremiah 32 provides a vivid picture of a theology of place in action.[9]

Under God's guidance, Jeremiah, who was in prison at the time, determined to purchase his cousin Hanamel's "vacant lot" in Anathoth. In human terms, what a foolish real estate deal! The field was behind "enemy" (Babylonian) lines with little prospect that its ownership would be honored. Certainly no "respectable" modern title company or bank would sign off on such a deal. But for Jeremiah, buying this piece of land was above all an act of hope in the face of despair, a renewal of normal cultural activity that witnessed to a greater reality.[10] In light of God's Word (Jer. 32:8–14), the investment in this land was a down payment on the Restorer's promises of a renewed city with its accompanying vibrant economic and cultural activity.

In microcosm, this captures something of the energizing spirit of CCD. Christian community development is about ministry in the overlooked and forgotten communities of our land, the throwaway places neglected and discarded by the powers that be. God's Word calls us to fully invest our lives and resources in them. It is about committing to the future based on the faith and hope that God has placed in our hearts.

Standing on the Shoulders

Vital as well to discerning God's call and ongoing formation is the role of mentor leaders. We have had the benefit of learning from seasoned leaders, succeeding in our work in great measure because we are building on the foundation of their lives and experiences. Certainly John Perkins is a mentor leader for us. For me (Mark), leaders such as Randy Nabors and Carl Ellis at New City Fellowship Church in Chattanooga, the late Lem Tucker of Voice of Calvary Ministries in Jackson, Mississippi, and Harvie Conn of Westminster Theological Seminary in Philadelphia were highly influential as well. For me (Noel), Wayne Gordon really encouraged my development in Christian community development ministry. Wayne and I still spend regular time together praying and talking, which is invaluable.

It is impossible to overstate the power of entrusting your life to another person committed to helping you succeed in ministry.

Mentors can save new community developers countless unnecessary trials by sharing with them their past experiences. If you are open, teachable, and eager to learn, a mentor will feel motivated to invest himself or herself even more fully in your life and ministry. I always took the initiative to seek Wayne out and let him know what I needed from him after he made it clear that he was open to that. While it takes humility to learn, it takes real commitment and character on the part of mentors to guide. Both are learning experiences that can deeply shape our ministry skills and character.[11]

Mentor ministries are critical as well. As is generally recognized today, we learn through models.[12] Models are how we organize and evaluate information. By defining, testing, and improving our picture of how ministries work as "models," we can gain invaluable perspectives on Christian community development. To this end, visiting and spending time with other ministries is essential. And so is staying in touch with them by being on their mailing lists. If ministry veterans want to stay creative and improve their efforts, they should continue lifelong learning by seeing and appreciating what others are doing. Try to visit regularly other churches and ministries, taking along key staff whenever possible. Look to bring back patterns, principles, and ideas that you can adapt, not cookie-cutter solutions, which may not match your context or gift/skill mix.

There is one danger, however, in working with an established leader or ministry. At times you will feel pressure to do things the way they do it or at their pace. Be careful to go slow—remember, they have been at it for years. Focus on the uniqueness and needs of your community and personal gifts and abilities; don't try to recreate someone else's experiences.

An important dynamic of our relationship with Lawndale was their desire to support, not control, our efforts at La Villita. Lawndale helped tremendously by sharing equipment such as tables and overhead projectors. Wayne also put me in contact with potential funding sources and gave credibility to our new work. A real sign of commitment and friendship is for someone to share funding contacts.

Understanding Community and City

Having made a commitment to relocate to a community of need in Baltimore, Allan Tibbels began our journey by researching the demographic data on Baltimore's neighborhoods. With statistical data analyzing those neighborhoods facing the greatest struggles, Allan and I spent a few days each week for several months visiting communities of need in Baltimore. This was a preliminary step that we augmented with much prayer and discussion as we decided where we would relocate.

Informed by broader understandings of racial and economic trends in Baltimore and rust belt cities, the questions we asked of the specific neighborhoods we visited were basic: What are the strengths of the community? What are its critical needs? Who is already involved in meeting needs in the community? What ways is the Lord already working in the community (Acts 18:9–10)? What change is the community undergoing? What are some of the ways we might be able to seek the shalom of the community if we lived there?

Effective ministry is rooted in a comprehensive understanding of the communities where we live and serve.[13] Learning about a community occurs through a variety of means and represents an ongoing process. Foremost, it must begin with bonding ourselves to the community where we will be ministering. As Manny Ortiz writes, "*Bonding* may be a strange term for many of us, but it is an extremely important concept for learning the urban context. . . . The best analogy to describe this process is that of a child being born and entering a new environment, a new culture, with new experiences, smells and sights."[14] Incarnation, sharing the world of our neighbors, calling where we live *home*, must be the guiding strategy to shaping a ministry agenda.

We must listen in a way that puts others first. Research must be empowering and in service of the liberation of community, not abstract (James 2:14–17; 1 John 3:17–18). And like Nehemiah, we should keep clearly in mind that community analysis should be undertaken in a strategic and appropriately cautious manner (Neh. 2:11–16). Infuse "research" with respect and the Golden Rule.

Urban areas are dynamic and complex settings. Thus careful research and exegesis is vital to understanding the place where God has called us. We should make wide but critical use of a variety of sources—census data, academic and foundation reports, ethnographic research, newspaper articles, and planning studies among them.[15] In addition to analyzing the external forces influencing the community (such as government and business) and attention to the city's history, the following is a preliminary list of areas important to understanding a community:

1. *Community History.* How has the present community been shaped by its past—social, political, demographic, and otherwise? What have been the turning points?
2. *Physical Layout.* What are the physical boundaries, significant buildings, types of housing, unique architectural features, important geographic landmarks, major transportation links, and locations of jobs? How do people define the geographic boundaries of their community? Where are the communities "within" the community?
3. *Neighborhood Assets and Resources.* What are the existing and potential strengths, capacities, "competitive advantages,"[16] and other assets of the community? What have been the past successes of the community?
4. *Indicators of Need.* In what ways is the community marginalized or distressed? What is the health status and economic profile of the community? Most importantly, as John Perkins reminds us, what are the *felt needs* of the community? What do the people of the community see as the real issues?
5. *Institutional Elements.* What organizations and agencies provide services and programs within the community? How are they perceived? Where are their operations conducted? What are their long-term plans?
6. *Community Dynamics.* What are the internal and external dynamics that help to drive community life? Who are the neighborhood opinion makers and stakeholders? What are the local "political" dynamics? Who is looked to as leadership?

7. *Religious Institutions.* What other congregations are present in the community? What is their role and ministry involvement in the community? What activities do other religious groups conduct?

8. *Neighboring Dynamics.* What are the existing webs of extended family and friendship networks? What role do neighborhood associations and other civic groups play within the community? What are the hopes, dreams, concerns, and driving themes of life in the community?

In La Villita, we found a community of approximately 100,000 people of which half were under twenty-two years of age. Educationally the population of our barrio created an unmet need for five additional elementary schools, and the local high school had a dropout rate of 75 percent. La Villita was a haven for active street gangs. The needs were great. On the other hand, La Villita was vibrant with life. There are over 850 Latino-owned businesses on our main street. Good brick buildings, a strong housing market, and strong Latino family strength made us excited about this "Little Village" God had called us to.

Learning about a community requires a great deal of hard effort. And it's work that should be continuous as well. Taking notes, keeping an ongoing file, and taking photographs of what you find are strongly encouraged. The most important research, however, comes from relationships and just being in the community. As Manny Ortiz reminds us, "It is relatively easy to become dull of hearing and heart to significant statistical data. Yet the intention is to create sensitivity and willingness to become part of God's great mission in the world."[17]

Beginning Involvement and Building a Team

Believing that it is the body of Christ that is best equipped to carry out ministry in the city, from the beginning we wanted in our respective works to keep the church at the center of our activities. In Baltimore, New Song formally began as a group of us worshiping together in my home. But that followed nearly two years of community relationship building, including volunteering at the recreation center operated by Pastor Renay Kelly and joining the Sandtown-Winchester Improvement Association led by long-time neighborhood leader Ella Johnson. It was primarily the Tibbels family, many neighborhood kids, and I, along with a few others, who helped get things going.

In Chicago, La Villita got started by connecting with people who had expressed an interest in helping to establish a church. Lawndale Church was the key here as a couple of health clinic staff became interested in our work, in addition to a missionary to Mexico City from Chicago, two ex–Eastern College students, and a doctor newly arrived from the Northwest. After six months of meeting weekly to pray, share dreams, and study the Scriptures as a core group, all of us had become involved in some sort of ministry of community involvement. Another significant event was the formation of a relationship with a young Dominican pastor, Roberto Guerrero, who was leading a group of Moody Bible College students who had established a church in a nearby suburb. Through our relationship and my sharing of the philosophy of the three Rs, Roberto formally dissolved their small church and encouraged its members to join La Villita.

My first formal involvement (Noel) in the neighborhood was volunteering at an elementary school a few blocks from our house. I taught an art class and tutored first grade. This gave me a relationship with the principal, who has since gone on to be deputy mayor for education in Chicago. Others were working at the Lawndale Clinic where the Latino patient load was growing every day. A Mexican man with a drinking problem became one of our first key connections, which led to the involvement of two men in our emerging ministry.

Everyone can and should play a role in the exciting work of CCD. Christian community development needs practitioners, organizers, technicians, funders, people who pray, and many others. It also needs "planters" or "initiators." To say that starting a participatory organization is a major undertaking is a profound understatement. It is a highly demanding calling requiring a firmly rooted spiritual commitment and passion for God and the rebirth of community.

Founders of ministries must be "catalyzers" who will work day and night to ensure that both the "big picture" and the details of each "little picture" keep going and growing. Thus, they need an entrepreneurial gift and skill mix. They must function as "ministry runners," a metaphor that suggests both marathon endurance and organizational responsibility. They must be involved in organizing people and building coalitions, initiating and seizing opportunities, introducing creative ideas, encouraging and involving other people, setting vision, raising funds, connecting resources with needs through networking, pastoring, building bridges with leaders from all sectors of the city, and so on.

Ministry catalyzers should work behind the scenes ideally, mostly staying out of the limelight. Their job is to put others first and work themselves out of a job (Mark 10:43–45). It involves accepting personal responsibility while celebrating the collaborative nature of Christian community development. "Come, let *us* rebuild," Nehemiah challenged the people. Successful CCD ministry projects are those in which, when we see the results, we recognize not only our own contributions, but everyone else's as well.

To this end, a principal task of ministry "initiators" involves building and attracting a high-quality community development leadership team and staff. Although the task of developing and maintaining a team of people to grow the ministry is very demanding, it is clearly the single most important area for developing a healthy ministry. As the image of the body of Christ makes clear (Rom. 12:4–8; 1 Cor. 12), we need one another to grow and serve. When this works, great things take place in the church and beyond in the lives of people (John 14:12–14; 17:23; Eph. 4:1–13). We all need the encouragement, unconditional love, and accountability of others. The founding team leadership must be secure enough in their calling to attract and lead people who are better skilled in many areas of community development and ministry than they are.

Key team members should share a deep and long-term commitment to the wholistic ministry and the three Rs, be characterized by Christian integrity and godliness, have the ability to think critically and creatively, be committed to personal discipleship, be team players, have cross-cultural gifts, and be flexible and able to deal with ambiguity in such issues as roles and timing. Ideally, teams should be as multidisciplinary as possible, drawing the highest quality leadership from such fields as business and finance, medicine, construction, education, organization, and pastoral ministry.

Team leaders need to allow other leaders to have responsibility, authority, and creative space. Team members need to know that they have the trust and respect necessary for them to do their work. Only time and honest, biblical patterns of communication will keep all of us maturing in these areas, particularly in cross-cultural situations (Eph. 4:2–6, 15–16, 25–27, 29–32). But this is what Christian community development is all about—new relationships for the sake of the kingdom.

The three ongoing tasks of team leaders, usually but not always the founding "visionary" leaders, should be to: (1) keep an unwavering eye on the overall vision (the "big picture") and the quality of the ministry ("the little pictures"); (2) keep the financial, technical, and spiritual resources flowing, which will equip people for ministry (Eph. 4:11–13); and (3) remind everyone that our attention should not be on the crisis or success of the moment, but rather on the reality of a living, sovereign God and his longterm purposes.

The team needs to be able to listen to the community and learn together, setting aside our stereotypes and biases. The worst situation would be to have an empowered team that gets things done, yet fails to empower the community. This happens when we treat our neighbors as objects, not neighbors. And it takes place when we accept the rational, programmatic, and impersonal values and forces of our culture into our ministries.

There is another great danger to team ministry, however. There is a real potential to become ingrown. The reason for starting a CCD ministry is to follow Christ by seeking the shalom of the city to which he has called you (Jer. 29:7). Often, however, there may be relocated team members who sincerely believe that the ministry is there to meet their needs first. Thus, they don't bond with the community and distract the energy and attention of the leadership. Great pastoral sensitivity is needed here, but so is a strong stance. The longer the problem is allowed to fester, the harder it will ultimately be to solve.

Leadership Is the Community

Neighborhood or indigenous leadership development should be thoroughly thought out from the start. In Baltimore, we didn't consider our core group to have developed until indigenous leadership was in place. Leadership development is not a way to accomplish ministry, it *is* the ministry. We must believe that viable community leadership already exists and needs only to be identified and encouraged to flourish. Leadership development is not someone taking on a ministry job.

In Baltimore our experience has been that the best staff will be men and women who have come through the ministry. For example, Orlando Mobuary (who has been involved with us for many years and is now an electrician with Sandtown Habitat) and Janice Jamison (Sandtown Habitat's dynamic office manager), were first Habitat homeowners. Chanel Boone, a superb preschool teacher in New Song's Learning Center, first got involved through having her child in the program. The list could go on for pages! All of us need time and opportunity to grow into God's calling upon our lives.

Very recently in Chicago, we had the opportunity to hire two Mexican staff from our church to help direct our children's ministry and our housing program. They had never worked in a church, so the transition to full-time ministry positions proved very stretching. It was crucial that I learned to invest the time and energy our new staff needed.

Whether neighborhood or relocated leadership, as Edgar J. Elliston and J. Timothy Kauffman point out in their book *Developing Leaders for Urban Ministries*, equipping leaders involves issues of content, skill, and being.[18] Because Christian community development ministry is so intensive, the emergence of a full-time staff is highly likely. A problem arises when church members may not feel as important to the ministry as the staff. Holding forth the missiological challenge that *every* believer, united to Christ—who is prophet, priest, and king (Heb. 1:1–3)—has a royal, priestly, and prophetic calling (1 Peter 2:9–10) has powerful implications for the life of the church.[19] It is exciting to see how God's Word and the life of the church can shape leaders.

This past Christmas I shared with the body how I made a special holiday salsa substituting cranberries for tomatoes. The reaction I got was not very surprising: "That's not really salsa." Mexicans should know! I went on to share how in many ways I had been too focused on doing the ministry and not enough on helping us understand what it means first to "be" God's people and his redeemed body. That's like making salsa without the tomatoes!

Starting Out

Particularly in the early days of ministry, the main task is to build relationships and learn to love the community where God has placed you (Ps. 48).[20] Relationships are the heart of God's shalom and are the true bridges to change.[21] We are called to be friends (John 15:12–15), not service providers or saviors. Though there will be occasions for miscommunication, remember that love covers over a multitude of sins! A deep and wide relational base in the community provides the strong foundation for all of the ministry that will take place. Learning to love the community means enjoying not only the people, but the streets, stores, sounds, and character of the community. Internally, it means coming to the point in your heart where there is no place else you would rather live!

For the first two years of New Song, all we did was "hang out" in the neighborhood. All the exciting things that are taking place in our church today can be seen as fruit of that time. For example, it was through some of the young people that we got to know that we met LaVerne Cooper, who is now co-executive director of our housing ministry. Early on at community association meetings we met Elder Clyde Harris and his wife Amelia, both of whom are deeply engaged in the work of rebuilding Sandtown. Isaac Newman and Fitt Bennett befriended us and introduced us to many people we now know and love deeply.

The importance of staying focused on the vision and ministry of the church cannot be overstated.[22] There will be countless potential distractions of your time and energy. A way to stay focused is to agree up front on vision and priorities. Early on, both New Song and La Villita set forth guiding priorities to:

1. Focus on our neighborhood
2. Reach people who are not committed to a church
3. Focus on young people and leadership development
4. Be a place where the gospel of reconciliation can be practiced
5. Be wholistic by holding to the three Rs and maintaining our church base
6. Create an environment where the gifts of the kingdom flourish
7. Accomplish our mission with the highest excellence
8. Keep God's message of grace central

Once such a framework is in place, we can learn when to say no, when to go for an opportunity, and when to adapt and change. These core commitments flavor the way we do everything from worship to staff development to health programs. They are the rallying points that will keep our churches visionary and cutting-edge over the long haul. Personal and corporate opportunity does not mean calling. Be willing and ready to turn down everything from speaking requests to program dollars if it will not help you fulfill your ministry goals. Guard carefully your time and energy.

Try to place a fence around the time you need to genuinely understand community felt needs and proceed at a proper pace. Give the community time to know and accept you. Think big, but be patient and proceed at a teaspoon pace initially. Later, if God so blesses, you will think big and act on a larger scale!

A clear vision holds people together through hard times. La Villita is a nondenominational, bilingual, and multicultural church. Even the Latinos were not from the same culture, although the majority of our group was Mexican. We discovered a variety of differences and issues of which language was a major one. We named the church La Villita Community Church, which emphasized both the bilingual and community focus of our vision. We also took a very important symbol in our barrio, a beautiful arch on the east end of La Villita, and used it in our logo to identify our church with our barrio.

Selecting a focus area, organizing the appropriate structure, and doing early ministry projects extremely well have numerous lasting benefits. If you spread out your energy and don't concentrate, you will be ineffective. Instead of doing a great many ministry projects early on, focus on being in your community and doing small things with excellence. Let ministry emerge naturally. This can actually help you with funding, as potential financial partners are attracted to works with a successful track record. And make sure that you invest your own funds before requesting others to support you. This will demonstrate your commitment. It's important to have an outside financial audit each year to ensure public integrity.

Working Together

Following core group development and vision establishment, Christian community development begins to take on the task of rebuilding the community. How do you know when to begin the ministries and projects that will give shape and focus to community reweaving efforts?

First, we should begin to share our core vision of the three Rs with everybody we meet, just as Nehemiah did. Create a broad-based network and partnership among your neighbors and in the public and private spheres. Obviously, in this stage and all others, guard your tendency to impose your plans and programs.

Having shared our core vision, we need to work together to develop a plan contextual to our community. Everyone has an important contribution to make. In our early years at New Song, we did a community planning process during a series of evening services. From housing to health care to economic development to education, we agreed that God was calling us to a comprehensive rebuilding effort. At La Villita, our plans revolved around our ministry to children. With the many children in our community, a large number of people in our body with a background in education, and many motivated parents, we knew this had to be a focus area.

Nehemiah was careful to help set goals and seek victories that they could achieve together. Note as well that the goal of rebuilding the wall of Jerusalem was tangible, energizing, and highly focused.

In the vocabulary of goal setting, it was easy to understand, audacious, and compelling. In other words, it was something that people could gather around and join in. In Sandtown, there were 1,000 vacant houses, 250 in our focus area. So we started an affiliate of Habitat for Humanity and set a goal of eliminating vacant housing in our focus area. Such a huge undertaking began with completing one house and building on that success.

A study of Nehemiah 3 points to a clear movement from individual vision to community activity. Nehemiah organized the community into at least forty different units, delegating authority to fit the task. "Some were to repair the wall near their home, shop or place of employment, which appealed to their enlightened self-interest to motivate them to protect that which was important to them. Nehemiah's evident concern for people and skill in organizing groups is revealed in the way in which leaders and groups are listed along with the section(s) each unit completed. While most political leaders tend to record the significance of their accomplishments, here it is the work of the people that is highlighted."[23]

An important problem-solving tool in community development is the pedagogy of reflection and action, a process through which people analyze their situation and together craft strategies to address what they determine are needs. Beginning with the basic felt needs and appropriate solutions, it builds in analysis and action to deeper levels of systemic evaluation of the political, social, and religious systems and projects and actions. Robert Linthicum describes it this way:

> It is simply the recognition that when people act, their action then affects the way they think about action. Likewise, reflecting in a new way creates receptivity for further and more adventurous action. Thus, action and reflection feed upon each other, with each action leading to a deeper and more insightful reflection which, in turn, leads to more courageous action. Thus, a spiral is created, with action pushing toward reflection which results in a more decisive action which in turn causes deeper and more analytical reflection which leads to further action, and thus to reflection. So the spiral drives deeper and deeper.[24]

Reflection and action should be viewed as a continual cycle of ministry advancement. We can see this dynamic at work throughout the

Book of Nehemiah. With the confidence obtained through the rebuilding of the wall, they moved on to address deeper issues relating to their social, political, and spiritual lives.

Keeping the Church at the Heart

Even though your model of the church may be developmental, for liability, organizational, and funding reasons, most congregations start a 501(c)(3) nonprofit corporation to carry out their community development initiatives. How do you keep such development ministries rooted in the life of the local church that started them?

First, continually cast the biblical vision of church-based Christian community development. Through regular Scripture reflection, sharing other models of ministry, and celebrating shared victories, vision can remain fresh and growing. Church and development ministry leadership praying and strategizing around shared vision is a must. How you structure or organize your efforts should flow out of the gifts and abilities of those involved.

Second, build in from the start structural connections between the church and development work. There are a variety of ways to accomplish this. Perhaps the easiest and most effective is to have the church appoint some portion of board members. In this area of legal issues, one should work closely with an attorney knowledgeable in nonprofit law. Whatever form you decide upon should involve the establishment of a robust structural center around which dynamic ministries can flow. The ethos of the center must be servant values. If there is strong unity within our Christian community and ministry vision is set in place, we can affirm the diversity of gifts and ministries. Christian community development needs both a strong unifying center and diverse outlets to unleash kingdom gifts. This is the calling of the church!

Third, keep the focus of the church on investing its resources (financial and human) in the community; look for ways to use your assets. One way to do this is to mortgage the building to grow a key ministry. Risk builds commitment and shows commitment.

Finally, structural connections are no guarantee that the relationship will be a healthy one. It will take maturity of commitment and sensitivity on the part of church leadership, boards, staff, and congregation to hold a wholistic ministry together.

Facing Tests and Trials

The work of bringing about lasting community change is not easy. Along the way, there will be many tests and watershed events. Outward tests will include finances, finding program space, and developing leadership. Inward tests will include periods of great doubt and struggle. At times, team dynamics will be a trial and test. Because differences will arise, the up-front relational commitment of the team to one another is critical. Not being able to get along together is perhaps the single greatest danger, one that no doubt the "powers" will try to use to damage Christian ministry.

Know from the beginning that success in ministry will not always earn you friends (Acts 16:16–19). Slum landlords will oppose you. The social service, health care, and political landscapes are changing dramatically, bringing shifting economic realities and new turf concerns. Doing the right thing at an increasing scale will be seen as a business threat by many. Add in the usual issues facing a Christian body, the physical stress and potential cost of development work, the conflict our hearts may still have over kingdom versus dominant culture values, and the strains of organization growth, and the task is rightly seen as overwhelming. Again, this is why absolute commitment and conviction are essential.

The rebuilding of Jerusalem threatened the political and economic hegemony of Samaria. A shift of power was taking place. Sanballat and associates moved from ridiculing the workers (Neh. 4:1–3) to organizing an attack (4:7–8) to plotting an infiltration (4:11–12, 15) to stirring discontent through isolation (4:2–3).[25] Changes in power bring conflict and animosity, both from within and without. The apostle Paul reminds us that our struggle is not against flesh and blood but spiritual powers (Eph. 6:12). Our goal is not to defeat others, but to see God's shalom touch every area of urban life.

Keep an eye out for defining moments, watershed events in the life of the ministry. One such moment for each of our churches was the purchase of our main building. A few months after La Villita had been meeting as a church in a day care center, I walked into a large building in the heart of La Villita located on the dividing line between the two gang nations in our barrio. Discovering that it was available for purchase, I began dreaming immediately about all the things we could do with it. We began plans to purchase it immediately, but a process we thought would take a few months took three years.

The issue became a great rallying point for our body as we prayed and talked about it. As time went on and the building could still not be purchased, we even reluctantly looked at other buildings. But finally it became ours! The deep encouragement of others helped me through the process. It was wonderful when we finally held our open house to celebrate what God had given us. Surely, God demonstrated his power and faithfulness to us in the barrio of La Villita.

In Sandtown, we have seen God constantly make himself known. From the provision of buildings to funds to new partnerships to Wy Plummer and Steve Smallman joining the work and becoming co-pastors, God's mercy and timing have always been just what we needed for our spiritual development. It has been painful beyond description but also rewarding beyond words.

Celebrating God as Rebuilder

From creation to the exodus to the cross to the resurrection of Jesus, the Bible is an account of God's redemptive deeds and his interpretation of them. Psalms such as 78, 105, 106, 135, and 136 particularly focus on remembering the "wonderful acts" of God's salvation (Ps. 105:2).[26] Christian community development should regularly celebrate the wonderful acts of God today as he is at work through us rebuilding communities of need (Ps. 127:1).

Remembering and telling the story of the ministry builds confidence, increases spiritual commitment, and keeps God at the center. This was true for God's people in the rebuilding of Jerusalem (Neh. 9). Such activities as times of testimony in the worship service, vibrant building and house dedications, banquet dinners celebrating successes, graduations, and a corporate journal should be built in from the start. Christian community development is about celebrating God's goodness and power. And it draws people into his living presence.

Recognize the importance of living by God's grace when you make mistakes as well. We all make them! True success only comes at great cost and usually with many errors made along the way. Most importantly, be willing to learn from your mistakes and change where needed. Look to God to sustain you during the great times and the hard times.

The Ongoing Task

We have only sketched some of the key issues in getting started. There are many ministry issues that arise between the beginning of the rebuilding process and its completion. Yet it remains true that a new work begun well is a ministry that continually grows and expands. If not, it will die. Growth is the challenge and test.

The Key Elements of Creating a Christian Community Development Ministry

- Starting a ministry that bears fruit over the long haul has more to do with calling, vision, passion, focus, bonding, and relationships than with funding or developing effective programs.
- Urban areas are dynamic and complex settings. Make a concerted effort to bond with and thoroughly understand the community where God has called you to serve.
- Although the task of developing and maintaining a team of people to grow the ministry is very demanding, it is clearly the single most important area for developing a healthy ministry.
- The importance of staying focused on the vision and ministry of the church cannot be overstated. Agree up front on vision and priorities and reinforce them regularly.

- Remembering and telling the story of the ministry builds confidence, increases spiritual commitment, and keeps God at the center. It reminds us that God is with us through our trials and tests.

Paul's question concerning urban incarnational ministry in his day is ours today: "Who is equal to such a task?" (2 Cor. 2:16). What a humbling privilege and opportunity we have to be the body of Christ, sent by God into a broken and hurting world. Let us embrace the challenge of starting new churches and development ministries![27]

In Conclusion

John M. Perkins

In Matthew chapter 5, Jesus is very clear about the role of his followers in society. We are to be salt to an unseasoned world and light in a sea of darkness. Sometimes we have not taken that exhortation seriously, especially when it has meant living and working in neglected neighborhoods. Christian community development is a courageous and creative way for Christians to be that salt and light in those places that the world sees as dark and unsavory.

The Book of Esther is a constant reminder of the type of attitude and courage that we must have when we are faced with a serious crisis. The crisis that the Jews faced in the days of Mordecai was not unlike the challenges that we face in our inner cities today. Many of the Jews had made it into the mainstream of the society and were doing well. But meanwhile there was a conspiracy that could, to put it mildly, undermine everything they had accomplished.

Esther, the product of a broken family and raised by her uncle, had achieved "success." Her example and that of her uncle Mordecai offers us a picture of the type of leadership that we as the people of God must be willing to demonstrate in order to bring healing to our broken society.

Extended family structure. Although Esther's mother and father had died, Mordecai took on the responsibility of raising her. He not only took her in but he raised her as his own daughter.

They had a strategy. Had Esther revealed her ethnic background, she could have been rejected before being given a chance. Therefore, Mordecai instructed her not to make known her ethnic identity until the proper time.

Strong family values. Even after she was queen, "Esther obeyed Mordecai just as when she was brought up by him." Had the family ties been weak, Esther would have been swallowed up by her individual success.

Esther never lost sight of who she was. Mordecai sent messages from the "hood" to keep Esther informed and to remind her of her duty to her people. "Think not that in the king's palace you will escape any more than all the other Jews. For if you keep silence at such a time as this, relief and deliverance will rise for the Jews from another quarter. . . . And who knows whether you have not come to the kingdom for such a time as this?"

Esther understood that this was a spiritual battle. Before she went in to the king, she had everyone fast and pray for three days. Only then did she feel peace about risking her life.

Esther responded to the challenge with courage. When the time came to act and to reveal her true identity, Esther was mentally and spiritually prepared. She said, "Though it is against the law, I will go in to the king, and if I perish, I perish."

God is calling on more of us to have the courage and the conviction of Mordecai and Esther. The more dangerous our cities get, the more middle-class Christians are running for their lives. Are we going to leave these desperate places to the Muslims? The Christian Community Development Association is not willing to abandon our cities just because we might have to place our lives on the line.

The questions for Christians today are the same type of questions that Mordecai put to Esther. Are we willing to sacrifice some of our individual ambitions in order to intercede on the behalf of those who are at risk? Are we willing to be salt and light in the places that need it the most? Do we really believe that our God is able to protect us and our families when we follow him into the places that others are fleeing?

The people of the Christian Community Development Association and many other Christians around this country and the world are answering *yes* to these questions.

And who knows whether God has brought the Christian community development movement into existence "for such a time as this."

About CCDA

More and more Christians are discovering the simple truth that people empowered by God are the most effective solution for the spiritual and economic development of the poor.

In 1989, Dr. John Perkins called together a group of Christian leaders from across America who shared a commitment to express the love of Christ to America's poor communities—not at arm's length, but at the grassroots level. An association was formed, and CCDA held its first annual conference in Chicago in 1989. CCDA has grown from 37 founding organizations to over 3,000 individuals and 300 churches and ministries in 35 states and more than 100 cities.

CCDA is not an organization, but an association of like-minded Christian churches, ministries, families, and individuals who encourage and learn from one another. Through CCDA, committed people of God working in the trenches among America's poor discover that they are not alone.

Members of CCDA are engaged in activities from evangelism to housing, from creating jobs to working with youth. The membership of CCDA is interracial and the leaders of its member ministries are heavily drawn from America's minority communities.

So whether you have been working in the trenches for years, are wondering how to get started, or simply have a concern to see God's love made visible among the poor—come join the people of CCDA as we encourage and learn from one another.

CCDA is governed by a diverse board of directors representing churches and ministries across the United States. CCDA is funded through membership dues and private gifts. It abides by the financial policies of the Evangelical Council for Financial Accountability.

Mission

CCDA's mission is to develop a strong fellowship of those involved in Christian community development. We desire to support and encourage existing Christian community developers and their ministries and help establish new Christian community development efforts.

What Are the Benefits of Joining CCDA?

Encouragement
People at the front lines need encouragement to sustain their efforts over the long haul. In CCDA you will find like-minded people who wrestle with tough issues like raising a family in the inner city, building interracial churches, nurturing children without fathers, and starting inner city businesses.

Ministry Support
- Regular training seminars in your region offering technical assistance
- On-site and phone consultations
- Evaluations of your programs from seasoned practitioners
- Restorer newsletter with "how-to" articles, funding information, biblical guidance, and more
- Job referral service

Networking Opportunities
- Annual national convention
- Directory of CCDA member organizations with program overviews, training programs, and regional and program cross-references
- Networking with seasoned practitioners with expertise in all phases of Christian community development

Who Are the Members of CCDA?

CCDA draws its membership from all across the United States, and its board of directors is representative of that diversity.

Board of Directors

Dr. John Perkins, Foundation for Reconciliation & Development, Pasadena, Calif., *chairman*

Rev. Wayne Gordon, Lawndale Community Church, Chicago, Ill., *president*

Rev. Noel Castellanos, LaVillita Community Church, Chicago, Ill., *vice chairman*

Mr. Ted Travis, Neighborhood Ministries, Denver, Colo., *secretary*

Dr. Robert Sturkey, A.R.E., Copley, Ohio, *treasurer*

Ms. Cheryl Appeline, Habitat for Humanity, Philadelphia, Pa.

Rev. Bill Brown, Trinity Christian Community, New Orleans, La.

Mrs. Edith Davis, Spring Arbor College, Jackson, Mich.

Ms. Yvonne Dodd, Hope for New York, New York, N.Y.

Mr. Harvey Drake Jr., Emerald City Outreach Ministries, Seattle, Wash.

Mrs. Donna Holt, Belleville, Ill.

Mr. Glen Kehrein, Circle Urban Ministries, Chicago, Ill.

Dr. Robert Lupton, FCS Urban Ministries, Atlanta, Ga.

Mr. Steve Morris, World Impact, Fresno, Calif.

Rev. Herman Moten, Christian Resource Center, Tampa, Fla.

Dr. Mary Nelson, Bethel New Life, Chicago, Ill.

Rev. Elizar Pagan, Discipleship Chapel, Inc., Brooklyn, N.Y.

Mr. Spencer Perkins, *Urban Family* Magazine, Jackson, Miss.

Mr. H. Spees, Youth for Christ, Fresno, Calif.

Mr. Jim Swearingen, Urban Concern, Columbus, Ohio.

Mr. B. T. Vangsoolatda, Lao Christian Church, Brookfield, Wis.

Mr. Robert Woolfolk, Community Outreach Service Center, Denver, Colo.

Dr. Gloria Yancy, Christian Believers, Richmond, Calif.

Advisory Board

Ms. Kathy Dudley, Voice of Hope Ministries, Dallas, Tex.

Rev. Ron Spann, Church of the Messiah, Detroit, Mich.

Rev. Haman Cross Jr., Rosedale Park Baptist Church, Detroit, Mich.

Dr. Keith Phillips, World Impact, Los Angeles, Calif.

Rev. Dolphus Weary, Mendenhall Ministries, Mendenhall, Miss.

Dr. Vera Mae Perkins, Foundation for Reconciliation & Development, Pasadena, Calif.

Dr. Ray Bakke, International Urban Associates, Chicago, Ill.
Dr. Ron Sider, Eastern College, St. Davids, Pa.

Statement of Faith

The Lord Jesus Christ, God's Son, redeems us through his death and resurrection and empowers us by the Holy Spirit. The Bible is God's Word and through it we are called to live out justice, reconciliation, and redemption. The church nurtures God's people as they gather in community to carry out God's Word.

For More Information or to Join CCDA

Contact the CCDA headquarters at

CCDA
3827 W. Ogden Ave.
Chicago, IL 60623
Phone: 312/762–0994
Fax: 312/762–5772

CCDA Member Organizations

Alabama

(The) Center for Urban Missions, Birmingham
Greater Mt. Calvary Baptist Church, Leeds
Lafayette Street United Methodist Church, Dothan
(The) National Black Church Family Council, Inc., Butler
(The) New City Church, Birmingham
Overcomers Ministries/Solomons Porch, Birmingham

Arizona

Baptist Foundation of Arizona, Phoenix
Palabra de Garcia, Mesa
Seeds of Hope, Inc., Casa Grande

Arkansas

STEP, Inc., Little Rock

California

California Recovery Facility, Oakland
Christian Believers, Richmond
Christian Challenge of Modesto, Modesto
CityTeam Ministries, San Jose
Discover the World, Pasadena
(The) Downtown Church, Fresno
Evangelicals for Social Action, Fresno
Gilead Group, Oakland
Harambee Christian Family Center, Pasadena
Harbor House, Oakland
Hope Now for Youth, Inc., Fresno
Innerchange, Fullerton
John M. Perkins Foundation for Reconciliation & Development, Pasadena

P. F. Bresee Foundation, Los Angeles
San Francisco Leadership Foundation, San Francisco
Vineyard Christian Fellowship, Pomona
World Impact, Inc., Los Angeles
World Vision, Monrovia

Colorado

Christian Corps International, Inc., Aurora
Church in the City, Denver
Community Outreach Service Center, Denver
Compassion International, Colorado Springs
Evangelical Concern of Denver, Inc., Denver
Hope Communities, Inc., Denver
Mercy Ministries, Denver
Mile High Ministries, Denver
Neighborhood Ministries, Denver
Young Life's Multiethnic & Urban Ministries, Denver

Florida

Christian Resource Center, Tampa
Springfield Ecumenical Ministries, Jacksonville
Trinity Episcopal Church of Vero Beach, Inc., Vero Beach

Georgia

FCS Urban Ministries, Atlanta
Koinonia Partners, Americus
MAP International, Brunswick
Perimeter Ministries, Inc., Atlanta
Summerhill Neighborhood Development Corporation, Atlanta

Illinois

Anvil Community Development Corporation, Rockford
Bethany Brethren Community Center, Chicago
Bethel New Life, Inc., Chicago
Breakthrough Urban Ministries, Inc., Chicago
Chicago Lawn Alliance Church, Chicago
Chicago Metro Baptist Association, Oak Park
Christian Center for Urban Studies, Chicago
Christian Friendliness Association, Moline

Christians Helping Inspire Local Development, Lake Bluff
Circle Christian Development Corporation, Chicago
Circle Urban Ministries, Chicago
Common Ground Community Youth Center, Chicago
Cornerstone Community Outreach, Chicago
Douglass-Tubman Youth Ministries, Inc., Chicago
Emmaus Ministries, Chicago
First Presbyterian Church of Aurora, Aurora
Families In Touch, Waukegan
Family Care Network, Chicago
Haynes Miracle Temple Church, East St. Louis
Here's Life Inner-City Chicago, Chicago
Hope for Kids, Inc., East St. Louis
Inner City Agapé Ministries, Chicago
Inner City Impact, Chicago
International Teams, Prospect Heights
Judson Baptist Church, Oak Park
La Villita Community Church, Chicago
LaSalle Street Church, Chicago
Lawndale Christian Development Corporation, Chicago
Lawndale Christian Health Center, Chicago
Lawndale Christian Reformed Church, Chicago
Lawndale Community Church, Chicago
MidAmerica Leadership Foundation, Chicago
Morning Star Baptist Church, Harvey
National City Ministries, Wheaton
Oakton Community Church, Evanston
Outreach Community Ministries, Inc., Wheaton
Reba Place Church, Evanston
Restoration Ministries, Inc., Harvey
Riverwoods Christian Center, St. Charles
Rock of Our Salvation EFC, Chicago
Roseland Christian Ministries, Chicago
Salem Evangelical Free Church, Chicago
Spirit of God Fellowship, South Holland

Indiana

Abundant Life Ministries, Fort Wayne
Broadway Christian Church, Fort Wayne
Community Fellowship Ministries, Inc., Indianapolis

Impact Ministries, Evansville
Ray Bird Ministries, South Bend
Shepherd Community Ministries, Indianapolis
Tabernacle Presbyterian Church, Indianapolis

Iowa

ACTOM, Inc., Des Moines
Good Samaritan Urban Ministries, Des Moines
Justice For All, Rock Valley
Olivet Neighborhood Mission, Cedar Rapids

Kansas

Hilltop EFC, Wichita

Louisiana

Desire Street Ministries, New Orleans
Trinity Christian Community, New Orleans

Maryland

Community Outreach Center, Bel Air
Faith Christian Fellowship, Baltimore
New Song Community Church, Baltimore

Massachusetts

Christian Economic Coalition, Dorchester
Emmanuel Gospel Center, Boston

Michigan

Christ Church Episcopal, Grosse Pointe
Christian Reformed World Relief Committee, Grand Rapids
Church of the Messiah, Detroit
Church of the Messiah Housing Corporation, Detroit
Empower, Detroit
Focus: HOPE, Detroit
Highland Park Community Outreach, Highland Park
Holy Ghost Full Gospel Baptist Church, Detroit
Inner City Christian Federation, Grand Rapids
John 3:16 Ministries, Albion
Join Our Youth, Grand Rapids

Joy of Jesus, Detroit
Kalamazoo Deacon's Conference, Kalamazoo
New City Resources, Inc., Jackson
(The) Other Way Ministries, Grand Rapids
Rosedale Park Baptist Church, Detroit
Vinedresser Ministries, Inc., Grand Rapids
Wellspring, Detroit

Minnesota

Bethlehem Baptist Church, Minneapolis
Hospitality House Boys and Girls Clubs, Inc., Minneapolis
Mission America, Minneapolis
North Minneapolis Christian Fellowship, Minneapolis
Park Avenue Urban Program and Leadership Foundation, Minneapolis
Urban Ventures Leadership Foundation, Minneapolis

Mississippi

Antioch Community, Jackson
Canton Bible Baptist Church, Canton
Cary Christian Center, Inc., Cary
Mendenhall Ministries, Mendenhall
(The) Myers Foundation, Inc., Tchula
New Horizon Baptist Church, Jackson
New Lake Outreach Ministries, Jackson
Quitman County Development Corporation, Marks
Voice of Calvary Fellowship, Jackson
Voice of Calvary Ministries, Jackson

Missouri

Are You Committed, Kansas City
Carver Christian Academy, Kansas City
Fellowship of Urban Youth Ministries, Kansas City
Independence Boulevard Church, Kansas City
Inner City Christian Church, St. Louis
Kids Across America Kamp, Branson
National Coalition for Pioneering Black America, Wentzville
Sunshine Mission, Inc., St. Louis

Montana

Montana Rescue Mission, Billings

New Jersey

Aslan Youth Ministries, Red Bank
Life Line Emergency Shelter, Trenton
Madison Avenue Christian Reformed Church, Peterson
New City Church, Jersey City

New Mexico

Baptist Neighborhood Center, Albuquerque

New York

Africa Inland Mission, Pearl River
Christ to the Community Church, Brooklyn
(The) Family Restoration Project, Inc., Rochester
HARKhomes, New York City
Here's Life Inner City, New York City
New Life Fellowship, Corona
Rehoboth Open Bible Church, Brooklyn
Urban Christian Ministries, Buffalo

North Carolina

Building Together Ministries, Raleigh
Winston-Salem Bible College, Winston-Salem

Ohio

Because He Cares, Inc., Akron
Christ's Community in College Hill, Cincinnati
Community of the Servant, Dayton
Home Ministries (CMA) Church, Dayton
LOVE Inc. of Greater Akron, Akron
Love Center Mission/Harvesting Our Samaria, Cincinnati
Operation Jochebed, Akron
Rhema Christian Center, Columbus
St. Patrick's Episcopal Church, Lebanon
TAPS (Teens Against Pre-Marital Sex), Cincinnati
University Bible Church, Columbus
Urban Concern, Inc., Columbus
Urban Mission Ministry, Steubenville
Urban Vision, Akron

Oklahoma

(The) Burbridge Foundation, Oklahoma City
Hope Outreach, Inc., Enid

Pennsylvania

Acts Ministries, Philadelphia
Allegheny Center Alliance Church, Pittsburgh
Center for Urban Resources, Philadelphia
Center for Urban Theological Studies, Philadelphia
Christian Community Health Fellowship, Philadelphia
Diamond Street Community Center, Philadelphia
Eastern College Graduate Programs, St. Davids
Evangelical Environmental Network, Wynnewood
Evangelicals for Social Action, Wynnewood
Fleischmann Memorial Baptist Church, Philadelphia
Hosanna House, Inc., Wilkinsburg
Kingdomworks, Philadelphia
Philadelphia Leadership Foundation, Philadelphia
(The) Pittsburgh Project, Pittsburgh
Wadworth Air Evangelical Church, Cadville

Tennessee

Emerald Avenue Urban Youth and Leadership Foundation, Knoxville
Knoxville Leadership Foundation, Knoxville
Memphis Leadership Foundation, Memphis
Operation R.O.C.K., Memphis
(The) Resource Foundation, Nashville
United Methodist Metro Office of Urban Ministries, Memphis
Urban Community Vision, Knoxville

Texas

Common Ground Ministries, Waxahachie
Leadership Network Foundation, Tyler
Mission Waco, Waco
Oak Cliff Bible Fellowship, Dallas
Operation Relief, Dallas
Project "Ginomai," Austin
Reconciliation Outreach/Mission Corps, Dallas
Texas Baptist Home for Children, Waxahachie

(The) Urban Alternative, Dallas
Voice of Hope Ministries, Dallas

Virginia

Enterprise Development International, Arlington
In-Touch Ministries, Richmond
Operation Breaking Through, Newport News
Project Light, Virginia Beach

Washington

Covenant Housing Association, Seattle
Emerald City Outreach, Seattle
Northwest Leadership Foundation, Seattle
Northwest Urban Ministries, Seattle

Washington, D.C.

Jubilee Enterprise of Greater Washington, Inc., Washington, D.C.
Servant Leadership School and Festival Center, Washington, D.C.

Wisconsin

Anchored to the Rock Ministries, Racine
Eastbrook Church, Milwaukee
Elmbrook Church, Brookfield
(The) Nehemiah Community Development Corporation, Madison

Other Countries

All Ontario Diaconal Conference, St. Catherines, Ontario, Canada
Broken Wall Community of Reconciliation Trust, Cape Town, South Africa
Edmonton Native Healing Centre, Edmonton, Alberta, Canada
National Society of Hope, Kelowna, British Columbia, Canada

Notes

Chapter 2: *Toward a Theology of Christian Community Development*

1. George Barna, *The Power of Vision* (Ventura, Calif.: Regal Books, 1992), 28.
2. William Julius Wilson, *The Truly Disadvantaged: The Inner City, the Underclass, and Public Policy* (Chicago: The University of Chicago Press, 1990), 21.
3. John Perkins, *A Quiet Revolution* (Waco: Word Books, 1976), 13.
4. Ray Bakke, *The Urban Christian* (Downers Grove, Ill.: InterVarsity Press, 1987), 32–33.
5. Ibid., 160.
6. William Pannell, *Evangelism from the Bottom Up* (Grand Rapids: Zondervan Publishing House, 1992), 14.
7. Dietrich Bonhoeffer, *The Cost of Discipleship* (New York: Macmillan Publishing Co., 1963), 78.
8. John Perkins, *Beyond Charity* (Grand Rapids: Baker Book House, 1993), 80.
9. Pannell, *Evangelism from the Bottom Up*, 37.
10. John R. W. Stott, *Christian Mission in the Modern World* (Downers Grove, Ill.: InterVarsity Press, 1975), 27.
11. Ibid., 30.
12. Perkins, *Beyond Charity*, 120.
13. Stott, *Christian Mission in the Modern World*, 30.

Chapter 3: *Understanding Poverty*

1. Lawrence O. Richards, *Expository Dictionary of Bible Words* (Grand Rapids: Zondervan Publishing House, 1985), see "Wealth/Riches/Possessions."
2. Perkins, *A Quiet Revolution*, 87.
3. Ibid., 88.
4. Wilson, *The Truly Disadvantaged*, 11.
5. Ibid.
6. Daniel Bell, *The Coming of Post-Industrial Society* (New York: Basic Books, 1976), 409.
7. John Naisbitt, *Megatrends* (New York: Warner Books, 1982), 26.
8. Eugene Rivers, "On the Responsibility of Intellectuals in the Age of Crack," *Boston Review* (October 1992), 3.
9. Wilson, *The Truly Disadvantaged*, 46.
10. Lerone Bennett Jr., "The Crisis of the Black Spirit," *Ebony* (October 1977), see also Cornel West, *Race Matters* (New York: Vintage Books, 1994), chap. 1.
11. Rivers, "On the Responsibility of Intellectuals," 3.
12. Pannell, *Evangelism from the Bottom Up*, 11.
13. Perkins, *Beyond Charity*, 18.

Chapter 6: *Reconciliation*

1. Raleigh Washington and Glen Kehrein, *Breaking Down Walls: A Model for Reconciliation in an Age of Racial Strife* (Chicago: Moody Press, 1993).

Chapter 7: *Redistribution*

1. Perkins, *Beyond Charity*, 119.
2. Robert D. Lupton, *Return Flight: Community Development through Reneighboring Our Cities* (Atlanta: FCS Urban Ministries, 1993), 36.
3. See chapter 9 of this book, "Indigenous Leadership Development" by Wayne Gordon, for clues as to how to develop local leadership.
4. John Perkins, *With Justice for All* (Ventura, Calif.: Regal, 1982), 179.

Chapter 9: *Indigenous Leadership Development*

1. Jawanza Kunjufu, *Countering the Conspiracy to Destroy Black Boys*, vol. 3 (Chicago: African American Images, 1990).

Chapter 11: *How to Start a Christian Community Development Ministry*

1. This phrase is from Cornelius Plantiga Jr., *Not the Way It's Supposed to Be: A Breviary of Sin* (Grand Rapids: William B. Eerdmans Publishing, 1995).
2. For a context setting overview of CCDA's opportunities, see Harvie M. Conn, *The American City and the Evangelical Church* (Grand Rapids: Baker Book House, 1994).
3. On how ministry is to be understood as an invitation to participate in God's reign, see the excellent work by Tom Sine, *Why Settle for More and Miss the Best?* (Waco: Word Books, 1987) and C. René Padilla, *Mission between the Times: Essays on the Kingdom* (Grand Rapids: William B. Eerdmans Publishing, 1985), 186–99. For a more detailed exegetical study of God's reign, see Herman Ridderbos, *The Coming of the Kingdom* (Philadelphia: Presbyterian and Reformed, 1976).
4. See for example such "call" texts as Exodus 18:13–27, 1 Corinthians 2, and Hebrews 11:24–27.
5. Martin Marty, "Can We Still Hear the Call?" in *Health Progress* 76, no. 1 (January–February 1995): 19.
6. Robert C. Linthicum, *City of God, City of Satan: A Biblical Theology of the Urban Church* (Grand Rapids: Zondervan Publishing House, 1991), 196.
7. This theme runs throughout his writing. For an extended exploration, see Lupton, *Return Flight*.
8. On this implication of the image of God, see the important essay by Nicholas Wolterstorff, "The Wounds of God: Calvin's Theology of Social Injustice," *The Reformed Journal* 37, no. 6 (June 1987): 14–22.
9. Thanks to Dr. Stephen Fowl of Loyola College (Baltimore) for this approach to the text. For a similar and very insightful look at this passage see Brian J. Walsh, *Subversive Christianity: Imaging God in a Dangerous Time* (Bristol, Great Britain: Regius, 1992), 85–93.
10. Ibid., 87.
11. See Manuel Ortiz, *The Hispanic Challenge: Opportunities Confronting the Church* (Downers Grove, Ill.: InterVarsity Press, 1993), 165–77 and Paul D. Stanley and J. Robert Clinton, *Connecting: The Mentoring Relationships You Need to Succeed in Life* (Colorado

Springs: NavPress, 1992). On the concept of "in-ministry" development, see Charles Van Engen, "Shifting Paradigms in Ministry Formation," *Perspectives* 9, no. 8 (October 1994): 15–17.

12. See for example the recent popular management text, Peter M. Senge, *The Fifth Discipline: The Art and Practice of the Learning Organization* (New York: Doubleday Currency, 1990), 174–204.

13. Most helpful is John P. Kretzmann and John L. McKnight, *Building Communities from the Inside Out: A Path toward Finding and Mobilizing a Community's Assets* (Evanston: Center for Urban Affairs and Policy Research, Neighborhood Innovations Network, Northwestern University, 1993). Two other very valuable resources are Harvie M. Conn, comp., *Urban Church Research Methods: Methods and Models* (Philadelphia: Westminster Theological Seminary, 1985), which is available from the seminary bookstore, and Alan J. Roxburgh, *A Workbook for Understanding Community* (1993), available for purchase from the author at 7 Edenbridge Ct., Dundas, Ontario, Canada L9H 3Y2.

14. Manuel Ortiz, "Being Disciples: Incarnational Christians in the City," in *Discipling the City*, 2d ed., Roger S. Greenway, ed. (Grand Rapids: Baker Book House, 1992), 92.

15. Harvie M. Conn, "Tools for Looking at the City," *Urban Mission* 8:4 (March 1991): 3–5. In today's changing health care environment, most hospital planning departments have collected a wealth of data that CCD practitioners would find helpful.

16. A reference to the inner city business development ideas of Harvard Business School Professor Michael E. Porter. See his "The Competitive Advantage of the Inner City" in *Harvard Business Review* (May–June 1995): 55–71.

17. Manuel Ortiz, "The Dilemma of Demographics," *The Bulletin of Westminster Theological Seminary* 27, no. 2 (1988): 4.

18. Edgar J. Elliston and J. Timothy Kauffman, *Developing Leaders for Urban Ministries* (New York: Peter Lang, 1993), 211–53.

19. Guillermo Cook, *The Expectation of the Poor: Latin American Basic Ecclesial Communities in Protestant Perspective* (Maryknoll: Orbis Books, 1985), 237–40.

20. Linthicum, *City of God, City of Satan*, 28–38.

21. See further Paul E. Hiebert, "Anthropological Insights for Whole Ministries," in *Christian Relief and Development: Developing Workers for Christian Ministry*, Edgar J. Elliston, ed. (Waco: Word Books, 1989), 75–76, 79–81.

22. From the management side of things, an excellent resource on this and other issues is James C. Collins and William C. Lazier, *Beyond Entrepreneurship: Turning Your Business into an Enduring Great Company* (New York: Prentice-Hall, 1992). Thanks to Dick Kaufmann of Redeemer Church in New York for this reference.

23. Kenneth Tollefson and H. G. M. Williamson, "Nehemiah as Cultural Revitalization: An Anthropological Perspective," *Journal for the Study of the Old Testament* 56 (1992): 51.

24. Robert C. Linthicum, *Empowering the Poor: Community Organizing among the City's "Rag, Tag and Bobtail"* (Monrovia: MARC, 1991), 61.

25. Tollefson and Williamson, "Nehemiah as Cultural Revitalization," 52–53.

26. Tremper Longman III, *How to Read the Psalms* (Downers Grove, Ill.: InterVarsity Press, 1988), 32.

27. I (Mark) am most grateful to Allan Tibbels for his comments on this paper. My portion of this paper reflects our shared views on CCD ministry. Its shortcomings, however, belong solely to me.

The Call and Task of Christian Community Development

A Resource Guide

Mark R. Gornik

Making use of what others have written about Christian community development, urban ministry, and racial reconciliation is an important part of sharpening our ministry formation. Fortunately, compared to ten or twenty years ago, there now exists a tremendous body of very helpful written resources for the ministry practitioner.

Listed here are resources that may help you as you weigh the next ministry steps within your context and situation. This is not a comprehensive or technical guide to CCD (such as would be needed in a more focused look at the fields of education, health care, housing, and economic development). Rather, this is an attempt to provide an overview of some of the more important general works in this area, each one introducing still other resources.

Don't limit yourself to learning from written or even visual materials (such as films or videos) alone. Many of the best stories and insights have yet to find their way into print—they are localized in the lives of pastors, developers, and congregations globally. They are there for you to find and learn from, and the annual CCDA conference is one of the best settings for getting started.

The listing of a book, of course, does not mean an endorsement. But each resource offers unique and important insights, perspectives, or foundational concepts that could be helpful to your ministry. Not all of the materials cited are written from a Christian perspective, but they are all helpful in raising and exploring the critical issues this book addresses.

Good reading, studying, and implementation!

General Bibliographies

Hartley, Loyde. *Cities and Churches: An International Bibliography: 1800–1991*, 3 vols. (ATLA Bibliography Series, 31), Metuchen, N.J.: Scarecrow Press, 1992.

Hunsberger, George R., Yohannes Mengsteab, and Craig Van Gelder. "Selected Annotated Bibliography on Missiology: Multicultural Ministry in North America," *Missiology: An International Review* XXI, no. 4 (October 1993), 501–3.

Stockwell, Clinton E. "The City, Urban Mission and Social Justice: Selected Resources." *Transformation*, 9, no. 2 (April/June 1992), 24–32.

Getting Started: Introductory Works on the Church, Community, and Wholistic Ministry

Bakke, Ray J., with Jim Hart. *The Urban Christian: Effective Ministry in Today's Urban World.* Downers Grove: InterVarsity Press, 1987.

Berger, Peter L., and Richard John Neuhaus. *To Empower People: The Role of Mediating Structures in Public Policy.* Washington, D.C.: American Enterprise Institute for Public Policy Research, 1977.

Bosch, David J. *Transforming Mission: Paradigm Shifts in Theology of Mission.* Maryknoll, N.Y.: Orbis Books, 1991.

Claerbaut, David. *Urban Ministry.* Grand Rapids: Zondervan Publishing House,1983.

Conn, Harvie M. *The American City and the Evangelical Church: A Historical Overview.* Grand Rapids: Baker Book House, 1994.

_____. *A Clarified Vision for Urban Mission: Dispelling the Urban Stereotypes.* Grand Rapids: Zondervan Publishing House, 1987.

_____. *Evangelism: Doing Justice and Preaching Grace.* Grand Rapids: Zondervan Publishing House, 1982.

Costas, Orlando E. *Christ Outside the Gate: Mission Beyond Christendom.* Maryknoll, N.Y.: Orbis Books, 1984.

_____. *Liberating News: A Theology of Contextual Evangelization.* Grand Rapids: William B. Eerdmans Publishing, 1989.

Ellis, Carl F., Jr. *Beyond Liberation: The Gospel in the Black American Experience.* Downers Grove: InterVarsity Press, 1983.

Elliston, Edgar J., and J. Timothy Kauffman. *Developing Leaders for Urban Ministries.* New York: Peter Lang, 1993.

Fuller, Millard. *The Theology of the Hammer.* Macon, Ga.: Smyth & Helwys, 1994.

Greenway, Roger S., ed. *Discipling the City: A Comprehensive Approach to Urban Mission.* 2d ed. Grand Rapids: Baker Book House, 1992.

Grigg, Viv. *Cry of the Urban Poor.* Monrovia, Calif.: Mission Advanced Research and Communication Center, 1992.

Keller, Timothy J. *Ministries of Mercy: The Call of the Jericho Road.* Grand Rapids: Zondervan Publishing House, 1989.

Lincoln, C. Eric, and Lawrence H. Mamiya. *The Black Church in the African American Experience.* Durham, N.C.: Duke University Press, 1990.

Linthicum, Robert C. *Empowering the Poor: Community Organizing Among the City's "Rag Tag and Bobtail."* Monrovia, Calif.: Mission Advanced Research and Communication Center, 1991.

Lupton, Robert D. *Return Flight: Community Development through Reneighboring Our Cities.* Atlanta: FCS Urban Ministries, 1993.

_____. *Theirs Is the Kingdom: Celebrating the Gospel in Urban America.* San Francisco: Harper and Row, 1989.

Meyers, Eleanor Scott, ed. *Envisioning the New City: A Reader on Urban Ministry.* Louisville: Westminster/John Knox Press, 1992.

Nouwen, Henri J. M. *In the Name of Jesus: Reflections on Christian Leadership.* New York: Crossroad Publishing, 1989.

Olasky, Marvin. *The Tragedy of American Compassion.* Rev. ed. Wheaton, Ill.: Crossway, 1995.

Ortiz, Manuel. *The Hispanic Challenge: Opportunities Confronting the Church.* Downers Grove: InterVarsity Press, 1993.

Padilla, C. Rene. *Mission Between the Times.* Grand Rapids: William B. Eerdmans Publishing, 1985.

Pannell, William J. *Evangelism from the Bottom Up.* Grand Rapids: Zondervan Publishing House, 1992.

Perkins, John M. *Beyond Charity: The Call to Christian Community Development.* Grand Rapids: Baker Book House, 1993.

_____. *A Quiet Revolution.* Waco: Word, 1986.

_____. *With Justice for All.* Ventura, Calif.: Regal, 1982.

Price, Peter. *The Church as the Kingdom: A New Way of Being the Church*. London: Marshall Pickering, 1987.

Raboteau, Albert J. *A Fire in the Bones: Reflections on African-American Religious History*. Boston: Beacon Press, 1995.

Ryan, William. *Blaming the Victim*. Rev. ed. New York: Vintage, 1976.

Sider, Ronald J. *One Sided Christianity: Uniting the Church to Heal a Lost and Broken World*. Grand Rapids: Zondervan Publishing House; San Francisco: HarperSanFrancisco, 1993.

Sine, Tom. *Wild Hope*. Dallas: Word, 1991.

Wallis, Jim. *The Soul of Politics*. New York: The New Press; Maryknoll, N.Y.: Orbis Books, 1994.

Warren, Rachelle B., and Donald I. Warren. *The Neighborhood Organizer's Handbook*. Notre Dame: The University of Notre Dame Press, 1977.

The City: Changing Context and Developments for Mission and Ministry

Abraham, Laurie Kaye. *Mama Might Be Better Off Dead: The Failure of Health Care in Urban America*. Chicago: The University of Chicago Press, 1993.

Anderson, Elijah. *Streetwise: Race, Class, and Change in an Urban Community*. Chicago: The University of Chicago Press, 1990.

Cisneros, Henry G. *Interwoven Destinies: Cities and the Nation*. New York: W. W. Norton & Company, 1993.

Currie, Elliott. *Reckoning: Drugs, the Cities, and the American Future*. New York: Hill and Wang, 1993.

Dogan, Mattei, and John D. Kasarda, eds. *The Metropolis Era: A World of Giant Cities*. Vol. 1. Newbury Park: Sage Publications, 1988.

———. *The Metropolis Era: Mega-Cities*. Vol. 2. Newbury Park: Sage Publications, 1988.

Duneier, Mitchell. *Slim's Table: Race, Respectability, and Masculinity*. Chicago: The University of Chicago Press, 1992.

Fainstein, Susan S., Ian Gordon, and Michael Harloe, eds. *Divided Cities: London and New York in the Contemporary World*. London: Blackwell, 1992.

Gratz, Roberta Brandes. *The Living City*. New York: Simon and Schuster, 1989.

Gulick, John. *The Humanity of Cities: An Introduction to Urban Societies*. Granby, Mass.: Bergin and Garvey, 1989.

Hartshorn, Truman. *Interpreting the City: An Urban Geography.* 2d ed. New York: John Wiley and Sons, 1992.

Jacobs, Jane. *The Death and Life of Great American Cities.* New York: The Modern Library, 1993.

Jencks, Christopher. *Rethinking Social Policy: Race, Poverty and the Underclass.* Cambridge, Mass.: Harvard University Press, 1992.

Katz, Michael B., ed. *The "Underclass" Debate: Views from History.* Princeton, N.J.: Princeton University Press, 1993.

Massey, Douglas S., and Nancy A. Denton. *American Apartheid: Segregation and the Making of the Underclass.* Cambridge, Mass.: Harvard University Press, 1993.

McKnight, John. *The Careless Society: Community and Its Counterfeits.* New York: Basic Books, 1995.

Myers, Bryant L. *The Changing Shape of World Mission.* Monrovia, Calif.: Mission Advanced Research and Communication Center, 1993.

Palen, J. John. *The Urban World.* 3d ed. New York: McGraw-Hill, 1987.

Peirce, Neal R. *Citistates: How Urban America Can Prosper in a Competitive World.* Washington, D.C.: Seven Locks Press, 1993.

Roberts, Sam. *Who We Are: A Portrait of America Based on the Latest U.S. Census.* New York: Times Books, 1993.

Rusk, David. *Cities without Suburbs.* Washington, D.C.: Woodrow Wilson Center Press, 1993.

Sassen, Saskia. *The Global City: New York, London, Tokyo.* Princeton, N.J.: Princeton University Press, 1991.

Shorris, Earl. *Latinos: A Biography of the People.* New York: W. W. Norton & Co., 1992.

Whyte, William H. *City: Rediscovering the Center.* New York: Doubleday, 1988.

Williams, Terry, and William Kornblum. *The Uptown Kids: Struggle and Hope in the Projects.* New York: Grosset/Putnam, 1994.

Wilson, William Julius. *The Truly Disadvantaged: The Inner City, the Underclass, and Public Policy.* Chicago: The University of Chicago Press, 1987.

Community Development: Biblical and Theological Resources

Brueggemann, Walter. *Using God's Resources Wisely: Isaiah and Urban Possibility.* Louisville: Westminster/John Knox Press, 1993.

Conn, Harvie M. *Bible Studies on World Evangelization and the Simple Lifestyle.* Phillipsburg, N.J.: Presbyterian and Reformed Publishing, 1981.

Gill, Athol. *Life on the Road: The Gospel Basis for a Messianic Lifestyle.* Australia: Lancer Books, 1989.

Linthicum, Robert C. *City of God, City of Satan: A Biblical Theology of the Urban Church.* Grand Rapids: Zondervan Publishing House, 1991.

McAlpine, Thomas H. *Facing the Powers: What Are the Options?* Monrovia, Calif.: Mission Advanced Research and Communication Center, 1991.

Meeks, Wayne A. *The First Urban Christians: The Social World of the Apostle Paul.* New Haven, Conn.: Yale University Press, 1983.

Mott, Stephen Charles. *Biblical Ethics and Social Change.* New York: Oxford University Press, 1982.

Mouw, Richard J. *When the Kings Come Marching In: Isaiah and the New Jerusalem.* Grand Rapids: William B. Eerdmans Publishing, 1983.

Murray, Stuart. *City Vision: A Biblical View.* London: Daybreak, 1990.

Noble, Lowell. *SocioTheology.* Available from Voice of Calvary, 1987.

Tidball, Derek. *The Social Context of the New Testament: A Sociological Analysis.* Grand Rapids: Zondervan Publishing House, 1984.

Van Engen, Charles, Dean S. Gilliland, and Paul Pierson, eds. *The Good News of the Kingdom: Mission Theology for the Third Millennium.* Maryknoll, N.Y.: Orbis Books, 1993.

Van Engen, Charles, and Jude Tiersma, eds. *God So Loves the City: Seeking a Theology for Urban Mission.* Monrovia, Calif.: Mission Advanced Research and Communication Center, 1994.

Villafane, Eldin. *The Liberating Spirit: Toward an Hispanic American Pentecostal Social Ethic.* Grand Rapids: William B. Eerdmans Publishing, 1993.

Winter, Bruce W. *Seek the Welfare of the City: Christians as Benefactors and Citizens.* Vol. 1 of *First-Century Christians in the Graeco-Roman World.* Grand Rapids: William B. Eerdmans Publishing; Carlise, England: Paternoster, 1994.

Wolterstorff, Nicholas. *Until Justice and Peace Embrace.* Grand Rapids: William B. Eerdmans Publishing, 1983.

Wright, Christopher J. H. *An Eye for an Eye: The Place of Old Testament Ethics Today.* Downers Grove: InterVarsity Press, 1983.

Learning from Others: Case Studies of Ministries

Barry, Patrick. *Rebuilding the Walls: A Nuts and Bolts Guide to the Community Development Methods of Bethel New Life, Inc., in Chicago.* Chicago: Bethel New Life, 1989.

Caes, David, ed. *Caring for the Least of These.* Scottdale, Pa.: Herald Press, 1992.

Freedman, Samuel G. *Upon This Rock: The Miracles of a Black Church.* New York: HarperCollins, 1993.

Guskind, Robert, and Neal Peirce. *Against the Tide: The New Community Corporation 1968–1993.* Newark: New Community Corporation.

Hilfiker, David. *Not All of Us Are Saints: A Doctor's Journey with the Poor.* New York: Hill and Wang, 1994.

O'Connor, Elizabeth. *Servant Leaders, Servant Structures.* Washington, D.C.: The Servant Leadership School, 1991.

Perkins, John, with Jo Kadlecek. *Resurrecting Hope.* Ventura, Calif.: Regal Books, 1995.

Schaller, Lyle. *Center City Churches: The New Urban Frontier.* Nashville: Abingdon Press, 1993.

Shabecoff, Alice. *Rebuilding Our Communities: How Churches Can Provide, Support, and Finance Quality Housing for Low-Income Families.* Monrovia, Calif.: World Vision, 1992.

Sider, Ronald J. *Cup of Water, Bread of Life: Inspiring Stories about Overcoming Lopsided Christianity.* Grand Rapids: Zondervan Publishing House, 1994.

Reconciliation, Multicultural Dynamics, and the Church

Branch, Taylor. *Parting the Waters: America in the King Years, 1954–63.* New York: Simon and Schuster, 1988.

Cone, James H. Martin. *Malcolm and America: A Dream or a Nightmare.* Maryknoll, N.Y.: Orbis Books, 1991.

Dawson, John. *Healing America's Wounds.* Ventura, Calif.: Regal, 1994.

Elmer, Duane. *Cross-Cultural Conflict: Building Relationships for Effective Ministry.* Downers Grove: InterVarsity Press, 1993.

Hacker, Andrew. *Two Nations: Black and White, Separate, Hostile, Unequal.* New York: Scribners, 1992.

Loury, Glenn C. *One by One from the Inside Out: Essays and Reviews on Race and Responsibility in America.* New York: The Free Press, 1995.

Mouw, Richard J. *Uncommon Decency: Christian Civility in an Uncivil World.* Downers Grove: InterVarsity Press, 1992.

Ortiz, Manuel. *The Multi-Ethnic Church in the United States.* Downers Grove: InterVarsity Press, forthcoming 1996.

Pannell, William. *The Coming Race Wars? A Cry for Reconciliation.* Grand Rapids: Zondervan Publishing House, 1993.

Perkins, John. *Let Justice Roll Down.* Glendale, Calif.: Regal, 1976.

Perkins, John, and Thomas A. Tarrants III with David Wimbish. *He's My Brother: Former Racial Foes Offer Strategy for Reconciliation.* Grand Rapids: Chosen Books, 1994.

Perkins, Spencer, and Chris Rice. *More Than Equals: Racial Healing for the Sake of the Gospel.* Downers Grove: InterVarsity Press, 1993.

Skinner, Tom. *How Black Is the Gospel?* Philadelphia and New York: J. B. Lippincott, 1970.

Stroupe, Nibs, and Inez Fleming. *While We Run This Race: Confronting the Power of Racism in a Southern Church.* Maryknoll, N.Y.: Orbis Books, 1995.

Washington, Raleigh, and Glen Kehrein. *Breaking Down Walls: A Model for Reconciliation in an Age of Racial Strife.* Chicago: Moody Press, 1993.

Weary, Dolphus. *I Ain't Comin' Back.* Wheaton, Ill.: Tyndale, 1990.

West, Cornel. *Race Matters.* Boston: Beacon Press, 1993.

Further Resources

There are an increasing number of journals devoted to social policy and urban issues such as health care, planning, and design. *Architecture, City Journal, Urban Affairs Review,* and *Journal of Urban History* are just a few and can usually be found in college or university libraries. Specialty publications such as in the field of health care and education frequently cover relevant subjects. Newsletters published by associations, organizations, and corporations are another excellent place to gather useful and timely information.

The National Congress for Community Economic Development (NCCED) newsletter, *Resources,* is up-to-date and provides very useful resource material. For more information, write NCCED, 875 Connecticut Ave. N.W. #524, Washington, DC 20009.

The Enterprise Foundation is another valuable resource for publications specifically related to housing programs. Their address is 10227 Wincopin Circle, Suite 500, Columbia, MD 21044.

Among Christian publications, the following are among the best resources:

Health and Development. 803 North 64th St., P.O. Box 12548, Philadelphia, PA 19151-0548. A publication of Christian Community Health Fellowship, a sister national network of CCDA, *Health and Development* is an excellent resource for health professionals serving among the poor as well as for other ministry practitioners.

IUA. International Urban Associates, 5151 N. Clark St., 2nd Floor, Chicago, IL 60640-2829. A newsletter with a global urban focus, this publication of Ray Bakke's International Urban Associates in Chicago is always challenging and insightful.

Prism. 10 East Lancaster Ave., Wynnewood, PA 19096. Published by Evangelicals for Social Action, *Prism* aims to help Christians integrate evangelism and social transformation.

Sojourners. 2401 15th St. NW, Washington, DC 20009. Edited by Jim Wallis, *Sojourners* serves the Christian community with a deeply rooted Christian perspective on faith, politics, and culture.

Together: A Journal of World Vision. World Vision, 121 E. Huntington Dr., Monrovia, CA 91016-3400. A quarterly publication of World Vision International, *Together* is intended to bring encouragement and stimulus to Christians who serve the poor by offering God's wholeness from a developmental commitment.

Transformation. 6 East Lancaster Ave., Wynnewood, PA 19096. An international evangelical dialogue on mission and ethics, *Transformation* covers a wide spectrum of topics certain to be of interest to community development practitioners.

Urban Family and *The Reconciler.* 1909 Robinson St., Jackson, MS 39209. *Urban Family* is a one-of-a-kind publication, celebrating the African American urban family and providing high-quality articles about how the Christian faith applies to city living. *The Reconciler*, a companion resource of sorts, is a newsletter for people serious about the demands of racial reconciliation.

Urban Mission. P.O. Box 27009, Philadelphia, PA 19118. Edited by Harvie Conn of Westminster Theological Seminary, *Urban Mission* provides essential articles on the church and the city. It is global in focus, unique as a journal.

A terrific resource not to be neglected are your local newspaper(s) and business journal(s). Keep an eye out for the work of syndicated columnists such as William Raspberry and Neal Peirce who focus on urban issues. And though the *Wall Street Journal* and the *New York Times* are East Coast newspapers, one can follow significant debates and trends at an in-depth level by reading them. They are often available at local libraries.

Last but certainly not least is the value of learning through novels such as Ralph Ellison's *Invisible Man*. Literature can make real for the practitioner many of the emotional, spiritual, and other daily experiences of community ministry in a much more powerful way than "textbooks" can. And they are invaluable for cultural analysis. Of great assistance here is Robert Coles, *The Call of Stories: Teaching and the Moral Imagination*, Boston: Houghton Mifflin Company, 1989.

Contributing Authors

Noel Castellanos is the pastor of La Villita Community Church, in "Little Village," a Mexican American neighborhood on Chicago's West Side. The interracial church, started in 1990, partners with Lawndale Community Church, located in a nearby Black neighborhood.

Wayne L. Gordon is founder of Lawndale Community Church on Chicago's West Side. Today Wayne serves as co-pastor at Lawndale with Carey Casey. Wayne's burden is developing Black Christian leaders from Lawndale. For example, over seventy-five youth have graduated from his church's programs to go on to college. Wayne is a graduate of Wheaton College and serves as president of the Christian Community Development Association. He has also recently authored *Real Hope for Chicago,* the inspiring story of Lawndale.

Mark R. Gornik, raised in the Baltimore area, is the founding pastor of New Song Community Church (Presbyterian Church in America), located in the West Baltimore neighborhood of Sandtown-Winchester, where he has lived since 1986. New Song was started in 1986 with Allan and Susan Tibbels and has been the "soil" for the creation of a "family of ministries" that includes Sandtown Habitat for Humanity, New Song Community Learning Center, New Song Family Health Center, and EDEN Jobs. Mark is a graduate of Covenant College and Westminster Theological Seminary (Philadelphia).

Glen Kehrein is the executive director of Circle Urban Ministries, a multifaceted Christian community development organization, founded in 1973, that partners with Rock of Our Salvation Evangelical Free Church in outreach to Chicago's Austin community. Glen and Rock Church pastor Raleigh Washington are authors of *Breaking Down Walls: A Model of Reconciliation in an Age of Racial Strife.* Glen is a graduate of Moody Bible Institute.

Bob and **Peggy Lupton** live in Atlanta, where in 1978 Bob founded FCS Urban Ministries, a Christian coalition of community services. Bob is the author of *Theirs Is the Kingdom* and *Return Flight.*

Mary Nelson moved to inner city Chicago to join her pastor brother at Bethel Lutheran Church in the turmoil of the 1960s. Bethel Church founded Bethel New Life, Inc., in 1979, and Mary became the founding president of BNL. This community-based development corporation, with a staff of four hundred and a $6.6 million budget, is making a significant economic impact on the Garfield

Park neighborhood through housing, business development, education, health care, and other creative enterprises.

Lowell Noble taught sociology and anthropology for more than twenty-five years at Spring Arbor College in Spring Arbor, Michigan. He is the author of *Sociotheology.*

John M. Perkins, considered the founder of Christian community development, founded three church-based ministries among the poor in Mississippi and California. He is the publisher of *Urban Family* magazine, chairman of the Christian Community Development Association, and board member of World Vision and Prison Fellowship. John's books include *Let Justice Roll Down, A Quiet Revolution, With Justice for All, Beyond Charity,* and *He's My Brother,* co-authored with Tom Tarrants.

Spencer Perkins and **Chris Rice** have been partners for more than a decade in the ministry of racial reconciliation. They are members of Antioch—an interracial Christian community that is part of Voice of Calvary Fellowship in Jackson, Mississippi. They are authors of *More Than Equals: Racial Healing for the Sake of the Gospel,* and editors of *Urban Family* magazine and *The Reconciler,* a publication for Christians serious about racial healing.

Vera Mae Perkins pioneered in Christian community development alongside her husband John, getting three ministries off the ground, enduring the challenge of the 1960s civil rights movement in Mississippi, and raising eight children in the process. Vera's heart for children has touched the lives of thousands in Mississippi and California through child evangelism and Good News Bible Clubs.

Ronald Clifton Potter and his family are members of Antioch Community and Voice of Calvary Fellowship Church in Jackson, Mississippi. He is a native of Chicago, attended Rutgers University, received an M.Div. at Turner Seminary in Atlanta, and pursued doctoral studies at Drew University. He has been assistant professor of Christian Thought and Contemporary Culture at the Center for Urban Theological Studies and is an ordained elder in the AME church.

Phil Reed has served for twenty years as senior pastor of Voice of Calvary Fellowship, an interracial congregation reaching the inner city in Jackson, Mississippi. Phil is a graduate of Reformed Theological Seminary.

Gloria Yancy returned to the Richmond, California, neighborhood where she grew up to found Christian Believers, a ministry to ex-offenders, addicts, and at-risk children.